Big Sur Country
Ventana Wilderness

Jeffrey P. Schaffer

Acknowledgments

Foremost, I would like to thank Ross and Helen Thackeray, who on many occasions opened their home to me after a hard, exhausting day's work. A large dinner, hot shower, clean bed and glass of sherry sure did wonders in preparing me for another grueling day in the field. It is to them that I affectionately dedicate this book.

Richard D. Zechentmayer (U.S. Forest Service) reviewed the book's two introductory chapters, Donald C. Ross (U.S. Geological Survey) reviewed the geology subchapter, and Steffani Jarrett, John Magee and Glen McGowan (all State Park employees) reviewed chapters 10–14.

In creating the final product, I've tried to be as accurate as possible, though in every book, a few errors seem to creep in, and I bear responsibility for any that occur.

FIRST EDITION May 1988 Fifth printing October 1995
Second printing June 1989 Sixth printing April 1998
Third printing January 1992 Seventh printing August 2000
Fourth printing February 1994 **Eighth printing May 2002**

Cover photograph copyright © 1988 by David Muench
All other photographs by Jeffrey P. Schaffer
Field mapping on U.S. Geological Survey 7.5' topographic maps by Jeffrey P. Schaffer
Topographic maps compiled from U.S. Geological Survey 7.5' topographic maps; amended by
   Jeffrey P. Schaffer, Noëlle Imperatore, and Larry B. Van Dyke
Book design by Jeffrey P. Schaffer
Cover design by Larry B. Van Dyke
Library of Congress Card Catalog Number 88-40007
International Standard Book Number 0-89997-083-4

Manufactured in the United States of America

Published by **Wilderness Press**
              1200 5th Street
              Berkeley, CA 94710
              (800) 443-7227; FAX (510) 558-1696
              mail@wildernesspress.com
              www.wildernesspress.com

              Contact us for a free catalog

Front cover: Calla lilies along lower Doud Creek. Photo © 1988 by David Muench
Title page: Pine Valley Camp

Library of Congress Cataloging in Publication Data
Schaffer, Jeffrey P.
      Hiking the Big Sur Country.
      Bibliography: p.
      Includes index.
         1. Hiking—California—Ventana Wilderness—
Guide-books. 2. Hiking—California—Big Sur Coast
National Scenic Area—Guide-books. 3. Natural history—
California—Ventana Wilderness. 4. Natural history—
California—Big Sur Coast National Scenic Area.
5. Ventana Wilderness (Calif.)—Guide-books. 6. Big
Sur Coast National Scenic Area (Calif.)—Guide-books.
I. Title.
GV199.42.C22V467   1988   917.94'78   88-40007
ISBN 0-89997-083-4

Contents

Introductory Chapters

Part 1: Ventana Wilderness

Part 2: State Lands of the Big Sur Coast

Contents

Hiking in the backcountry entails unavoidable risk that every hiker assumes and must be aware of and respect. The fact that a trail is described in this book is not a representation that it will be safe for you. Trails vary greatly in difficulty and in the degree of conditioning and agility one needs to enjoy them safely. On some hikes routes may have changed or conditions may have deteriorated since the descriptions were written. Also trail conditions can change even from day to day, owing to weather and other factors. A trail that is safe on a dry day or for a highly conditioned, agile, properly equipped hiker may be completely unsafe for someone else or unsafe under adverse weather conditions.

You can minimize your risks on the trail by being knowledgeable, prepared and alert. There is not space in this book for a general treatise on safety in the mountains, but there are a number of good books and public courses on the subject and you should take advantage of them to increase your knowledge. Just as important, you should always be aware of your own limitations and of conditions existing when and where you are hiking. If conditions are dangerous, or if you are not prepared to deal with them safely, choose a different hike! It's better to have wasted a drive than to be the subject of a mountain rescue.

These warnings are not intended to scare you off the trails. Millions of people have safe and enjoyable hikes every year. However, one element of the beauty, freedom and excitement of the wilderness is the presence of risks that do not confront us at home. When you hike you assume those risks. They can be met safely, but only if you exercise your own independent judgment and common sense.

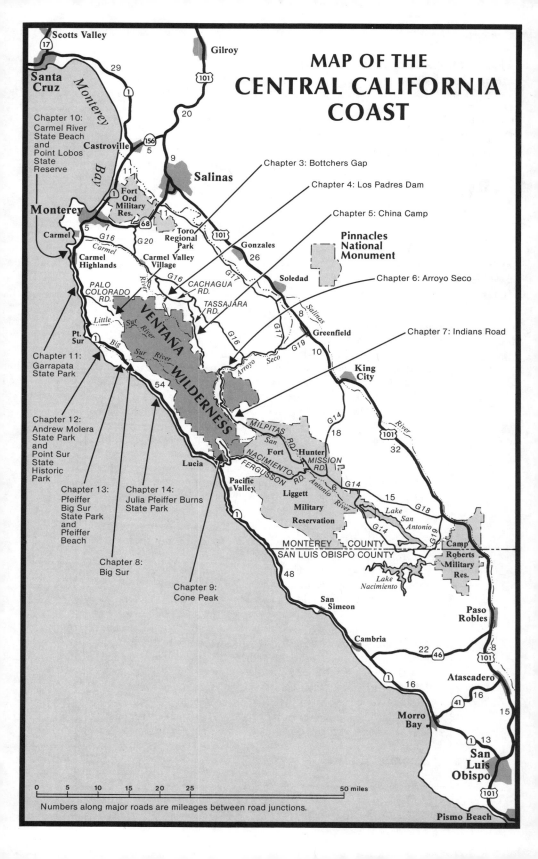

MAP OF THE CENTRAL CALIFORNIA COAST

Scotts Valley
17
Gilroy
101
Santa Cruz
29
1
20
Monterey Bay
156
5
Castroville
9
11
Salinas
Chapter 10: Carmel River State Beach and Point Lobos State Reserve
Monterey
1 Fort Ord Military Res.
68
11
Toro Regional Park
Chapter 3: Bottchers Gap
Chapter 4: Los Padres Dam
Carmel
5 7
G16
G20
Carmel Valley Village
101
Gonzales
26
Chapter 5: China Camp
Carmel Highlands
Carmel River
G16
CACHAGUA RD.
Soledad
Pinnacles National Monument
PALO COLORADO RD.
TASSAJARA RD.
Salinas
G17
Chapter 6: Arroyo Seco
Little Sur River
VENTANA
G16
G17
G19
Greenfield
Pt. Sur
1
Big Sur River
WILDERNESS
Arroyo Seco
8
10
Chapter 7: Indians Road
Chapter 11: Garrapata State Park
54
King City
Chapter 12: Andrew Molera State Park and Point Sur State Historic Park
MILPITAS RD.
San Antonio River
G14
18
101
River
32
Chapter 13: Pfeiffer Big Sur State Park and Pfeiffer Beach
Lucia
NACIMIENTO-FERGUSSON RD.
Fort Hunter MISSION RD.
Chapter 14: Julia Pfeiffer Burns State Park
Pacific Valley
1
G14
Liggett Military Reservation
6
15
G18
Chapter 8: Big Sur
Lake San Antonio
G14
G19
Camp Roberts Military Res.
MONTEREY COUNTY
SAN LUIS OBISPO COUNTY
Chapter 9: Cone Peak
48
Lake Nacimiento
Paso Robles
San Simeon
Cambria
22
46
8
101
1
16
Atascadero
41
16
15
Morro Bay
1
13
San Luis Obispo
101
Pismo Beach

0 5 10 15 20 25   50 miles

Numbers along major roads are mileages between road junctions.

Chapter 1: Introduction

The Big Sur Country

What is the Big Sur Country? Most geographers would probably equate it to the Santa Lucia Range. This is a rugged, youthful range rising from a stretch of central California's coastline that extends from about Carmel, in the north, to about San Simeon, in the south. This stretch, as measured along State Highway 1, is 90 miles long. I've chosen a more restrictive definition, which I feel is more appropriate for hikers,* namely *Ventana Wilderness and its adjacent coastal lands.* My definition covers about 40% less coastline: just the 54-mile stretch from the Carmel Valley Road, in Carmel, south to the Nacimiento-Fergusson Road, in absolutely the middle of nowhere. With this definition, Pfeiffer Big Sur State Park lies midway along the stretch, and to many people this park, with its adjacent resorts, is synonymous with Big Sur.

For a few reasons I haven't covered the part of the range south of the Nacimiento-Fergusson Road, that is, south of Ventana Wilderness. First, that area lacks trails east of the crest, since that land is part of Fort Hunter Liggett, which is also known as the Hunter Liggett Military Reservation. Second, the crest is considerably lower and less esthetically appealing. Third, being lower this land has significantly less precipitation, and year-round water can be harder to find; there are no major rivers. Fourth, there are no coastal state parks with trail systems. Finally, the few trails in the area are hardly used, especially by residents of the San Francisco and Monterey bay areas, who constitute the vast majority of hikers using Big Sur's trails. For them this southern land is not worth the extra driving, especially since more attractive lands lie closer to home.

How long does it take to drive to the Big Sur Country? From San Jose, which is in the southern part of the San Francisco Bay Area,

you'll reach the northern trailheads in about 2 hours and the most isolated southern ones, along Cone Peak Road, in about 3½ hours. If you're driving from San Francisco or Oakland, add another hour. From San Luis Obispo, you'll reach the southern trailheads in about 2 hours and the northern ones in about 3 hours. If you're driving from Santa Barbara, add about 2 hours; from Los Angeles, add about 4 hours. The central-coast map on the opposite page shows the location of the Big Sur Country and the mileages between major points.

Salinas and Monterey Peninsula residents benefit most, since Ventana Wilderness and the state lands are so close. Some of these residents can even reach trailheads at or near Highway 1 by bus. The Monterey-Salinas Transit Line 22 (BIG SUR) serves Carmel, Point Lobos State Reserve, Carmel Highlands, Garrapata Beach, Bixby Creek Bridge (north end of the Coast Road), Point Sur Light Station, Andrew Molera State Park (south end

---

*Throughout the book I use the term *hikers,* but the book is equally meant for *equestrians.* Saying "hikers and equestrians" many times is cumbersome, and not being an equestrian, I prefer using "hiker." I'm not doing this to slight equestrians, for I strongly feel that they have as much right to the wilderness as do hikers.

of the Coast Road), Big Sur resorts and Pfeiffer Big Sur State Park. During the tourist season, lasting from about May through early September, the bus runs twice daily. The rest of the year it runs only on weekends. For a current schedule, phone the Monterey-Salinas Transit at (408) 899-2555.

The Big Sur Country appeals more to northern Californians because of its proximity, and because it is the only sizable area near the Bay Area offering a four-season wilderness-camping experience. When the High Sierra is under snow, which it usually is for about 8 months of the year, Bay Area residents can find solace at one of about four dozen backcountry camps in Ventana Wilderness and adjacent Forest Service lands. Southern Californians, on the other hand, needen't drive to Ventana Wilderness for a fall, winter or spring wilderness-camping experience, since their part of the state is blessed with many suitable four-season wildernesses.

Ventana Wilderness The name *Ventana* is Spanish for window. Just where there was a window is a mystery. According to a legend, there was once a natural bridge connecting the two adjacent summits of Ventana Double Cone, and until it fell, there existed a natural window. However, there is absolutely no evidence that a bridge existed there in the last few thousand years. If a bridge existed, it would more likely have spanned a deep cleft between Ventana Double Cone and its western outlier. However, there are dozens, maybe hundreds, of windows in cliffs and islets along the Big Sur coast, and perhaps they were responsible for the name the early Spaniards gave to the area.

Ventana Wilderness—the prime hiking area in the Big Sur Country and the main subject of this guidebook—straddles the higher part of the Santa Lucia Range. This relatively obscure range is only about one third as high as the celebrated Sierra Nevada, which rightly has been called the *Gentle Wilderness*. One might infer from this phrase that the Santa Lucia Range must be three times gentler, but it is not. The range plunges to the Pacific Ocean at a gradient similar to the mighty eastern escarpment of the Sierra Nevada. Indeed, the drop from 5,155' Cone Peak to the sea is slightly steeper than the 8,000' drop from the Sierra's highest point—14,494' Mt. Whitney—to the west edge of Owens Valley.

What this means for you, the hiker, is a wilderness experience that is, mile for mile, as rugged as any in the Sierra Nevada. If you are backpacking at the rate of about 10 miles per day, you can expect to average 2000 to 3000' of daily elevation change, and there are some 10-mile stretches where you may average 4000 to 5000'. Ventana Wilderness is not gentle; if anything, it is formidable. It is easy to overexert yourself there, so don't plan heroic hiking days. Doing so invites trouble, including the possibility of going lame.

The wilderness is very formidable when it comes to cross-country hiking. The vegetation—particularly the chaparral, which dominates the landscape—is in most places so dense that most routes are practically impossible. You can tediously work your way along streams, but you'll be stopped short trying to traverse most slopes and ridgecrests. Once, after attempting to map an abandoned trail, I headed cross-country ½ mile to the Pine Ridge Trail. *Two hours* later I reached it. The moral is to keep to the trails.

Not all the trails in this approximately 320-square-mile-wilderness have major climbs and descents. Some are relatively easy, including the two most popular routes in the wilderness: the upper Pine Ridge Trail/Carmel River Trail, which leaves China Camp and goes almost 19 miles down to Los Padres Reservoir; and the lower Pine Ridge Trail, which goes 9½ miles up the Big Sur River to Sykes Camp. Together these two routes probably receive about 90% of the wilderness' traffic, even though they only make up about 10% of its trail system. Hiking along the other trails, I rarely met anyone. While this is great for a wilderness experience, it is a real liability if you are hiking alone and get injured.

The trail system consists of about 260 miles of trails and closed roads in and about the wilderness, though soon after I mapped these, the Ventana Wilderness Mounted Assistance Group began resurrecting the Black Cone Trail. This and several other trails had been closed by dense brush that sprang up in the wake of the 1977 Marble-Cone fire, which had razed much of the wilderness' vegetation. If the volunteer group succeeds in opening all these trails, there will be about 20 more miles in the system.

State Lands of the Big Sur Coast This is a second, ancillary hiking area in the Big Sur Country. Two of these state lands—Point Lobos and Pfeiffer Big Sur—*each* receive far more visitation than does Ventana. However, for most people, Point Lobos is a tourist attraction to photograph, and Pfeiffer Big Sur is a camping and picnic area to relax in. It's too bad most folks don't think of these lands as hiking areas, for there are plenty of routes. All told, there are about 45 miles of trails and closed roads in the state lands of the Big Sur Coast. Andrew Molera State Park, just north of Pfeiffer Big Sur, has the lion's share of the trails—about 20 miles' worth—yet these are lightly used. Although many of its trails are suitable for hikers, joggers, equestrians and bicyclists, it seems that, at least on summer weekends, surfers taking short trails to the beach are the primary users.

The state units are relatively small, 7.4-square-mile Andrew Molera—easily the largest—accounting for almost half of the total lands. Consequently the trails are short, the longest being under 3½ miles long and many being under a mile long. Therefore, these lands aren't suited for backcountry camping. *Indeed, all trails and roads on state lands are day-use only.* There are no backcountry campsites. Though the trails are short, some are among the steepest to be found in the Big Sur Country. All the steep trails are found in three units—Garrapata, Andrew Molera and Julia Pfeiffer Burns state parks—and all climb east from Highway 1. However, most of the trails lie west of Highway 1, and most them do very little climbing.

Particularly in Garrapata State Park, the westside trails offer coast access. *Be aware that the Big Sur surf is dangerous, even in calm weather.* The water is cold, ranging from the low 50s in winter to the mid or high 50s in summer. If you're swept out by a riptide, you'll last only a few minutes before hypothermia starts setting in, so think twice about getting wet. Watch the wave pattern for 5 or 10 minutes to see if it's tricky. At Carmel River State Beach I saw a series of harmless 2–3′ waves suddenly followed by a potent 6′ wave. And where the surf crashes against rocks or cliffs, the danger of being swept away is greater. Even in calm weather, a rogue wave can easily send spray 30′ into the air. In rough weather, particularly after a series of storms, waves may repeatedly drench the tops of 50′ high cliffs. Avoid becoming a fatality statistic by respecting the power of the surf.

The Route Chapters

If you are unfamiliar with the attractions of Ventana Wilderness, then read the following chapter synopses, which present the highlights of each area. Introductions at the start of each hiking route in every chapter fill you in on the details. As shown on the map opposite page 1, these chapters are arranged in two northwest-to-southeast sequences. Chapters 3–7 cover the "dry lands" of Ventana Wilderness, which extend from its north part to its southeast part, while Chapters 8–9 cover its "fog-prone lands" above the west coast. Each route chapter covers trails originating from either one trailhead or from several relatively close trailheads.

Chapters 10–14 cover the state lands of the Big Sur Coast, and these too are arranged in a northwest-to-southeast sequence. Each of these relatively short chapters has a general introduction, so they are not duplicated below.

Chapter 3: Bottchers Gap From the fault-line gap you can hike into two different environments. First, you can climb east to brushy viewpoints having sweeping panoramas, these best viewed from about November through April, when coastal fog is unlikely. On clear days, you'll see from Mt. Carmel's summit virtually all of Monterey Bay. I prefer to visit this area in mid-February to mid-April, when wildflowers and ceanothus bushes fill the landscape with color and aroma. From Devils Peak you can continue south to Ventana Double Cone, the highest summit in the north half of the wilderness that can be reached by trail. The second major-route choice is to descend south to streamside, redwood-shaded camps, which are pleasant retreats from summer's heat. No wonder Pico Blanco Boy Scout Camp was located in this area.

Chapter 4: Los Padres Dam The Carmel River Trail—easily the chapter's most attractive route—heads up the river to generally roomy camps that are inviting in spring, summer and fall. Summer afternoons can be quite oppressive, but shallow "swimming holes" offer respite. During winter, when the river canyon's floor is cold and damp and the river is flood-prone, you can climb west on the sunny Big Pines Trail to two fine winter camps. From either you can continue west down to Bottchers Gap, concluding a ridgecrest transect of the northern part of the wilderness.

Chapter 5: China Camp Spacious, easily reached Pine Valley is the usual goal from this trailhead. A large, pine-shaded camp below sandstone cliffs is a worthy year-round goal, particularly for rock climbers. Winter camping is on the cold side, but still tolerable, since there is plenty of open space to warm oneself on a sunny day. The road to the trailhead may be closed during storms, due to fallen trees or small mudslides, but it is rapidly re-opened, since there are residences along the road. From spring to fall, the Carmel River and Miller Canyon trails offer enjoyable riverside routes, which are the best in the wilderness. Year-round, the Pine Ridge Trail offers a fine though demanding wilderness transect, one across highly varied topography and diverse vegetation. Another route, the brushy Church Creek Trail, rollercoasters across the most dramatic sandstone outcrops in the wilderness.

Chapter 6: Arroyo Seco This area has only one main route, the Marble Peak Trail. Climbing west, it mimics Chapter 4's Carmel River Trail, but at a more subdued scale. It makes numerous creek crossings on its way past camps to Indian Valley, an analog of Pine Valley (both are fire-scarred, but the damage was particularly severe in Indian Valley). This route is a third good transect of the wilderness, at least in late spring and after the first rains in early fall. Summer and early fall are either too hot or too dry, and from about mid-November through April or May, Indians Road, the access road to the trailhead, may be gated. However, if you're willing to walk several extra miles to the trailhead, you'll be richly rewarded in March and early April with a cornucopia of flowering plants.

Chapter 7: Indians Road Like the Marble Peak Trail in the previous chapter, the Lost Valley Trail climbs to Indian Valley. And like that route, its trailhead is on the seasonally gated Indians Road. Most hikers take the trail only as far as Lost Valley, which was torched as badly as Indian Valley, but at least has a wonderful year-round stream flowing through it. The valley has one of the best winter camps, which justifies hiking the several extra miles along Indian Road to reach the trailhead. Near the start of Indian Road, the Santa Lucia Trail begins a climb to the highest summit in the Santa Lucia Range, Junipero Serra Peak. On clear days you can see not only most of the range, but also a vast stretch of ocean and part of the Sierra Nevada crest. The relatively short Arroyo Seco Trail has two camps that are acceptable in all but the winter season. Finally, near the trailhead you'll see The Rocks—the most massive sandstone formation in the Big Sur Country—vaulting up toward the heavens. They are a fine assemblage for exploring, scrambling or climbing.

Chapter 8: Big Sur The Pine Ridge Trail, climbing east from the Big Sur Forest Service Station, is easily the most popular trail in the wilderness, for it takes you to spacious camps along the Big Sur River, which has swimming holes that are very inviting during summer. Unlike Chapter 4's Carmel River Trail, the Pine Ridge Trail doesn't proceed up along the floor of the river's canyon, but rather "leaps" from one river camp to another, making you work to earn your just reward. The Mt. Manuel Trail is quite different. This waterless and brushy, though well-engineered, route climbs to one of the area's finer viewpoints. Finally, the Coast Ridge Road starts its climb south from the Big Sur locale. On a fogless day, it's certainly worth hiking, even if you climb just several miles up it to the Coast Ridge. However, by heading south along it, you're offered myriad views of the wilderness to the east and coast lands to the west.

Chapter 9: Cone Peak The easily reached Cone Peak summit is a popular day hike, and no wonder, for it is arguably the finest viewpoint in the Santa Lucia Range. Below the summit is the start of the Coast Ridge Trail, which advances north along the ridge, spinning off side trails to lightly used, shady camps before reaching the Coast Ridge Road. Not far south of the summit are trailheads for the San Antonio and Vicente Flat trails. Both lead to spacious camps, Fresno Camp along the San Antonio Trail being easily reached and therefore ideal for a young pack of troopers. However, Vicente Flat Camp is a year-round stellar attraction. In winter it's best reached by starting from the lower end of the Vicente Flat Trail, which begins at Highway 1.

Using This Guidebook

As mentioned above, I've divided this book's routes into two parts: Ventana Wilderness and state lands of the Big Sur Coast. Since the trails and closed roads of the state lands are day-use only, you need very little planning and preparation for them. Consequently, in that second part I've kept preliminary comments to a minimum. Ventana Wilderness is another story. Enjoying a backpack trip in it requires that you plan your trip well. Foremost, this depends on selecting a route suited to the time of year *and* to your condition. It also depends partly on how well you handle the area's potential adversities, such as bad weather and nagging flies. The rest of this chapter covers potential problems and their solutions, and it also covers proper hiking and camping practices in the wilderness.

Each Ventana Wilderness chapter is based on routes emanating from a single trailhead or from two or more nearby trailheads. Each route has a two-letter code that is the same for all the routes in a given chapter. The two letters refer to the trailhead. For example, the code in Chapter 3 is **BG,** for **B**ottchers **G**ap. The routes shown on this book's topographic maps have such markings, which allow you to readily identify what route or routes to take to go from point A to point B. I say *routes* instead of *trails* because most of them consist of two or more trails, and some of them consist of both trails and limited-access roads.

Title The title of each Ventana Wilderness route is in fact a synopsis, for it includes the starting point, the ending point, all the camps to be found along the way, and all the trails and/or roads taken.

Distances Immediately below the title are the distances to all the route's major points. A route often consists of a main trail with lateral trails. Since you might want to skip some of these lateral trails, I've indented them to set them apart. Where lateral trails have branching trails, these branches are indented farther.

Maps Below the distances is a list of the topographic maps that show the route. If you are skilled at map interpretation, you can get a good idea of how much ascent and descent are along a route. However, you don't need to be a map expert, since each route description contains a number of points (trail junctions, camps, summits, creek crossings, etc.), each with an elevation and the distance from the previous point; hence you can determine the net gain or loss between two points.

A few words need to be said about mileages and maps. With a Brunton pocket transit, I surveyed the trails and roads and drew them as accurately as possible on 7.5′ topo maps. Then to determine mileages, I measured the lengths of the lines I had drawn. If a topo map is accurate, I can get values within 2 or 3% of the true figures—in other words, the same accuracy one gets by pushing a footage wheel. But what if the topo map is inaccurate? This, unfortunately, is true for every topographic map covering Ventana Wilderness. Having mapped over 4,000 miles of trail in my 16-year career, I've gotten to know when *my* mapping is in error—and needs to be redone—and when the *map itself* is in error.

Each topo map is a mosaic of errors, such as one section drawn 10% too large, while the adjacent one, in compensation, is drawn 10% too small. So, over distances of one to several miles, my figures can be up to 10% off. However, over longer distances, the maps errors balance out, and so do my mileages. Take, for example, the Pine Ridge Trail, eastbound from Big Sur. A Sierra Club measurement, made with a footage wheel (usually accurate to within 2 or 3%, but fairly inaccurate where there are many fords or short

switchbacks), gets 4.3 miles to the Ventana Camp Trail junction; I get 3.9—9.3% less. They are probably right. Then they say the trail's total length is 23.0 miles, while I say it's 23.1, which is a discrepancy of less than ½ of 1%.

Map accuracy is even worse along short distances, such as between two gullies, which too often are shown up to 50% greater or 30% less than they really are. Perhaps more upsetting is the number of gullies *not* shown. It's very disconcerting when you're ducking in and out of a series of gullies and the topographic map shows not one of them. This oversight can be forgiven in areas of dense redwoods, where relatively small features are not visible in aerial photos. But in chaparral? It's inexcusable. Also, on many occasions I encountered contour lines out of orientation by 30° or more. This shouldn't happen even in redwood forests, but when you see it time and again in areas of brushy slopes, you begin to lose faith in U.S. Geological Survey maps.

Where I've had good topographic control in the field, I've remapped some incorrect contours for the maps in this book. But in general I've left the bad ones untouched, since in most cases correcting *each* offender would require extensive time surveying many acres of terrain. Consequently, I've drawn the trail to best fit these contours, so that you, when looking at the map, can determine whether the trail is going up or down. However, if you take a compass bearing, you may find the map trail, in a number of spots, to be 30° out of orientation. Having mapped the area, I can now understand why previous maps of the area were so inaccurate—all too often, the trail mappers (if indeed they did MAP and not just spot check) had no idea what was going on.

Trailhead After a route's list of maps comes directions to its trailhead. This section also includes vital information, such as location of gas stations, stores, restaurants, resorts, campgrounds and Forest Service stations.

Introduction If you're familiar with Ventana Wilderness, you may find the route introductions too long. However, the desirability of *every* route changes from season to season, making it, for example, fine in spring but miserable in summer. Consequently, I've taken pains to give not only a route's overview, but also to note how conditions along it change with seasons (see also the next section in this chapter, "The Hiking Seasons").

Description All route descriptions mention major points in **bold-face** type. These points are the same ones that appear in a route's distances. But most routes also mention *other* points, which are not set apart in special type. Each main point and each lesser point is followed by two sets of numbers, the first being the elevation of that point, and the second being the mileage since the previously mentioned point. By comparing elevations between two points, you can determine the *net* change. This is not the same as the total change, for there can be many minor ups and downs between two points of equal elevation. And if the ups and downs are steep or very steep, as along the Coast Ridge Trail, you'll expend more energy, because you'll have to brake on the downhill stretches.

So that you can assess how taxing a route is, I often mention the grade along stretches of trail. Grade (or gradient) is the amount of vertical gain or loss over a horizontal distance. For example, a 10% grade means you gain or lose 10 vertical feet over a horizontal distance of 100'. Mostly, I say a stretch has a gentle, moderate, steep or very steep grade. Gentle-to-moderate and moderate-to-steep refer to intermediate grades. The basic gradients are:

gentle	5%
moderate	10%
steep	15%
very steep	20%.

For the *average backpacker,* a gentle climb requires only a little more effort than walking on the level. A moderate climb requires quite a bit of effort, and though you may perspire, you can usually maintain a good pace. A steep climb requires a lot of effort, so your pace will be slower and your steps shorter. And if the ascent is long, you'll need a number of rests. A very steep climb will not only have you huffing and puffing, but also cursing and swearing. Finally, there are some excessively steep routes, a few even exceeding 30%, and these require caution while descending, since you almost slip down them even while trying to take a rest stop. For quite a number of sections and for a few entire trails, I give absolute gradient values. After you've done quite a bit of hiking in the Big Sur Country, you learn to respect the difference between, say, a protracted 14% grade and a protracted 17% one.

The Ventana Wilderness route descriptions also make detailed mention of the vegetation, which may help you determine a trail's desirability. For example, as mentioned below under "Problem Plants and Animals," oaks can present fly problems in hot weather, and chaparral can present tick problems in wet weather.

Lack of water along some routes and at a few camps can be a problem from as early as June until as late as November. Consequently, I point out all sources of water and their reliability. During the wet months, there can be too much water in places, and I point this out too.

I've also described *some* amenities of each camp. It's good to know in advance if the camp is large enough to hold your party, or if it may be too sunny, too shady or, most importantly, seasonally waterless. Most camps have at least one stove and one table, but vandalism or just the march of time can do these in, so generally I don't list every stove, fire ring, table or pit toilet a camp may hold. Some *official* camps are too small and inadequate, so along certain routes I've mentioned existing or potential use camps, which deserve development. Some existing unofficial camps are unnecessary or undesirable, and these aren't mentioned.

The Hiking Seasons

Although the Big Sur Country can be hiked in every month of the year, the visitation rate is anything but uniform. Part of this has to do with vacations and holidays, and part has to do with weather, which essentially has two periods: wet (from about November through March) and dry (from about April through October). Within the area, the rainfall pattern is highly variable, due to the varied topography. The coastline gets about 40 inches per year, but as storm clouds are forced up over the Coast Ridge, they drop a lot more rain, generally about 60 or more inches. (In some wet years, over 100 inches of precipitation have been recorded.) With less clouds, a storm drops less rain on Ventana's land east of the Coast Ridge. The eastern part of Ventana gets about 20–30 inches, and beyond that, the storm clouds descend into Salinas Valley, warming up as they do so, and thus becoming able to retain more moisture. Consequently, the valley is deprived of precious moisture, receiving only about 10–15 inches.

Each of the four seasons creates usage patterns in Ventana Wilderness that are different from those in the coastal state lands, and so these two areas will be discussed separately.

If the weather is pleasant, campers surge into the campgrounds bordering *Ventana Wilderness* on three- and four-day weekends, such as President's Day, Thanksgiving and sometimes even Christmas. Few people, however, backpack during these often cool and sometimes wet times. However, with the advent of spring, most of the major storms have passed, and temperatures become optimal for backpacking. Days warm into the 60s and 70s and sometimes even into the 80s. Spring break ("Easter vacation") can bring hikers to Ventana in droves.

From then until about Memorial Day, most trails receive their heaviest use—although many are seldom traveled during any time of year. In June, days typically warm into the 80s and sometimes into the 90s, the latter temperatures being too hot for strenuous backpacking but just right for lolling about in riverside camps. Consequently, backpackers mostly head to camps along the Big Sur and Carmel rivers. The Big Sur River in particular has some nice swimming holes, which can warm from the mid-40s in the morning to the mid-50s by afternoon of a day in March or April (and also in October). But by late spring and through at least late summer, the morning-afternoon temperatures will be about 10° warmer, so afternoon dips become quite enjoyable and refreshing.

In July the Sierra Nevada becomes essentially snow-free, and most backpackers abandon Ventana for higher, eastern lands. Despite Ventana's high temperatures, you can enjoy a summer backpack trip, even if you don't restrict yourself to the relatively cool Big Sur and Carmel river canyons, which can be fogbound in the morning. Plan to hit the trail early and reach a camp by noon. Most camps are shady, and the deeper the canyon, the cooler the temperature is likely to be. On a typical day from late spring through early fall, the afternoon temperature can be in the 70s at a shady creekside camp, but in the 80s on shady canyon slopes and adjacent ridges, and up to 100° on sunny slopes. In the sunshine, temperatures typically run about 20° higher (in winter, about 10° higher). So if you feel it's been 100° on a summer afternoon's trek, it probably has been, despite the fact your thermometer reads only in the low 80s at a shady rest stop.

When the air is stable, the temperature cools upward, usually at a lapse rate of about 3½° per 1000′ of elevation gain. So while King City in the Salinas Valley can be sweltering in the high 90s, your sunny viewpoint atop Junipero Serra Peak can be a fairly comfortable 80°. On the west side of the wilderness, however, the higher place may be warmer than the lower place, because coastal terrain below 2000′ is often fogbound and typically has summer temperatures only in the 60s and low 70s.

Nor does the lapse rate apply to nighttime temperatures. As temperatures fall in the evening, higher, cooler air begins to sink, and it displaces lower, warmer air, creating a temperature inversion. Hence, by sunrise the next morning, when the day's temperature is at its minimum, your camp can be significantly cooler than terrain just above you. On one early morning immediately before sunrise, I measured the temperature at Bee Camp and at the Coast Ridge, just 200′ above it. The camp was a surprising 10° degrees cooler. This can be an advantage in warm weather, when you don't mind the temperatures dropping into the 50s or even into the 40s. However, there can be one detriment, at least west of the Coast Ridge, as Bee Camp is: a large drop in temperature can cause quite a bit of dew to form on your tent. Inland, the air is drier, and condensation is considerably less. You can minimize condensation by pitching your tent under a shady tree rather than in the open.

Usually in November there's a pronounced change in the weather. Whereas days may have been in the 70s and nights in the 40s in late October, days are likely to be in the 60s and nights in the 30s by Thanksgiving. And furthermore, the rainy season has begun. Storms are sporadic at first, but certainly by mid-December they can come thick and fast, usually bringing rain but occasionally snow (which typically doesn't stay long on the ground). The area can have a series of storms lasting a week or two with virtually no letup between storms. But then, the wilderness can go for a similar time—or longer—without any precipitation. Winter days are usually in the 40s and 50s, nights in the 20s and 30s.

While this is too cold for most people, you can still have a fairly comfortable backpacking experience in the winter, if you have the proper clothing, sleeping bag and tent, and if you plan your itinerary carefully. First, confine your trip to two or three days, since the longer you stay out in the wilderness, the greater the chance you'll encounter a storm. If a five-day forecast calls for sunny weather, you're probably safe for the first three days. When you hike, start in midmorning, after the day has begun to warm, and where possible take trails along ridgecrests or sunny slopes rather than along canyon bottoms or shady slopes. Reach your destination in midafternoon, when you can set up camp in relative warmth. Choose a camp that is close to ridgecrests, such as Pat Spring, Pine Ridge or Cold Spring, for these will be considerably warmer than canyon-bottom camps (which also receive copious amounts of dew by morning). Not all the lower camps need to be avoided. For example, at Lost Valley, which has a broad bottom, the sun's rays can hit Lost Valley Camp quite early in the morning, soon chasing away the frigid sunrise temperatures.

By late February temperatures have warmed enough to permit some enjoyable backpacking. Most of the storms are now behind you, but still as late as April there can be a rogue storm that will paint at least the upper part of the wilderness white with snow. Basically, from October through May always check the weather report before you drive to the trailhead.

Weather is not so much of a concern if you plan to hike on the *coastal state lands,* since they are day-use only. You don't have to worry about being rained on. Regardless of the season, if the day's weather is acceptable to you, you can dress appropriately and enjoy a day hike. In January mornings average about 40° and afternoons about 60°. In July mornings average in the low 50s, afternoons in the high 60s. As you can see, there isn't much variation in temperature either daily or annually.

The wet months of the year, November through March, can be the best time of year to hike—if you do so on a sunny day. The problem with the warmer, dry months is that most of the days are foggy. (Ventana hikers, hoping for views of coast lands, will be quite frustrated; I've yet to see the ocean during the dry season.) Fog isn't too bad in April, but it increases in May and June. From July through September it's so thick that it sometimes doesn't burn off all day. When it does burn off, it's usually gone for only several hours, and then it rolls back in. I know that a few summer days are fogless, but I haven't had the luck to experience one. If you are a resident of either the San Francisco or the Monterey Bay areas, then you are perhaps used to summer fog and will feel at home. The fog begins to subside a bit in October, but it takes some really good rains to banish it for the year.

Problem Plants and Animals

In addition to planning for weather, you'll have to plan for possible encounters with certain undesirable plants and animals. The plants exist year-round, and you often can't avoid them; the animals tend to be quite seasonal, and you can take precautionary measures.

Poison oak First, virtually all the trails in Ventana Wilderness and some of the trails on state lands (particularly Andrew Molera and Pfeiffer Big Sur state parks) have poison oak along them. Fortunately, it rarely grows in dense clusters—though in several places I've had to wade through it. By being careful, you

can avoid most of it, but chances are that you'll still brush against some plants. If you are severely susceptible to it, you probably shouldn't hike at all in the wilderness, even in the winter, when most of the plant's leaves are gone, since you can still develop a rash by rubbing against its naked stems, which most hikers fail to recognize as poison oak.

Despite hiking about 600 miles through poison oak to map and research the area, I developed only a hint of rash. One reason is my body's relative immunity to the plant's chemicals, but another is that I wore long pants and changed them every day. The few extra pounds in your backpack are good insurance against several weeks of misery.

Poison oak has shiny leaves

Other brush I wasn't so lucky with another plant problem, which gave me a rash on three occasions, each rash lasting about 6 weeks. Unfortunately, I haven't identified the specific source, but the vegetation type is chaparral dominated by chamise. I suspect the culprit to be *warty-leaved ceanothus,* which has oily, aromatic, sawtoothed (arm-scratching) leaves. Chances are that you won't do as much intense bushwhacking as I did, and so I think there's only a slight chance you'll get the rash. Still, it doesn't hurt to carry a windbreaker or a long-sleeved shirt in your pack just in case you encounter a protracted overgrown stretch of trail. You needn't worry about occasional contacts with brush, at least as far as rashes are concerned.

Ticks It's through occasional contacts with brush that you are most likely to pick up ticks, which seem particularly fond of chamise—the most widespread plant in the Big Sur Country. I've also encountered these slow-moving, blood-sucking spider relatives on yerba santa (a plant that associates with chamise) and on lowly grasses and herbs. Over my extensive hiking—most of it outside the tick season—I picked up several hundred ticks, which is an intimidating amount, but an *average* of only one little beastie (about 3/16 inch long) every two miles. Ticks usually become prevalent after the first major rains, and then their numbers stay high through the rest of the rainy season. After that, their numbers dwindle, so that by July they aren't much of a problem.

A tick (lower left) always climbs *up*

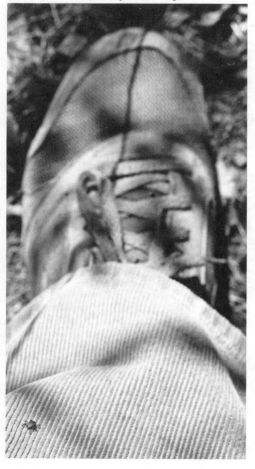

Regardless of the season, their numbers and their distribution are anything but regular. Under identical weather conditions (just after a storm, when ticks climb the wet vegetation), I hiked two similar trails, each passing through vast fields of chamise. On the first, the Lost Valley Trail, I garnered perhaps 100 ticks. Along the second, the Santa Lucia Trail, I got nary a one. But this was in 1987. I've found the Sierra Club's warnings about certain tick locales to be very inaccurate. Apparently tick populations fluctuate considerably from year to year, so one can't make specific caveats.

I've heard horror stories—none of them true—such as "ticks wait in ambush to jump out of trees onto hapless hikers." First of all, ticks can't jump, and if they could, their vision is so poor that they wouldn't even recognize you as a free meal. Still, of the hundreds of ticks that grabbed onto me as I brushed past them, the only two that were able to nibble my skin (before I removed them) were on the back of my neck. There is very little potential tick food up in trees, and long ago ticks evolved that were programmed not to climb more than about 3′ off the ground—about the height of chamise and the shoulder height of deer (a favorite target). Ticks, once they latch onto you, *always climb up* until they reach an exposed patch of skin. Because I wore long pants and had my shirt tucked in, the first patch was my neck.

Ticks take quite some time—about an hour or more—to burrow into your skin, so you don't have to get paranoid about brushing them off instantly. If you encounter ticks, check for them on you every few minutes. Where ticks are locally prevalent, I don my rain pants, which are smooth enough that ticks can't get a hold. (Had I discovered this early in my explorations, I would have picked up far fewer ticks.) Even out of the rainy, tick season, you ought to check for these brown burrowers about every half hour. The ones in Ventana Wilderness don't carry disease now, but there are diseased ticks in nearby areas, so Ventana's tick situation could change in the future. Ticks are encountered less often in the coast lands, not because they are less numerous, but because much fewer trails have protruding brush.

Flies There are a number of fly species in the area, some of them biting flies, but these are not very numerous and they are easy to swat. However, there is one small fly, which usually doesn't bite, but it is nevertheless especially vexing. It is present year-round, but is more numerous, and certainly more active, when temperatures rise into the 70s. You may encounter some of these flies on a sunny, warm winter's day, but from April through October you're more likely to encounter *hordes*. The hotter you get and the more you perspire, the more you'll attract them. On hot summer days, when you're particularly sweaty, you may have dozens of them swarming about your eyes, ears, nose and mouth. I've inadvertently swallowed a few while hiking through their favorite habitat, oaks and madrones, which unfortunately is where you like to take shady rest stops on hot days. You can minimize contact by hiking in the cool of the morning and by washing the sweat off your face at every opportunity.

Rattlesnakes   Like most animals, these poisonous snakes are most common in the spring when their food supply—mostly rodents—is at its peak. Consequently, you stand a greater chance of meeting them in this season. They can be hidden in trailside grass, or if the day is cool, they may be on a sunny patch of trail, trying to warm up. Motionless, they blend in with the surroundings, and you'll probably be right on top of one before it moves and gives you a startle. They are not very likely to be in shady redwood groves, but everywhere else you should stay alert. Predators tend to decimate their ranks by summer, and then as temperatures drop in fall, these cold-blooded creatures become quite sluggish. During this season, they also bask on trails, trying to keep warm. By the time winter sets in, they've usually migrated to a local den where, with perhaps dozens of other rattlers, they hibernate for the winter.

Some people's fear of rattlesnakes is almost rabid. Certainly, when one buzzes you unexpectedly on the trail, your adrenalin really shoots up. Still, dogs, cats and small children get bitten by rattlesnakes, and they *usually* live. If you're an adult in good health—particularly, no heart problems—then a snakebite almost surely won't kill you. Your chances of surviving are close to 100%. There are over a dozen variables affecting your body's reaction to the bite. One of them is that in about half the snakebite cases, the rattler injects little or no venom.

A rattlesnake sunbathing on a trail

But if you feel severe, immediate pain, you've probably been envenomated. Then, the main thing to do is to keep calm. I met a man who had been bitten on two occasions (neither in California), and he survived without treatment both times. Small children have a much greater risk, and I would think twice about bringing them into Ventana Wilderness. If you do bring along children, make sure an adult leads your group and "takes the heat." Rattlesnakes are pit vipers, a family of snakes having heat-sensitive pits, one on each side of the head. If you hike in shorts and tennis shoes, your exposed, likely warm calves make perfect targets for the heat-seeking snake. If you wear long pants, these make the target area—below the knee—more diffuse. They can only strike about one third of their 2–3' body length. Also, pants *may* partly deflect a rattler's strike, and hence result in less envenomation. High boots provide better protection.

Other animals   *Mosquitoes* are present in the wetter areas, particularly during spring, but they are rarely present in such numbers as to be a real nuisance. While they can transmit diseases, the chance of one doing so while it is sucking your blood is astronomically small.

Yellowjackets build nests under logs or in the ground, including trails. Despite hiking all this area's trails, I didn't get stung, perhaps because I almost always wore long pants. These wasps can be a minor nuisance at certain campsites. They go out of their way to sting you only if you disturb their nest. The nest colonies swell to large populations in late summer, so if you are allergic to bee stings, be particularly cautious at this time of year.

Rodents, skunks and bats may be rabid or carry the plague, but as with mosquitoes the chance of being bitten by a diseased mammal is astronomically small.

Finally, *Giardia lamblia* is a microorganism that in the 1980s became established in the Big Sur River, and it could get established elsewhere due to contaminated humans defecating near water. In the '80s, I drank from many water sources, ranging from slimy seeps to the Big Sur River, and not once got sick, but you may not be as lucky. If you drink *untreated* contaminated water, it will take a week or two for you to develop the characteristic symptoms of giardiasis (jee-ar-dye-a-sis): diarrhea, gas, loss of appetite, abdominal cramps and bloating. This gastrointestinal disease rarely causes death; still, you should call a doctor. If indeed you do have giardiasis and you suspect you got it from this area, tell the Forest Service.

What to Carry

If you've done a lot of backpacking, you'll know what to carry. However, I think I ought to mention two items—clothes and tents.

Clothes   You can rightly conclude from the previous section that I advocate wearing long pants. Still, most hikers seem to prefer shorts. They do have their advantages, which you must weigh against the aforementioned liabilities. Mainly, you'll stay cooler and less sweaty in warm weather. Also, if you're a strong hiker and cover 15+ miles a day, you'll get far less chafing. 'Then too, there can be a time when you feel a sudden attack of diarrhea—usually due to overexertion—and then getting shorts down and off your boots is far more easier than getting long pants off. Finally, if you're going to make a lot of tricky boulderhops, such as along the Carmel River in spring, shorts are a definite advantage. You can jump farther, and if you slip, you probably won't get wet above the knees—the maximum depth of typical crossings. With pants, you have to roll them above the knees or face the consequences. On my backpacks, I bring both pants and shorts. I also bring two pairs of shoes: boots for hiking, and lightweight shoes for walking about camp or making short day hikes from camp.

Bring an assortment of clothes to suit the temperature. In early morning you may need a hooded sweatshirt or a windbreaker, a shirt and a T shirt, but two hours later you may strip down to just the T shirt. Also consider bringing along raingear, even in the dry season. Rain pants, donned over shorts, provide good protection from brush and ticks, and a poncho will double as a groundcloth for your tent.

Tents   Too often hikers leave tents at home in the dry season, particularly in summer, when rainfall is very unlikely. While the main purpose of a tent is to keep you dry, in Ventana Wilderness a tent serves a more important purpose: it allows you to get a good night's sleep. Conditions here are quite different from in the High Sierra, for all kinds of creepy, crawly creatures come out at night. If you don't mind

A tarantula on the Carmel River Trail

squirrels, mice, toads, salamanders, tarantulas or scorpions skirting about you, or even getting into your sleeping bag, leave your tent at home. Most camps are located among oaks, whose acorns mature in autumn. Then there's another reason to use a tent, for the acorns drop all night long. It's amazing how many acorns an oak has! It can drop one or more a minute, and it's disconcerting to have them dropping all about you, if not directly on your head.

Wilderness Ethic

The following information is based largely on the Forest Service's rules and recommendations.

Group size   The largest your group can be is 25 individuals. Before you start, leave an itinerary with someone, particularly if you are traveling alone (not recommended!) so that rescue groups know where to look if you're past due.

Traveling   Pack and saddle stock have the right-of-way; hikers must move off the trail.

Stay on the trail unless it's impossible to do so, such as when a fallen tree blocks the route. Also, avoid the strong temptation to cut switchbacks, since this can lead to serious erosion problems and to risk of injury. Switchbacks can be very time-consuming to construct or repair. A trail crew could spend a day rebuilding one, or the same day clearing several miles of brush along a trail. Since volunteer labor is in short supply, obviously the latter task is a better use of their time.

If you smoke, please stop in an area clear of vegetation. Be sure the ashes are out before you leave that area. Don't travel and smoke at the same time.

Silence   Enjoy the blend of wildland silence and natural sounds. Keep trail and camp talk down so you don't disturb other wilderness visitors or spook wildlife you might otherwise see along the way.

Campsites   At most of the dozens of camps, you'll probably be the only party present, and even at the most popular ones, there are usually sites available. Therefore, use an existing site in the camp rather than brush out a new one, which would have further impact on the environment.

Campfires   In 1977 most of Ventana Wilderness and part of the adjoining lands were devastated by the lightning-initiated Marble-Cone fire. This burned for 21 days, destroying vegetation on about 280 square miles of land.

In 1985 two more lightning-initiated fires torched 104 square miles. More commonly, however, fires are started by careless campers, and an unwatched campfire could cause another conflagration. Fires are permitted only in fire rings or stoves at official camps. During the dry season, from about May to October or November, a permit (and a shovel) is required for a fire. As fire danger increases, fire use may be restricted to backpack stoves only, and in critical times all fires may be banned. For a permit, east-side users should contact the Forest Service district office in King City (phone: (408) 385-5434), while west-side users should get one from the Big Sur Station (phone: (408) 667-2423), about ½ mile south of the entrance to Pfeiffer Big Sur State Park.

When fire use is authorized, please observe the following measures to protect the wilderness' resources.

Use only dead, downed wood. Never break branches from a standing tree, even if the tree is dead. Use as little wood as necessary; bonfires are out of place.

Extinguish your campfire at least ½ hour before you start to break camp. First let it die down, then pour water over the wood and ashes and spread soil over that. Mix soil, water and ashes until the fire is positively out. Never just bury a fire with soil, for it can still smoulder for hours and then possibly escape. Before you leave camp, double check the ground within 50′ of the fire to detect any sparks or embers that may have escaped.

Sanitation Keep soap and detergent out of streams. You and others need that water for cooking and drinking. Long ago I discovered I could get along fine without soap. However, if you're prone to poison-oak rashes, you may want to bring along some medicated soap. If so, bathe with water from a pot; don't lather up in a stream. Also wash dishes and clothes in a pot, and then dispose of the wastewater on rocky soil at least 100′ from stream or spring.

If a pit toilet isn't handy, dig a hole—about 8–10″ wide by 6–8″ deep—at least 100′ away from any source of water.

Do not bury trash, since some animals will dig it up. Rather, burn it in campsite stoves or fire rings. You must pack out unburnable materials, such as cans, bottles and foil, so think twice about what you plan to carry in.

Before leaving camp, clean it up and scout the area to be sure you leave nothing behind.

Also try to pack out any trash left by inconsiderate campers. Make the site look as if no one had been there.

Pack Stock and Horses These can severely damage soil and vegetation if not properly cared for. Bring in a good supply of ration pellets. Forage is scarce in most areas, and stock need to eat as well as you do. Avoid tying animals to trees, since they paw up roots and strip bark, which can kill the tree. Picketing is a good method for managing stock.

Maintaining the Trails

Particularly in Ventana Wilderness, trails can use a helping hand. There are two things you can do. The simplest—and what I routinely do, even while mapping—is to kick or brush aside boulders, branches and other debris on the trail. This takes a minimal effort. In a few places where the trail is vague, you can also scruff out a bit of tread with your boot to make the route more visible. And if a backcountry camp is messy, take a few minutes to clean it up.

The second thing requires more of a commitment: do volunteer trail work. Since the 1977 Marble-Cone fire, virtually all of Ventana's trail maintenance has been performed by volunteers. If you can spend a day, a weekend, or longer working on trails, contact the Ventana Wilderness Mounted Assistance Group. Since the leadership in this organization can change, contact the Forest Service district office in King City (phone: (408) 385-5434) for the person to call. The group is an association of horse owners dedicated to maintaining Ventana's trails. However, you needn't be an equestrian to work with these volunteers. If you plan to spend a few days working in the wilderness, they'll pack you in and carry you out. If you'd rather work just a day or so, going in on foot, contact the group anyway, since they know what trails need the most work and what tools are required.

Having done volunteer work for several years in the Sierra Nevada, I can say that you get a splendid feeling of accomplishment after every day's work. Also, by doing work, you come to realize just how much effort is required, and you take on a deeper appreciation of trails.

Chapter 2: Natural History

Geology

Along a few routes—the Church Creek Trail in particular—the rocks leap up at you and you can't fail to marvel at the geology. But over most of the area the rocks are masked, hidden by forest or chaparral. Naturally, this cover has frustrated geologists trying to decipher the area's faults and rock units. From the visitor's standpoint, the 1977 Marble-Cone fire, which burned most of the wilderness, was a disaster. But from the geologist's standpoint, it was a golden opportunity, for it temporarily eliminated the nearly impenetrable brush, thereby facilitating field work. Then, one year after the fire, the Forest Service commissioned aerial photographs, which greatly aided geologists' efforts. From their efforts I've compiled the following geologic story, one that is likely to change as more details are known.

About several hundred million years ago, river-borne sediments from a mountain range in what is now Mexico were being deposited to the west, along the coast. In time, these sediments solidified to become layers of sandstone, siltstone and limestone. Much later, one large piece of the earth's crust underrode much of what is now Mexico, compressing and folding these sediments. The compression also created high temperatures and pressures, which changed the sediments into the schist, gneiss, granofels and marble rocks that we see today. Collectively, these metamorphosed sediments are called metasediments. These are now the oldest rocks in the Santa Lucia Range, and they make up a sizable portion of it. One metasediment, marble, is metamorphosed limestone, and it is readily identified as a white-to-gray rock with a sugary texture. While not too common, it has nevertheless produced some dramatic landforms. Just west of Ventana Wilderness stands a particularly large hunk of marble, Pico Blanco. However, most of the range's metasedimentary rocks are gneiss and granofels, which can closely resemble the much younger granitic rock that occupies a sizable part of the range.

About 100 million years ago, a large piece of the earth's crust (known as a plate) dove under the west coast of Mexico. With increasing depth and pressure, the plate began to melt, and the molten material incorporated overlying, continental rocks, changing its composition. In time, perhaps over millions of years, this molten material gradually solidified as various kinds of granitic rock several miles beneath the Mexican landscape. Such rocks also pervade today's Sierra Nevada landscape, and are commonly called granite. (In that range and in our Santa Lucia Range few are true granites. There are many kinds of granitic rocks, granite being only one of them, and in both ranges the commonest type of granitic rock is granodiorite.)

By about 65 million years ago, at the demise of the dinosaurs and the start of the most recent geologic era, the metasediments and granites started a ride on a northward-drifting plate, the Salinian block, reaching the current location after perhaps 1500 miles of travel. The ride is by no means over, for the plate is only midway to the Pacific's major "garbage dump," Alaska, which the plate will ram and then become attached to—the fate of many earlier plates.

While this northward drifting is of little consequence to us, it definitely helped determine the distribution of plant species found in the Santa Lucia Range today.

From about the time the Salinian block began to drift north and up to a few million years ago, the Santa Lucia Range was anything but a mountain range. In its place was a basin that was receiving sediments—mostly sand, but also silt and boulders. In time, these became, respectively, sandstone, siltstone and conglomerate. Conglomerate is the least common, although at Point Lobos it is the dominant sedimentary rock, and it has eroded into dramatic outcrops.

A conglomerate cliff at Point Lobos State Reserve

The Salinian block today is more than its name would suggest: the area drained by the Salinas River and its tributaries. This is roughly its southern half. The block is bounded on the east by the San Andreas fault, on the west by another major fault, and on the south by the Transverse Ranges. The northern half of the block lies mostly offshore, and is poorly

known. However, the two major faults bounding the block appear to join just off the southern Mendocino coastline. From about 29 million years ago until about 4 or 5 million years ago, the Salinian block migrated smoothly northward, but then, apparently due to a clockwise rotation of the Pacific Ocean's crust, the block was jostled up. In our area, the Big Sur Country, the response was faulting and uplift: the Santa Lucia Range was born.

The faulting, still active today, is part vertical movement and part horizontal movement. The horizontal movement specifically is right-lateral, which means that as you look across the fault, features on the other side of it are shifted to the right. In California, the San Andreas fault is the best-known example of a right-lateral fault, but there are two other notable ones parallel to it. One is on the east side of the Santa Lucia Range, largely hidden beneath Salinas Valley's sediments, while the other is on the west side of the range, partly offshore and partly onshore. The most conspicuous onshore trace of this major fault is the faultline valley extending from Point Sur southeast to Big Sur. Lateral offset on the eastern fault may be about 30 miles; on the western one, about 80 miles.

Caught between these two right-lateral faults, the rising Santa Lucia Range fractured under the strain, and a series of somewhat parallel right-lateral faults developed. It was along these faults, where the rock was broken and easily eroded, that streams cut most effectively. Consequently, most of the major streams tend to parallel the coastline rather than descend directly to it. All but one of the major canyons have, like the coastline, a northwest-southeast orientation, the exception being the Willow Creek canyon. Willow Creek, flowing east, is cutting down along the only major east-west fault in Ventana Wilderness.

Pico Blanco, a massive mountain of marble, dominates the local landscape

The faults played a primary role in the evolution of the Santa Lucia's topography, and the rock types played a secondary role. Most of the highest summits are granite, which is not surprising, since this rock is usually the one that best resists weathering and erosion. Resistant types of metasedimentary rocks account for a few other high summits, notably Cone Peak. Since marble tends to erode quickly, you may be surprised to see several high, marbled summits such as Pico Blanco and Marble Peak. These exist in large part because streams aren't cutting into their flanks. Where streams do cut across massive marble deposits, deep, steep-sided canyons result, such as the Little Sur canyon just south of Pico Blanco and the three canyons of the Limekiln Creek drainage, below Cone Peak.

Most of the sedimentary rocks laid down atop the metasedimentary and granitic rocks were eroded away as the Santa Lucia Range was being uplifted. However, they have not only survived in the southeastern part of our area—Arroyo Seco and Indians Road (Chapters 6 and 7)—they dominate the landscape there. These sediments aren't uniform, and neither is the topography. Where thick beds of sandstone have been tilted upward, massive cliffs have formed, the best examples seen in a formation known as The Rocks. Shale, on the other hand, is at the other end of the resistance spectrum, and where this rock is extensive, streams can excavate large hollows, such as Lost and Indian valleys.

There is no reason to expect the pattern of faulting and uplift that has been occurring over the last several million years to change in the near future. Consequently, there is no reason to conclude that the Santa Lucia Range has topped out. Just how many thousands of feet the range will rise depends on a number of future variables—and these are a speculator's can of worms. One thing can be said: the growing western ridge will intercept increasing amounts of moisture—both winter storms and summer fog—thus making the central and eastern parts of the range increasingly drier, and this will affect the distribution of today's plant species.

Botany

In 1977 most of Ventana Wilderness and part of the adjoining lands were devastated by the lightning-initiated Marble-Cone fire. This burned for 21 days, destroying vegetation on about 280 square miles of land. In 1985 two more lightning-initiated fires torched 104 square miles. Are these isolated, freak events, or are large, natural fires part of the natural scene in Big Sur Country? This is an easily answered question, since most of the dominant vegetation is adapted to fire. Indeed, some species have adapted to fire so well that they can't propagate without it. Over most of Ventana Wilderness and even on some coastal foggy lands, the dominant vegetation is composed of fire-loving shrubs and trees. Hiking across most of Ventana's landscape, particularly its eastern half, I got the impression I was hiking in southern California's Santa Monica Mountains. Indeed, Nancy Dale's plant guide to the Santa Monica Mountains (see "Selected References") proved to be the most useful plant-identification guide.

But there's also a very different kind of vegetation, which is exemplified by redwoods. Hiking beneath these august giants in the coastal canyons, I could swear I was in north-western California. Early in this project I became fascinated by this sharp dichotomy of vegetation, which was unlike anything I had seen in the Cascade, the Sierra Nevada or the southern California ranges. From north to south, the vegetation there changes gradually, adapting to increasingly hotter and drier climates. But in Ventana Wilderness and adjacent coast lands, northern and southern species, adapted to very different conditions, literally grow side by side; there is no apparent gradation between the two vegetation types. Furthermore, among the northern plants there are about eight dozen species that grow no farther south than this area; among the southern ones there are about ten dozen that grow no farther north. How did this side-by-side combination of northern and southern plants arise?

The Big Sur Country, of course, didn't start out as a barren landscape that was subsequently invaded by northern and southern plants. To be sure, there were plants, but just what they were is a question, since fossil evidence is scant. For millions of years, our area was a rather uniform lowland, one blessed with a more equable climate. Winters were warmer and summers were wetter. The climate likely was too wet for many of today's shrubs and too warm for redwoods and their shade-loving wildflowers. Given the relatively uniform landscape and climate, we can infer that there were considerably fewer species than in today's area, which has a greater number of habitats for plants to exploit.

But uplift, beginning about 5 million years ago, disrupted this situation. At first, invasion

Summer fog cools the floor of the Carmel River's canyon while neighboring slopes swelter

by outside species was likely slow, but a profound climatic change occurred about 2½ million years ago, bringing mayhem to the native vegetation: the Ice Age began. (Currently we are in an interglacial period, and it's important to realize that more often than not, particularly in the last million years, the Big Sur Country has been appreciably colder than it is at present.) With the advent of the Ice Age, the southward current along our coast turned cold, initiating the pattern of summer fog that persists today.

It was likely in the last 2½ million years that most of the plant invasions occurred. This seems obvious for redwoods and their entourage of associated plants, since the climate had become cool enough and wet enough for their survival. Also, by the start of the Ice Age, the Big Sur Country had developed respectable canyons, which provided more shade and more ground water than did gently rolling terrain. What is not immediately obvious is why, as the range rose and temperatures cooled, the landscape became mostly covered with drought-tolerant brush and oaks. One would expect a preponderance of northern plants, but in reality, the southern plants dominate both in the number of species and in the number of individual plants.

This reversal of expectations is explained by another one: surprisingly, the landscape was becoming more fire-prone. Several environmental changes were involved. First, the overall climatic regime had switched to one of winter rains and summer droughts. Species that could survive dry months were given an advantage. Second, a rain shadow developed. As the range increased in height, the coastal lands received an increasing share of precipitation, depriving Ventana's eastern lands of their fair share.

Third, with the advent of summer fog, which was great for the redwoods, came the advent of an inversion layer. Under normal conditions, air temperatures decrease steadily upward, but not when fog is present. Instead, cool, foggy marine air is trapped under warmer, drier air. You'll experience this if you climb above the fog bank on a summer's day; in just a minute's hike above it, the temperature can rise 15°. So, while coastline plants stay cool and moist, most of the vegetation in the Big Sur Country swelters in hot, dry air.

Fourth, thunderstorms became commonplace. This is because, under proper conditions, moist air that is initially forced upward will take off by itself, rising to form cumulonimbus clouds, or thunderheads, which produce thunderstorms. As the Santa Lucia Range rose, thunderstorms became more common. These storms can occur in summer, when temperatures are at a maximum and soil moisture is at a minimum. It's not surprising that Ventana's most successful species, chamise, regenerates well in dry-season fires but does poorly in wet-season fires.

Fifth, the steepening of topography accelerated erosion, which in turn prevented the development of mature soils. Instead, shallow, primitive soils formed, holding considerably less ground water.

With all the above changes, the environment became very ripe for fires and for the southern, fire-loving plant species. But there is still one more consideration. A hot summer fire induces the formation of a water-repellent layer just below the surface. Then, when the winter rains come, the water can't percolate through this layer, so it erodes the topmost layer, which, having been burned, lacks protective vegetation. Thus the soil's ability to hold water is reduced even farther. It's no wonder one sees so many fire-and-drought-adapted plants in the Big Sur Country.

Modern man has disrupted the native vegetation of geologically recent time by the introduction—usually unintentional—of alien plants. In Ventana Wilderness, there are about 170 species. Earlier, Indians must have likewise introduced alien species, but at least these were relatively similar species, not aggressive exotics from all corners of the world, and so the impact was probably much less. These collective introductions probably wrought more havoc on the native vegetation than any other act of man, although in the previous century, accessible stands of redwoods and tanbark oaks were decimated for use in the construction and tanning industries. Fortunately most of the wilderness vegetation was dense brush on steep slopes, which was unappealing to loggers, cattlemen and most homesteaders. Despite man's travesties, I can't help but feel they paled in comparison to those wreaked on the pre-uplift native vegetation by the invading northern and southern species. I believe there were many extinctions.

The Santa Lucia fir appears to be a descendant of one of the original species, for like a relict species it lacks—both geographically and genetically—any close relatives. Also like many relict species, this bristlecone fir exists precariously in small, isolated stands. The endemic species of the Monterey and Point Lobos peninsulas also appear to be leftovers from less mountainous times. Endemics such as Monterey pine, Monterey cypress and Gowen cypress appear to be headed for extinction, at least in their native habitat, for that land is disappearing. The southern part of the Salinian block—essentially, the Santa Lucia Range—is "marching" inexorably into Monterey Bay, being eroded in the process by the relentless pounding of waves.

In the Big Sur Country, the "Ice Age newcomers" appear quite entrenched, making up most of the area's vegetation. The area's plants can be catalogued into several vegetation types, and botanists have produced different lists. Since there isn't absolute agreement, I've devised my own list, which is based on species I noted along all the area's trails. My vegetation types are: chaparral, oak woodland, tanbark-oak forest, pine woodland, riparian woodland, redwood forest and coast brush. The order of these types is *approximately* 1) from the most plentiful to the least plentiful, 2) from the east side to the west side, and 3) from drought-tolerant to water-loving. The first three vegetation types are well-adapted to fire, the fourth is partly adapted, and the last three are basically not adapted. The Monterey and Point Lobos peninsulas contain additional vegetation types, but since this area is peripheral to Ventana Wilderness and its adjacent coast lands, these types won't be discussed.

Chaparral This is certainly the dominant vegetation type in the Big Sur Country, particularly in Ventana Wilderness. Hiking a several-mile stretch of the Marble Peak Trail, you'll note that chaparral stretches as far as the eye can see. The predominant species of this fire-loving vegetation type is chamise, or greasewood, which is a drab member of the Rose family that has evergreen ¼″ needle leaves. It pays to learn this species, since it is the tick's favorite. Chamise often grows in pure stands, but it also associates with woolly-leaved manzanita, big-berry manzanita, buckbrush ceanothus and warty-leaved ceanothus. If you scrape against the last species, you'll know it, since its sawtoothed leaves can cut your skin and will leave a pungent odor. In this vegetation type, there are at least 7 other species of manzanita and at least 11 of ceanothus, these and several others making up the "hard" chaparral. Pushing even 100 yards through such woody brush is a major task. There is also "soft" chaparral, represented by sages, sagebrushes, sticky monkey flowers, and yerba santas. Two species usually go unnoticed except when blooming: bush poppy, which has large, yellow flowers, and woolly blue curls, which has clusters of small, pinkish-purple flowers. Coffeeberry and toyon are tall species—almost small trees—and intermediate in stiffness. These two are also found in the next vegetation type.

Warty-leaved ceanothus has blue flowers

Oak woodland   This is a heterogeneous, perhaps artificial vegetation type. Indeed, to botanists, oaks and associated species can be divided into several types, but to the vast majority of hikers, "oak woodland" will suffice. The live oaks—the ones that keep their leaves year-round—clearly dominate over the deciduous oaks. The latter are chiefly the valley oak, which is seen along with buckeyes on the lower, interior lands, and the black oak, which more often than not is seen along the higher ridges and slopes.

Live oaks can be hard to identify. There are three main species—coast, canyon and interior—and each can exist as a tree or as a shrub. As shrubs they resemble a true live-oak shrub, the scrub oak. Oak identification is complicated further, since some species will interbreed—even a live oak with a deciduous oak. Where live oaks exist as trees, they are often accompanied by madrones, which are tree analogs of manzanitas. These smooth, orangish-tan barked trees can locally dominate, and where they do, they often have an undesirable ground cover of poison oak.

Madrones have smooth, orangish-tan bark

Tanbark-oak forest   The tanbark oak is not a true oak (Quercus), but that's not why I set it apart. I've put it in a separate category because it grows in dense stands, forming a forest. The ground in a tanbark-oak forest is almost as shady as that in a redwood forest. Indeed, both vegetation types have a common associate, the bay tree (also known as California laurel and Oregon myrtle). The tanbark-oak forest also differs from the oak woodland in that it is fly-free rather than fly-prone.

Like the preceding vegetation types, tanbark oaks respond well to fires, which can cause nightmares to trail crews—or nightmares to hikers if the trail crews haven't been through. From the bases of charred snags, new vegetation sprouts, forming, after a few years, a dense, almost impenetrable shrub. Then the myriad snags begin to fall across the trail, and they can be even more of a detriment to visitors.

There is one shrub of note that occurs in the oak woodland, the tanbark-oak forest and the redwood forest. Usually it is a minor component in each, and indeed, in pre-fire transects of the Big Sur Country, it was hardly seen. But since the major fires, it has spread like an epidemic, and it too is a species that trail crews must constantly beat back. This shrub is *Ceanothus thyrsiflorus,* which is commonly called blue brush, blue blossom or California lilac. Because these names are ambiguous and can be applied to other species of ceanothus, I've given it the very descriptive name of green-stemmed ceanothus. Unlike most of its relatives, it is a soft shrub, which is fortunate, since you'll occasionally have to push through it. Surprisingly, ticks don't seem to like it (at least I never got one while wading through it).

Pine woodland   Like the oak woodland, this is a heterogeneous and certainly artificial vegetation type. I say "woodland" instead of "forest," because nowhere is the pines' coverage extensive; indeed, *no* conifer does well in our area. I've lumped four species of pine together, even though they usually grow separately, mostly among oaks. Knobcone pine prefers the driest environments, and it associates more with chaparral than oak. This short-lived, sparsely-needled pine, which has whorls of small cones along its branches—even at their bases—is very well adapted to fire, and so it should be plentiful. Instead, its numbers are as sparse as its needles, and because it is small and drab, it is easily missed.

Coulter pine is also drab, but it can grow quite high, making it quite conspicuous. More impressive than its height are its cones, which can be the size of a football (hence the alternate name, bigcone pine). It is found among live, black and tanbark oaks, and it sometimes associates with the sugar pine, which is very stately and also has large cones. The cones are long—a foot or so—but unlike the fat Coulter-pine cones, they are relatively narrow. Given time, the sugar pines will form a dense grove and shade out associated Coulter pines. However, Coulter pines do quite well after fires, which may be the main reason the sugar pines haven't increased their territory. Sugar pines prefer fairly steep, somewhat shady slopes, and they grow near only two of our area's highest summits, Junipero Serra Peak and Cone Peak.

The Santa Lucia fir mingles with sugar pines on the upper slopes of Cone Peak, but it also grows sparsely in the wilderness in canyons as well as on high places. Another conifer with a spotty distribution that makes no sense is the incense-cedar, which can be seen high on sunny Pine Ridge and along the shady Lost Valley Creek drainage. And while I'm at it, I might mention another species that defies cataloging: Whipple's yucca, also known as Our Lord's Candle and Spanish bayonet. It grows at all elevations in our area, from the dry eastern lands west to rocky outcrops above the crashing surf.

A yucca without its towering flower stalk

The ponderosa pine, which has yellowish, platy bark and small cones, is, like the sugar pine, a stately tree. It is also the conifer that was most ravaged by the 1977 Marble-Cone fire. Before that conflagration, walking through a stand of these lofty pines was a pleasant, almost religious, experience. Like the sugar pine, it tends to grow in scattered, fairly dense stands, preferably on ridges or gently sloped ground in the 3000–4000' range. As in the Sierra Nevada, the black oak is a favored associate.

Riparian woodland Most of Ventana's camps are along streams, the location of riparian woodland. Somewhat surprisingly, the trees shading most camps aren't the water-loving streamside trees, but rather are live oaks, madrones and bays, which will grow only up to the water's edge. The true streamside trees include white alder, big-leaf maple and sycamore, the two latter species also doing well in gullies that are dry most of the year. Black cottonwood grows along the Carmel River drainage, while Fremont's cottonwood grows along the Arroyo Seco and San Antonio River drainages. Willows are close relatives of cottonwoods, and these are found along with alders. In the wilderness, the willow species are mostly of a shrub form, but along lower drainages north and east of the wilderness, they are often trees. Other shrubs include spikenard, or elk clover, blackberry and poison oak. The latter two can grow in dense masses that are impediments to streamside travel.

Redwood forest The Santa Cruz Mountains, just north of Monterey Bay, is almost awash in a sea of redwoods and Douglas-firs. However, just south of the bay in the Santa Lucia Range, neither species is major. Although coast redwood, locally dominating coastal canyons, is the range's most successful conifer, it is not very plentiful compared to oaks and chaparral, though during glacial times it may considerably expand its numbers and its range. Growing along with this conifer are the area's least successful conifer and oak, the Douglas-fir and the giant (golden) chinquapin, respectively. The redwood grows up to about 2000' elevation, while the false fir grows to about 1000' and the false oak to about 500'. The difference in success in the two ranges is due largely to the fact that summer fog engulfs most of the lower, gentler Santa Cruz Mountains.

In the Santa Lucia's coastal, foggy canyons, redwoods are joined, at least near sea level, by red alders. However, the "palo colorado's" more common companions are bays and tanbark oaks. All prefer cool, well-watered ground, the redwood in particular, which seems to have an extravagant desire for water. Streams flowing down into a redwood grove can totally dry up before they leave it.

On the forest floor, shrubs, herbs and ferns grow in profuse numbers. Here you'll see California rosebay—a rhododendron—and thimbleberry along streams, and carpets of redwood sorrel elsewhere. Splashes of springtime color are provided by redwood violet, Pacific starflower, Andrews' clintonia, tiger lily and many other species. One of the showiest is Douglas' iris, which does equally well among redwoods and tanbark oaks.

Chaparral

Mammals western pipistrelle, pallid bat, Brasilian free-tailed bat, brush rabbit, California ground squirrel, Merriam chipmunk, California pocket mouse, Santa Cruz kangaroo rat, brush mouse, desert wood rat, coyote, ringtail, badger, spotted skunk, mountain lion, bobcat, mule deer

Birds turkey vulture, golden eagle (where open enough, such as Pine Valley and Lost Valley), California quail, Anna's hummingbird, wrentit, California thrasher, blue-gray gnatcatcher, orange-crowned warbler, Lazuli bunting, rufous-sided towhee, brown towhee, rufous-crowned sparrow, golden-crowned sparrow, fox sparrow

Reptiles western fence lizard, sagebrush lizard, side-blotched lizard, western whiptail, striped racer, common kingsnake, night snake, western rattlesnake

Oak and Pine Woodlands

Mammals fringed myotis, California myotis, hairy-winged myotis, long-eared myotis, Yuma myotis, hoary bat, red bat, silvery-haired bat, big brown bat, lump-nosed bat, Audubon cottontail, western gray squirrel, California mouse, gray fox, coyote, striped skunk, wild boar (introduced from Europe)

Birds Cooper's hawk, red-tailed hawk, red-shouldered hawk, American kestrel, band-tailed pigeon, mourning dove, western screech-owl, great horned owl, northern flicker, acorn woodpecker, Lewis' woodpecker, Nuttall's woodpecker, violet-green swallow, tree swallow, scrub jay, common raven, plain titmouse, white-breasted nuthatch, western bluebird, Hutton's vireo, orange-crowned warbler, black-throated gray warbler, Townsend's warbler, black-headed grosbeak

Reptiles western fence lizard, western skink, southern alligator lizard, gopher snake, common kingsnake, western rattlesnake

Amphibians arboreal salamander, California newt, western toad

Riparian Woodland

Mammals many bats, opossum, Pacific shrew, ornate shrew, western harvest mouse, deer mouse, dusky-footed woodrat, raccoon

Birds Cooper's hawk, western screech-owl, long-eared owl, belted kingfisher, downy woodpecker, white-headed woodpecker, black phoebe, willow flycatcher, violet-green swallow, tree swallow, plain titmouse, white-breasted nuthatch, American dipper, Bewick's wren, Swainson's thrush, Bell's vireo, warbling vireo, yellow warbler, yellow-breasted chat, Wilson's warbler, northern oriole, American goldfinch, lesser goldfinch, song sparrow

Reptiles ringneck snake, sharp-tailed snake, California mountain kingsnake, common garter snake, western aquatic garter snake, western rattlesnake

Amphibians Monterey ensatina, California slender salamander, Pacific treefrog, red-legged frog, foothill yellow-legged frog

Redwood and Tanbark-Oak Forest

Mammals Trowbridge shrew, shrew-mole

Birds western screech-owl, northern pygmy-owl, spotted owl, Vaux's swift, Allen's hummingbird, hairy woodpecker, Steller's jay, chestnut-backed chickadee, pygmy nuthatch, brown creeper, winter wren, American robin, varied thrush, hermit thrush, golden-crowned kinglet, red crossbill, dark-eyed junco

Reptiles northern alligator lizard, rubber boa

Coast Brush

Mammals black-tailed hare, California ground squirrel, Botta pocket gopher, California meadow mouse, coyote, long-tailed weasel, striped skunk

Birds osprey, bushtit, wrentit, Bewick's wren, California thrasher, western meadowlark, savannah sparrow, white-crowned sparrow

Reptiles California legless lizard, racer, western terrestrial garter snake, western rattlesnake.

Ventana Wilderness, which makes up the bulk of the Big Sur Country, has one more important species: man. Directly, his impact has been negligible compared to his impact in most of the state, for the wilderness has little to offer in economic terms. Indirectly, his impact is more substantial, for he has inadvertently introduced over 100 exotic plant species into the wilderness. And by his presence, he prevents the successful re-introduction of the area's largest bird, the California condor, which was once intimately associated with central California's coastal ranges.

Redwood sorrel is very common among redwoods

Coast brush Much of the coast lands have been cleared of the native vegetation to provide pasturage for cows. However, coast brush can still be investigated, particularly at Andrew Molera State Park, where there is quite an extensive growth. There, coyote brush—a sunflower that looks nothing like a typical sunflower—is the dominant species. Other prominent species include dune buckwheat, bush lupine and California sagebrush.

Zoology

Big Sur Country's animals, like its rocks, are mostly hidden by the vegetation. Birds are singing everywhere, but except for a few bold species, they stay hidden deep among the bushes or high in the oaks and conifers. Birders who rely on song rather than sight are at a definite advantage. It is risky to make generalizations about what birds you may see or hear, since many species migrate. You're almost certain to see the dark-eyed junco during the cool, wet months, but by the start of the dry season it has usually taken off north to better feeding grounds. In contrast, the California quail stays put, not only not leaving the Big Sur Country, but more specifically, not leaving its brush. In between these two extremes are species that may be present most or all of the year, and that may be found in two or more vegetation types.

Mammals, reptiles and amphibians generally stay put, though the larger mammals—mule deer in particular—can cover a good deal of territory in search of better food or weather. Most mammals are reclusive, and there are only a few kinds you'll likely see daily. Deer are large enough and common enough that you're almost bound to see several. Western gray squirrels are very abundant among oaks,

and they noisily announce your presence, as do their competitors, the scrub jays. At dusk, bats come out, particularly above major streams, where flying insects are at their greatest concentrations. But many if not most mammals forage at night. Regardless of where you camp in the country, you're almost certain to have a night visit by mice. These and sometimes other mammals, such as noisy raccoons, will rummage about your camp, and if you're not in your tent, they'll rummage about your sleeping bag.

After the ground is moistened by a storm, certain amphibians such as the California newt and the western toad, "hit the trail." More correctly, they head for water, since the advent of rain spurs them to mate and then lay eggs in it (some salamanders begin as aquatic larvae, the equivalent of frogs' and toads' tadpoles). Streams and stream banks are the preferred habitat of most amphibians. However, the California slender salamander, which doesn't require water for reproduction, can be found in almost any nook or cranny that offers protection from the hot summer sun. You generally find them under rotting logs.

Probably the most commonly seen vertebrates are reptiles, particularly lizards, which often take trailside sunbaths. Some snakes, notably rattlers, prefer to sun directly on the trail, since they prefer level ground to steep slopes. On hot summer days, rattlesnakes seek shade, and on cold winter days they're hibernating, so they are generally seen in spring and fall, particularly in spring, when they are most numerous.

The geography of animals is a subject even more vague than the geography of plants, due to their ability to move about and to exploit a number of habitats. Many animals can be found in most of the previously mentioned vegetation types. Therefore, the list of fairly common species I've compiled should be taken with a grain of salt. Still, if you're interested in identifying animals, you should find this list useful. I've omitted birds and mammals of shoreline and marine environments, which are largely beyond the scope of the book. Also, I've combined pine woodland with oak woodland and tanbark-oak forest with redwood forest since neither the pines nor the tanbark-oaks have an assemblage of unique species. You should be aware that except for the redwood and tanbark-oak forest vegetation type, all types have small-to-moderate amounts of grass. This is another vegetation type exploited by animals, particularly rodents and their many predators.

Part 1: Ventana Wilderness

Chapter 3: Bottchers Gap

BG-1

Bottchers Gap to Turner Creek, Pine Creek, Comings Camp, Big Pines Camp and Pat Spring Camp via Skinner Ridge, Big Pines and Ventana Trails

Distances

2.1 miles to Skinner Ridge viewpoint
2.8 miles to junction with Turner Creek Trail
    0.4 mile along trail to Apple Tree Camp
    1.5 miles along trail to Turner Creek Camp
3.8 miles to Devils Peak viewpoint
3.9 miles to junction with Mt. Carmel Trail
    0.8 mile along trail to Mt. Carmel
5.1 miles to junction with Comings Camp Trail
    0.4 mile along trail to Comings Camp
5.1 miles to junction with San Clemente Trail
    1.5 miles along trail to Pine Creek Camp
6.3 miles to junction with Ventana Trail
    1.0 mile along trail to Pat Spring and Pat Spring Camp
7.2 miles to junction with trail to Big Pines Camp
    0.1 mile along trail to Big Pines Camp

Maps 4 and 5

Trailhead From the junction of Carmel Valley Road (County Road G16) in Carmel, drive 11.4 miles south along State Highway 1 to a junction with Palo Colorado Road. If you're not carefully watching for this junction, you could drive past it. It is just 0.3 mile after a more obvious junction, one with Rocky Point Road, which descends a short distance to lavish Rocky Point Restaurant, overlooking the ocean. Head up narrow, paved Palo Colorado Road, climbing, descending and winding for 7.7 miles to road's end at Bottchers Gap Campground.

Introduction Depending on your willingness to hike—mostly uphill—you can attain three progressively farther viewpoints, each a suitable goal for day hiking: Skinner Ridge, Devils Peak and Mt. Carmel. If you're more interested in backpacking, you have a choice of seven camps, though the two secluded sites along the abandoned San Clemente Trail are unofficial. If your destination is either Big Pines or Pat Spring camp, you might consider an alternate route to it—from Los Padres Dam west up the Big Pines Trail (Chapter 4's Route LP-3). Though the dam's trailhead is 1100' lower than the Bottchers Gap trailhead and the route is appreciably longer, it does have 1000' less elevation gain, round trip. Still, the steeper route east from Bottchers Gap is undeniably more scenic.

The main route and its side trails can be enjoyed year-round, except during severe winter storms and prolonged summer drought. If you're hiking from July through October, you might first check with the Bottchers Gap Campground ranger to see if there's adequate water at your planned camping destinations. Be aware that there are no reliable trailside creeks or springs, though winter and spring hikers should find a flowing creek or two along the route's first 2 miles.

Left: Big Sur River below Ventana Camp (Chapter 8's Route BS-2)

Description Your route, initially signed as the Skinner Ridge Trail, begins from the upper left (northeast) corner of the paved parking area at Bottchers Gap Campground (elev. 2080'). The route climbs north, passing above the campground's walk-in sites, and live oaks quickly give way to chaparral. Along this open stretch, we're treated to views to both the northwest and the south. Northwest, we look down Mill Creek canyon and a couple of ridges beyond it to the ocean (when it's not fog-bound). This canyon is carved along part of the Palo Colorado Fault, which you more or less followed when you drove up the Palo Colorado Road to your trailhead. This major fault separates granitic rocks, on its northeast side, from metamorphic rocks. One of the most prominent outcrops of metamorphic rock lies to the south of us, towering over fault-formed Bottchers Gap: 3709' Pico Blanco. Its Spanish name means White Peak, which is very appropriate, for its mass is a huge chunk of light-gray marble—an estimated 600 million tons worth. Fortunately, this stately landmark hasn't been quarried, even though it lies within private land.

After a half mile of moderate ascent north, most of it along an abandoned jeep road, we round a ridge and then parallel a seasonal stretch of Mill Creek upstream. Our route is now a shady, though sometimes steep, trail, and it climbs generally east, up to a ridge. On it, a jeep road briefly replaces trail, and then, one mile from the trailhead, the trail tread resumes. Over the next mile we have an interesting though viewless route, the trail winding and ducking into gullies, and perhaps throwing off our orientation. Overall, the general plan of the trail is a northeast-to-southeast arc up to Skinner Ridge. On that ridge we wade through an open field of bracken ferns, then make a steep, brief climb northwest to a **Skinner Ridge viewpoint** (3370-2.1), which is to the left, just off the trail, by a grand madrone. This viewpoint is best in winter and early spring, when you'll experience an idyllic setting of vibrant, green grassy slopes and a distant, blue glistening ocean. During the dry season, the slopes are brown and the ocean is often obscured by a fog bank.

If you want more encompassing views, you can climb to Devils Peak. Be forewarned: the slope of your route so far has averaged 11½%; the route up to Devils Peak averages 15¾%. Toward that goal you stroll along Skinner Ridge, under a cover of madrones with a smattering of black oaks. Then you leave the ridge,

entering Ventana Wilderness as you begin a 280' drop, at a 17% gradient, to a saddle. It's these sizable, often steep drops we encounter along this route that make reaching Big Pines Camp or Pat Spring Camp such a chore; one's quick glance at a topo map easily underestimates the route's considerable ups and downs. At the saddle we meet the **Turner Creek Trail** (3180-0.7), which offers two appealing campsites.

Turner Creek Trail

From the saddle this trail, closely following the Church Creek Fault, swoops northwest down into a broad-floored draw. Due to a fairly dense canopy formed by mature madrones, the understory growth is minimal except for this species' fairly common associate, poison oak. The trail's gradient quickly relaxes to gentle, and then we come beside Turner Creek's seasonal headwater stream and follow it for a few minutes down to its union with a minor creeklet on our right. Here you spy creekside **Apple Tree Camp** (2920-0.4), just to the left. Nestled under several tall California bays and white alders, the camp's two relatively small sites are worthy goals in all but the driest months of the year. Even then, a short stretch of creek may trickle past the camp while the creek bed just above and below the camp may be dry.

To really be guaranteed water in summer, you'll have to continue down to Turner Creek Camp. You cross the creek immediately below Apple Tree Camp's lower site, only to recross in 200 yards after plowing through a dense understory of blackberries, thimbleberries, cow parsnips and, especially, poison oak. Soon we cross two seasonal, granite-bouldered creeklets in rapid succession and then our gently descending path heads westward. The ground cover generally becomes denser, and can encroach on the trail, though in spring the lavish display of wildflowers should more than make up for the minor inconvenience. Without much effort we breeze into grassy lawned **Turner Creek Camp** (2790-1.1), shaded by tall white alders and a spreading walnut.

Ahead, the trail quickly leaves the creek's bank, makes an initial climb, and 0.4 mile beyond the camp reaches a saddle. Here you're likely to find a NO TRESPASSING sign, for immediately west lies a private residence—at the end of private, gated Long Ridge road. This road, beginning from a saddle (signed THE HOIST) almost 4.0 miles up Palo Colorado Road, does provide an alternate route up to Turner Creek

Turner Creek Camp

Camp, though no one in his or her right mind would hike up this dry, shadeless, overly steep route.

Still, if you have an emergency and need to exit via this route, then you ought to know that from the saddle 0.4 mile west of the camp you'll find a trail branching left. This makes a short drop, then rambles about 250 yards west to a *steeply climbing* road, which gets you, in 100 panting yards, back up to the ridge road. You'll pass at least a half dozen minor spur roads, each with private residences, on your way out. The main, ridge-hugging road is quite obvious.

Back at the Turner Creek Trail junction atop a fault-formed saddle, the main route ahead is now signed BIG PINES TRAIL, although on the U.S.F.S. *Ventana Wilderness* map it is labeled SKINNER RIDGE TRAIL. The first 100 or so yards from the saddle are indeed trail but, just after entering brush, it joins a closed road. (On your return trip, the closed road can be more obvious, and it will take you through some undesirable brush before you reach the saddle junction.) At first the steep old road climbs mostly through tick-harboring chamise, but fortunately this strenuous, shadeless stretch has a generally wide tread. One can take a number of rests on this ascent, pausing to admire the ever-expanding panorama. After a 500′ elevation gain, our route turns from north to southeast at a minor ridge flecked with yuccas. This shorter tack gives way to an even shorter one north, which yields to an extremely steep final push up to **Devils Peak viewpoint** (4130-1.0).

Looking west from this narrow, chamise-clad ridge, you gaze beyond Long Ridge, well below you, toward the blue (or fog-obscured) Pacific. Although Long Ridge is a sizable divide separating Las Piedras (Spanish: *The Stones*) Canyon from its southern neighbor, the ridge's east end—closest to you—has very humble beginnings; you may find it difficult to locate. That lowly stretch of divide is where the Church Creek Fault crosses from Las Piedras Canyon into Turner Creek canyon, passing within yards of unseen Turner Creek Camp. The fault then follows the Turner Creek Trail up to the saddle on which you recently stood, and it descends into the Skinner Creek headwaters, giving rise to a fault south down Skinner Creek. The main fault continues southeast through two gaps—the second one sizable—before descending into the unseen Pine Creek drainage. Factually, of course, the faults aren't following the creeks and gaps; rather, the reverse is true: stream canyons and gaps in ridges develop along the fault-fractured rocks.

From west to south to southeast we see a deeply dissected basin, which is drained by the Little Sur River and its tributaries. Unmistakable Pico Blanco, soaring prominently to the south-southwest, divides the main Little Sur drainage from its South Fork drainage. Off to the southeast stands Ventana Double Cone, which is composed of two summits of nearly equal height that are anything but cone-shaped. From your vantage point Ventana Double Cone appears as the highest summit along a ridge, this summit being slightly notched in the middle and having rather steep slopes. If you gaze north along the ridge, you'll notice a deep gap in it, Puerto Suelo (Spanish: *Mountain Pass*). This gap, at the southwest (right) base of hulking Uncle Sam Mountain, is the result of the aforementioned Church Creek Fault, which continues 14 miles southeast to the east-west trending Willow Creek Fault.

If you're day hiking and looking for summit views, you might as well take in close-by Mt. Carmel. Head east on your nearly level trail to a close-by junction (4130-0.1) with the **Mt. Carmel Trail.**

Mt. Carmel Trail

This trail, branching left, immediately gives rise to a spur trail, right, which climbs 60 yards east to the true summit of Devils Peak. Enshrouded with black oaks, the summit is viewless, but this shady site makes a fine picnic spot on a hot summer's day. Folks have camped here, but with water nowhere near it, this is a less than desirable campsite.

The northbound Mt. Carmel Trail drops slightly to a ridge saddle, then hugs the ridge as it pursues its namesake. The vegetation is chiefly a dense stand of scrub oaks, with some manzanita and warty-leaved ceanothus adding variety. The oaks and brush crowd in and over the trail, but really aren't a problem for hikers. Equestrians, however, will likely be stopped unless a trail crew has recently cleared the brush. The oaks, being low, dense trees, totally hide the view, so that when you do reach flat-topped **Mt. Carmel** (4417-0.8), the 360° panorama instantly pops into view. Were it not for the fortuitous existence of a granitic outcrop, your view would be poor indeed; you'd have to bring a stepladder. Actually, some folks did something like this—they brought in and erected a section of telephone pole. Standing on the topmost spike of the leaning pole, you're only 3' higher than you are on the outcrop, which in no way enhances your views of distant features, but surprisingly does help quite a bit for closer ones.

Mt. Carmel's unique viewpoint

You've been introduced to some of the closer features seen from the Devils Peak viewpoint, which lies due south. An imaginary line due north touches the easternmost shore of Monterey Bay at Moss Landing, which is about 28½ miles distant. Off to the east, with a true bearing of 85°, is broad-topped, 4465' Palo Escrito (Spanish: *Tree with Carvings*) Peak, some 16½ miles away. This peak is the climax of the Sierra de Salinas (Spanish: *Salt Marsh Mountains*), an eastern component of the Santa Lucia Range that rises abruptly from the west side of unseen Salinas Valley. With these compass bearings established, you can identify other, mostly cultural features. Salinas, the largest city you see, is in the north-northeast, about 21 miles away. It is named for the nearby salt marshes at the mouth of the Salinas River, from which the Spanish commercially extracted salt. Carmel Valley Village, only 7¼ miles away, also lies along this line of sight, but is hidden, as are the lower parts of most of the canyons we see. The most distant city you're likely to see, given excellent visibility, is Santa Cruz, along the north shore of Monterey Bay. It is a hefty 43 miles away, on a north-northwest bearing. Just left of it and appreciably closer is the tip of the Monterey Peninsula, which is a mere 19 miles away. Viewing Carmel Bay, along the peninsula's south side, you can identify Pebble Beach and Carmel.

In former times a trail ran west-northwest from Mt. Carmel along the brushy ridge to Twin Peaks, which lies just beyond the forest boundary. You won't find a trace of the trail today. The ridge west from Twin Peaks separates Garrapata Creek Canyon from its smaller southern counterpart, Palo Colorado Canyon. The Spaniards named them well. Brushy *Garrapata* Creek Canyon has its ticks; *Palo Colorado* Canyon has its red sticks (redwoods).

From the Mt. Carmel Trail junction our main route, the Big Pines Trail, heads southeast, first crossing grassy, view-blessed slopes at the start of a major, 500' descent. Initially the descent across slopes and along a ridge is easy, but then the ridge drops, and the trail is forced to do likewise. Fortunately, at the steepest part the trail swings just east of the actual ridge, and we're treated to a shady, switchbacking descent to a minor saddle. From it we make a short climb to round a 3682' summit, pass through an even smaller saddle, and then have a leisurely descent, hiking through a grove of mature madrones shortly before we make a quick drop to a saddle. Here we meet the southbound **Comings Camp Trail** and the northbound **San Clemente Trail** (3500-1.2). The first is easily the more popular route, while the second, being essentially abandoned, offers a great deal of solitude. Both routes are parts of an old road that once provided access to Comings Camp.

Comings Camp Trail

If you like groves of madrones, you'll appreciate this trail and its main campsite. The shady trail makes a steep initial drop, traverses southeast across a gentle slope, reaches a minor gully, plunges south along it, and then turns east to level off at shady **Comings Camp** (3150-0.4), which is large enough to hold a Scout troop. A smaller, more open site lies about 130 yards down the trail, by a black oak at the edge of a willowy meadow. During the rainy months you may find water here. At other times, follow a faint trail 35 yards along the meadow's west side to a pipe spring.

San Clemente Trail

This route, which years ago ran several miles north to San Clemente Ridge, is now an abandoned road, and you may find a number of downed trees across it to clamber over or crawl under. Nevertheless, it is relatively easy to follow. The road north goes from fairly steep to very steep and, when not maintained, is heavily littered with leaves. The madrone leaves in particular are a problem on the steepest parts; you have to tread cautiously or risk a slip. Your steep descent ends just as you approach the headwaters of Pine Creek (2960-0.5). You now

head down-canyon and in about 100 yards cross seasonal Pine Creek. This crossing is ill-defined, so if you go about 200 yards and don't find it, cross anyway; you'll quickly find the old road just above the east bank. About 300 yards downstream you make your second crossing, one with a small camp beneath a black oak. If the creek's flowing you may not want to go farther.

Onward, you hike past bays, madrones, black oaks and an occasional ponderosa pine. Your feet skirt poison oak, blackberries, bracken ferns and occasional chain ferns. You'll pass a giant ponderosa pine, with a 5' wide trunk, along the west bank, between crossings six and seven. After crossing number eight, go about 300 yards, passing through dense ground cover immediately before reaching easily missed **Pine Creek Camp** (2590-1.0). A large tree fell across the site, obliterating most of this small camp. Still, there is room to pitch a tent.

If you plan to continue onward, you'll immediately cross and recross Pine Creek, then in 200 yards recross it again. From here the abandoned road rapidly dissolves away as it curves from northeast to north. At this curve, on a west-bank flat, is a small campsite ringed with poison oak. Immediately beyond it the creek briefly turns northwest, entering a small, picturesque gorge. Your route downstream is now definitely cross-country.

A large, spreading live oak east of the Comings Camp Trail junction

Beyond the saddle with trails to Comings Camp and Pine Creek Camp, the Big Pines Trail climbs rather steeply east up to a ridge, climbs gently to a south spur bearing a giant black oak, and then descends moderately northeast to a saddle with a northward view. You pass a large, spreading live oak as you start a climb east, then encounter ponderosa pines as you gain 240' while climbing around the open, grassy southern flank of a 4052' ridge summit. This gain yields to a 200' loss as you descend a moderately steep, though shady and switchbacking route, to a saddle. Unfortunately, steep lower slopes make the climb necessary, though it does offer you fine views, Pico Blanco as usual catching your attention. On the saddle is a conspicuous junction (3620-1.2), from which the **Ventana Trail** starts southeast along the long saddle. This is easily the more popular route, but the remainder of Big Pines Trail will be described first.

This trail leaves the ridge, executing a series of small switchbacks and dropping east into a bracken field before entering brushy ground on gentle slopes. Without recent trail maintenance, the route can be a bit obscure, but it goes about 90 yards through the brush to the headwaters of Danish Creek and follows it about 50 yards downstream before crossing it (3440-0.3). This vicinity used to be the site of Spaghetti Camp, but since the creek is reliable only during the wet season, it's probably all for the best that the camp is gone. The trail tread east from Danish Creek is quite obvious and is mostly an easy, rambling traverse with a final short descent to a trail junction (3370-0.4). From it a 0.5-mile-long lateral trail first descends 250 yards southwest to often-flowing Danish Creek before climbing up to the Ventana Trail.

The Big Pines Trail heads northeast, descending a minor ridge on a 220-yard course over to a junction (3350-0.2) with a **trail to Big Pines Camp.** (To continue east along the Big Pines Trail, follow—all in reverse—first Chapter 4's Route LP-3, then LP-2, and finally the first part of LP-1.) Here, beside a 2' broad stump, you start a rather steep descent, reaching a pleasant, one-tent site in 120 yards. However, the more pleasing, *real* **Big Pines Camp** (3290-0.1), with room for two tents, lies 70 yards below it, just above a short stretch of Danish Creek that is usually flowing even during summer and early fall. If not, then you'll have to head up the lateral trail to Pat Spring and hope for the best, or else backtrack several

miles and descend the Pine Creek Trail—not desirable.

Ventana Trail

Back at the long saddle the Ventana Trail runs about 180 yards southeast along a gently climbing ridge before veering left onto richly forested slopes. Madrones and tanbark oaks dominate over scattered ponderosa pines; then at the end of our traverse, live oaks become more common. Immediately before reaching the seasonal south branch of Danish Creek (3560-0.7), we meet the lateral trail from the Big Pines environs.

Upstream, we step across the south branch in 35 yards then, after 210 yards along it, reach a spacious camp under a large madrone. Another camp, not quite as desirable, lies just out of sight atop the flat saddle immediately northeast of the first camp. From November through May you can often get water from the adjacent creeklet, the south branch. If it's dry, you'll have to get water from nearby Pat Spring. Climb moderately southeast 270 yards up to a prominent saddle, then 80 yards beyond it to **Pat Spring.** If you're interested in **Pat Spring Camp** (3740-0.3), head 80 yards west from the saddle. This spacious camp, beneath a cover of live oaks, would be first-rate were it not located on sloping ground. The two lower, previously mentioned sites, being flat, will probably give you a better night's sleep. But Pat Spring Camp is closer to reliable water— Pat Spring. (**Two notes:** First, there is only one spring, contrary to all maps and signs; it seemingly flows out of granite bedrock on a dry slope dotted with yuccas. Did Moses pass by here? Second, the trail east from it is not the Ventana Trail, but rather a misleading spur to nowhere. More folks seem to erroneously follow it than the Ventana Trail, which climbs northeast from the Pat Spring saddle.)

Pat Spring

BG-2

Bottchers Gap to Little Pines Camp, Puerto Suelo, Lone Pine Camp, Hiding Camp and Ventana Double Cone via Skinner Ridge, Big Pines and Ventana Trails

Distances
 9.2 miles to Little Pines Camp
 11.0 miles to Puerto Suelo (saddle) and junction with Puerto Suelo Way
  2.6 miles along trail to Hiding Camp
 12.4 miles to Lone Pine Camp
 14.7 miles to Ventana Double Cone

Maps 4, 5 and 9

Trailhead Same as the Route BG-1 trailhead

Introduction The farther you travel from a trailhead, the fewer people you see, so 4853' Ventana Double Cone is one of the loneliest summits in Ventana Wilderness. It is also the highest peak within the wilderness that you can reach by trail. After the 1977 Marble-Cone fire, the 3.7 miles of trail from Puerto Suelo south to Ventana Double Cone became very overgrown, but fortunately in 1987 some volunteers cleared away most of the brush and fallen snags. Still, bring along a long-sleeved shirt or jacket just in case the brush has grown back some. You don't want to get scratched up by the sawtooth-leaved warty-leaved ceanothus, a common shrub here that proliferates after fires.

East of Pat Spring the route is waterless, though during and just after rains two or three creeklets may flow down the flanks of Uncle Sam Mountain. Also, from about November through May there is usually a flowing spring about 270 yards down Puerto Suelo Way, which begins from a saddle called Puerto Suelo. Though folks have camped here, most people bound for Ventana Double Cone would be wise to make it as a day hike from Pat Spring Camp, which amounts to about a 15-mile round trip. Leave early in the morning if you're doing this day hike in summer.

In my opinion the best time to hike this route is in March or April. During these months rainfall is not very likely, yet some seasonal streams may provide water. Also, the flowering vegetation is at its zenith. This includes both wildflowers and grasses, which can be vexing to those with allergy problems, but it also includes the two species of aromatic ceanothus that pervade the route. During these months, the ceanothus cloaks the slopes in a blanket of blue blossoms.

Description The previous route describes the first 7.3 miles of trail to the saddle near Pat Spring (elev. 3740'). The well-trod spur trail east to a water trough at solitary Pat Spring appears to be the correct route, but it isn't. Many a sorry hiker (including me, while mapping it) has continued eastward beyond the spring, only to find the trail's tread steadily dwindling into obscurity. So be sure you take the less obvious trail from the saddle, the one that climbs moderately northeast. At first you climb through a mature forest, but with elevation you meet increasing numbers of snags—the slopes below you were razed by the 1977 Marble-Cone fire. After ½ mile of climbing with a substantial 650' elevation gain, you top out on a ridge and have a revealing view north and east of a charred ghost forest that inhabits the slopes below you.

With no major climbing until Puerto Suelo, one can enjoy views southwest across the Little Sur drainage, which has Pico Blanco as its prime focal point. After ¼ mile of traversing, just past a cluster of ponderosa pines, our trail begins a generally descending route southeast to a saddle (3940-1.4). Ahead, we tackle a short, moderate, 120' gain, first past live oaks and then through brush, to breach a gap in a northeast outlier of 4189' Little Pines summit. Easy hiking follows, first a traverse through an open woodland of pine, oak, madrone and brush, then a drop briefly to a dry hollow that is the site of **Little Pines Camp** (3960-0.5). Before the Marble-Cone fire, this dry camp was probably an acceptable site, for one could work downslope, at least in the wet months, to find water. Unless a trail is cleared downslope, the brush below the flat, moderately large camp remains impenetrable, a quest for water inconceivable.

Onward, we crest a nearby low, broad divide, make a brief, gentle descent past snags and brush to a main-ridge saddle, and then, after a momentary ascent, find ourselves starting a long, gradual descent across the western flanks of Uncle Sam Mountain. The vegetation varies from grass to brush to trees (largely live oaks), and along this usually gentle-to-moderate descent we have ample opportunities to enjoy the views. Early on your descent you'll note Ventana Double Cone and an unnamed 4653' peak capping the horizon. Ventana Double Cone, your goal, is the left, slightly higher peak. After about ⅓ mile of descent, you pass an ephemeral creeklet, in another ⅓ mile pass a pair of similar creeklets, then in a final ⅓ mile pass one more. Expect water in one or more of them only from about December through March.

Beyond the last creeklet, you contour and then descend to **Puerto Suelo** (3530-1.8), the only deep cleft in your south-trending ridge. *Puerto Suelo* is Spanish for "a deeply cleft mountain saddle," which indeed this saddle is. It is eroding along the Church Creek Fault, which crosses the ridge at this point. On oak-and-madrone-shaded Puerto Suelo, there's enough level space for several people to make a dry camp. For water, one can head 270 yards down a fault-line trail, Puerto Suelo Way, to a seeping spring, which *usually* flows from November through May. If it's dry and you're out of water, you then face a 1400' drop, 1.6 miles long, down the trail to a crossing of reliable Uncle Sam Creek. Bring enough water!

The 2.6-mile route from Carmel River's **Hiding Camp** up to Puerto Suelo is described near the end of Chapter 4's Route LP-1 and will not be repeated here. Rather than climb Ventana Double Cone, you can descend this trail, follow the Carmel River 7.4 miles downstream, and then climb 7.1 miles up the Big Pines Trail to Big Pines Camp. Then, the total length of your semiloop route out of Bottchers Gap is about 35½ miles—36½ miles if you also revisit Pat Spring Camp.

The trail to Ventana Double Cone first climbs moderately 0.2 mile past snags to a switchback. Beyond it you have several inspiring views, both east and west, before you finally pass a 4366' ridge summit and cross its southeast ridge (4300-1.1). You then parallel the main ridge down to a saddle, which is near **Lone Pine Camp** (3990-0.3). The fire basically obliterated the camp, which is now overgrown, so folks occasionally attempt to camp on the tiny saddle, which will cosily accommodate two persons. From the saddle the spur trail starts southeast down a shallow gully, then quickly veers right, away from it. About 200 yards from the saddle, the trail passes just above the charred remains of what

was once one of the most majestic ponderosa pines in the wilderness. Momentarily you'll reach a gully, which you can descend about 300 yards cross-country to water—in *wet* season only!

Beyond the Lone Pine Camp saddle the trail crosses a broad stretch of ridge, then in 0.4 mile starts a serious climb. If you've had brush problems so far, these now diminish considerably, and from a quickly reached switchback you have an enticing view south toward Ventana Double Cone. Next, you make a moderate climb ¼ mile east to another switchback, this one with a fine view of the Carmel River watershed. Another climbing, ¼-mile segment, this one south, guides us up to a minor plateau. Ahead, fire damage is minimal. We now pass mature live oaks, madrones and a few Coulter pines. These pines have needles grouped in threes, like those of the ponderosas we saw earlier on our route, but the Coulter's cones are the size of footballs, hence the alternate name, bigcone pine.

With only a mile to go, we resume our climb south up to a dry, narrow, granitic ridgecrest, along which ceanothus and scrub oak return as our trailside companions. We quickly leave the crest, then momentarily touch it at a minor cleft, through which we have a view east. Several minutes later we touch the north toe of Ventana Double Cone's north summit and have a real botanical treat—our first Santa Lucia fir. Also known as the bristlecone fir, this species occurs naturally *only* in Monterey County's Santa Lucia Range.

A gentle-to-moderate, scenic climb along east-facing slopes leads us to the saddle separating the two summits, and we're atop the southern one in about two minutes. Atop **Ventana Double Cone** (4853-2.3) you'll find remnants of the foundation of a fire-lookout station plus a makeshift emergency bivouac shelter (basically, a windbreak). Since trailside views have been so plentiful along your climb, your summit views pull no surprises. Nevertheless, being able to scan the northern half of Ventana Wilderness in one fell swoop is quite exhilarating.

The highest peaks lie to the southeast. A ridge from your summit extends in that direction, connecting you to 4727' Ventana Cone, a mere 2 miles away. This peak barely scratches the horizon. From it, another ridge continues east-southeast, connecting that peak to 4965' South Ventana Cone, another 2½ miles away. This peak stands left of and just above Ventana

Summit view west toward Pico Blanco (center) and the fog-enshrouded coast

Cone's summit. The highest peak to be seen—indeed, the highest peak in California's central Coast Ranges—is just right of Ventana Cone, standing conspicuously higher than any other summit—5862' Junipero Serra Peak, a healthy 19½ miles away. But Cone Peak, surmounting a long ridge to the right of Junipero Serra, is even more distant—20¾ miles. What's so interesting about Cone Peak is something you can't see—it lies very close to the ocean. From the ocean the land rises to the peak's 5155' summit in only 3.2 miles—a 30½% gradient, which is steeper than the High Sierra's mighty eastern escarpment that towers over Owens Valley. And the Santa Lucia is still a youthful, rising range—something to think about.

BG-3

Bottchers Gap to Little Sur Camp, Pico Blanco Boy Scout Camp, Jackson Camp, Pico Blanco Camp, Launtz Creek Camp, Vado Camp, Manuel Peak and Big Sur via Pico Blanco BSA Road, Little Sur Trail and Mt. Manuel Trail

Distances

1.8 miles to junction with Little Sur Camp Trail

    0.8 mile along trail to Little Sur Camp

3.6 miles to footbridge across Little Sur River in Pico Blanco Boy Scout Camp

3.9 miles to junction with eastbound Little Sur Trail

    1.2 miles along trail to Jackson Camp

5.3 miles to junction with Mt. Manuel Trail

    1.2 miles along trail to junction with trail to Pico Blanco Camp

    0.1 mile along trail to Pico Blanco Camp

6.9 miles to Launtz Creek Camp

7.8 miles to junction with trail to Vado Camp

    70 yards along trail to Vado Camp

12.7 miles to Manuel Peak's viewpoint, summit 3379

17.5 miles to junction with Oak Grove Trail

18.1 miles to Pfeiffer Big Sur trailhead

Maps   3, 4, 8 and 12

Trailhead   Same as the BG-1 trailhead

Introduction   This route visits four camps that are located among redwoods. If you like shady sites, these may be for you. A fifth, Pico Blanco Camp, is my favorite, in part because it is sunny, but mostly because it is along the lip of a redwood-forested gorge that contains a large swimming hole and an attendant, splashing fall. Since the pool's temperature ranges from the low 40s to high 50s, depending on time of year, you won't want to take an extended swim. From about mid-June through mid-August, all sites may receive moderate-to-heavy use, when children and adults are hiking out of Pico Blanco Boy Scout Camp. Hence, to better your chances at finding an available campsite, try another time of year (except for "spring break," when college students may be hiking in the area).

All camps should be accessible year-round, except during major storms. Problems with poison oak, ticks, etc. should be minimal. However, if you continue beyond Vado Camp toward Pfeiffer Big Sur State Park, you'll encounter lots of brush, additional poison oak, springtime ticks and, from about June through November, very little water. The only folks who would sanely consider this southern half of the route are those who must take it in order to complete a grand loop of the wilderness, such as from Bottchers Gap south to Pfeiffer Big Sur State Park, east to Pine Valley, north to Los Padres Reservoir and west back to the gap.

Bottchers Gap Campground

Description From Bottchers Gap (elev. 2080′) start south down the obvious, gated road toward Pico Blanco Boy Scout Camp. After ⅓ mile of shady descent, we meet a minor, gated road that climbs northwest, then in ¼ mile come to our first switchback. From it we have a noteworthy view of Pico Blanco, a prodigious peak of marble that lords it over the often fogbound Little Sur River canyon. Next we head north, enter a redwood forest, hairpin south and then reach another switchback. At its east side you'll find the start of the **Little Sur Camp Trail** (1230-1.8).

Little Sur Camp Trail

This essentially viewless trail starts south along a ridge shaded by live oaks and Douglas-firs. Poison oak locally adorns the trailside. The moderate-to-steep trail switchbacks eastward down into a shadier forest, then descends west at an easier grade before debouching at **Little Sur Camp** (670-0.8). The camp is fairly small, having only two somewhat cramped sites. Considering how close the camp is to the trailhead and to Pico Blanco Boy Scout Camp, the sites could be full when you arrive at them, so don't visit the sites during spring vacation or the summer months.

In summer 1987, when I mapped the trail to the camp, I was serenaded along the route by roosters up at the Scout Camp's ranger station—hardly a call of the wilderness. You can get a better wilderness experience by heading cross-country ½ mile or so down the Little Sur River and looking for campsites where the canyon floor widens. Beyond, the canyon constricts, and here you leave the National Forest. Don't continue downstream, first, because it's dangerous to do so, and second, because it's posted private property.

Past the switchback with the start of the Little Sur Camp Trail, we descend northward back into the redwood forest, switchback and cross a fault-line creek, and then traverse in and out of several gullies over to the Scout Camp's ranger station (1100-0.9). Ahead, our closed road on private land descends to the northern confines of Pico Blanco Boy Scout Camp, which is operated by the Monterey Bay Area Council B.S.A. The road gently roller-coasters south past the camp's structures and spur roads, and then, just before it plunges across the Little Sur River, you'll reach a **footbridge across the river to Pico Blanco Boy Scout Camp** proper (820-0.9). Just upstream from the bridge you'll meet a hairpin turn in a road. The left branch of the road parallels the river upstream, quickly crossing it. You take the right branch, which climbs a bit up to a nearby large structure, the central kitchen. Just a minute or two past it, your road makes a hairpin turn right and then snakes westward, climbing steeply for 160 yards to a junction with the **eastbound Little Sur Trail** (1080-0.3).

Little Sur Trail to Jackson Camp

This trail branches left from the road, makes a mildly fluctuating traverse south-southeast to a usually flowing creeklet (1120-0.7), and from it soon starts a fairly steady descent to a bench above the canyon floor. Here you leave the B.S.A. land, enter Ventana Wilderness, and make a short, steep drop north to adjacent **Jackson Camp** (930-0.5), along the south bank of the Little Sur River. A use trail from Pico Blanco Boy Scout Camp ascends along the river to this camp, so for most of the summer you may have visitors. If so, continue cross-country upriver until you find peace of mind.

Onward, you could follow the steep road a bit, but it's much better to take a right-branching trail, the Little Sur Trail, which climbs south. Initially it switchbacks up to the steep road, but then diverges from it and climbs, steeply at times, up an amorphous, viewless route past tanbark oaks, madrones and other trees that fester with flies on warm days. You're likely to lose your sense of orientation as you strive for the top, and the grossly inaccurate contours on the map don't help matters either (lacking topographic controls, I've mapped for best fit). Your fairly exhausting climb ends at a minor crest point (elev. 2194'), where among live oak and poison oak you have a pleasant view east up the Little Sur drainage. Next, in two minutes you meander along the crest to a junction with the **Mt. Manuel Trail** (2090-1.4). This trail starts along the crest toward Launtz Creek and Vado camps, but first I'll describe a continuation of the Little Sur Trail to Pico Blanco Camp.

Little Sur Trail to Pico Blanco Camp

This branches right, and descends all too steeply—at about a 20% gradient—to a usually dry crossing of a redwood-lined creeklet (1780-0.3) just beyond ramshackle Byles Camp, on private land. At times the camp has had spring water, but none was present when I hiked past it in the dry summer of '87. Beyond the camp's shacks the Little Sur Trail soon curves west through chaparral, but this is quickly replaced mostly with grass as our trail starts a traverse

south across the lower slopes of Pico Blanco. Its grassy, almost desertlike slopes are due to the peak's composition—marble. Rainfall tends to sink into the marble monolith rather than remain in the overlying soil.

We climb to a sloping bench, coming quite close to a conspicuous private road, which traverses the peak's slopes just above us. Next we descend south to three short switchback legs, then turn southwest. By the turn the trail is quite exposed, and a fall would likely be fatal, so watch your footing. Across safer ground we make a rubbly descent ¼ mile southwest to a junction (1385-0.9) with a **trail to Pico Blanco Camp.** The camp actually has three separate, official sites, and we pass the first in about a minute. From it the trail splits, and you can take either fork across a grassy slope to a site in **Pico Blanco Camp** proper (1300-0.1). Both sites are located along a forested brink of a minor gorge, and from the down-canyon site a footpath descends up-canyon. It is quickly joined by a steep footpath from the other site, and after a minute's walk, you drop (or fall, if you're not careful) to a swimming hole in a grotto at the base of a waterfall. The pool is certainly wide and deep enough for swimming, but with temperatures warming to the high 50s *at best,* your swim will be a short one. This redwood-shaded grotto, along the South Fork Little Sur River, is unquestionably one of the most beautiful spots in the wilderness.

To continue west on the Little Sur Trail, see Route BG-4, which describes the trail in an eastward direction.

Launtz Creek and Vado camps pale in comparison to Pico Blanco Camp's ambience, but both are located in creekside, redwood settings. Bound for either, start along the crest on the Mt. Manuel Trail. After a brief climb up to a minor high point, you quickly leave the crest and then have several views southwest down the South Fork canyon, which is framed by Pico Blanco and a northern outlier of Post Summit. Beyond these, live oaks give way to green-stemmed ceanothus and then to chamise as you wind in and out of minor gullies on a well-graded descent to a major, north-trending gully. This you descend briefly south past stately redwoods to **Launtz Creek Camp** (1910-1.6), along the north bank of its namesake creek. The very shady camp is small, holding at best three tents in cramped, gently sloping sites. But the water flows year-round, which is more than can be said of Vado Camp.

Launtz Creek Camp

If you're bound for that camp, you'll make an easy crossing of Launtz Creek, ascend for a minute up-canyon, then switchback southwest for a fairly short climb. After a few minutes you level off on slopes of the South Fork canyon and soon make a well-graded descent to its floor. Here you cross the South Fork Little Sur River. In the next ¼ mile you make two more crossings and then continue 130 yards up-canyon to a switchback, where there's a junction (1780-0.9) with a **trail to Vado Camp.** You immediately cross the South Fork, which can be dry in summer and fall, and follow the use trail over to a bench on the south side of an east-climbing gully. There lies **Vado Camp** (elev. 1800′), complete with table and stove, and just a bit more spacious than Launtz Creek Camp. I prefer it to Launtz Creek Camp, though when the South Fork is dry, heading a couple of minutes downstream to get water can be a nuisance.

Most folks won't want to continue farther and, judging from the trail's condition ahead, few do. If you're one of those diehard souls bound for Pfeiffer Big Sur State Park, you'll first make a switchbacking ascent west and then head south for a well-graded (though not well-maintained) ascending traverse. You duck in and out of three redwood-shaded gullies before arriving at a fourth (2280-1.6). There, by an unofficial one-tent camp, you may find water flowing down a creekbed. If not, follow your ears for a moment up the gully to a small, trickling fall. You've gone about 9½ miles from

your trailhead and have about 8½ more to go. From June through November, the stretch ahead *may be bone dry,* so carry at least one quart of water. (In the opposite direction on a hot summer day, two or three quarts may be in order.)

Onward, you continue the well-graded, poorly maintained, ascending traverse, sometimes through dense stands of green-stemmed ceanothus, sometimes past poison oak and, after ducking into a sizable gully, you soon pop into a major one. Unless the trail has been upgraded, your tread up it will appear to be little more than a deer path. From the head of the gully, at a point about 400′ below a long saddle between Post Summit and Manuel Peak (that is, Cabezo Prieto ridge), the trail angles east up the side of the gully to a quickly reached switchback (2640-0.8). From it a trail once went east to Tin House Camp, though in 1987 the trail was definitely abandoned (probably for the better).

Now you begin a series of well-graded switchbacks, these in amazingly good condition considering the low degree of trail maintenance. Views appear as you climb slopes above Cabezo Prieto (Spanish for *Dark Head*), which stretches just to the west, and as you almost top point 3554, about 1.1 miles past the start of the former spur trail, the trail becomes overgrown with brush. Staying just south of the point, you push about 100 yards east through this brush—the result of the 1977 fire—then emerge onto a narrow crest with views north and east into the wilderness and south and west to the ocean (or its fog bank).

For over a half mile, your crest trail offers you views, but then as you approach Manuel Peak proper, which is only a little higher than any other spot on the crest, you re-enter dense brush, again the result of the 1977 fire. For almost a half mile you make a viewless push past scrub oaks, manzanitas, warty ceanothus, yerba santa and occasional madrones. One hopes the brush will have been cleared before you pass by. The brush ends at the first saddle south of the peak, and from it you top a minor point, drop to a second saddle, and then make a brief climb to **Manuel Peak's** *real* **viewpoint** (3379-2.5). From it you see, on a fogless day, the California coast extending south from Point Sur. Ahead, the trail is good, well-traveled, and almost entirely downhill. This stretch down to the trailhead—a good day hike—is described in the reverse direction in Chapter 8's Route BS-1.

BG-4

Coast Road to Pico Blanco Camp via Little Sur Trail

Distances

5.9 miles to junction with trail to Pico Blanco Camp

0.1 mile along trail to Pico Blanco Camp

Maps 7 and 8

Trailhead A small turnout for several cars is located on the east side of the Coast Road about 40 yards north of a mile 6.5 sign. Signs occur at ½-mile intervals along this 10.3-mile road, starting from its north end. However, they are easily missed by those starting from the south end, which is the best way to the trailhead (shorter distance, less climb and drop, less chance in winter of road closure due to falling trees and washouts). Starting from the south end, you drive 3.8 miles, first making a long climb to a grassy ridge, then descending past brush and finally descending about ⅓ mile into forest. If you reach a major gully, you've driven about 50 yards too far.

The north end of Coast Road leaves State Highway 1 beside the north end of the Bixby Creek Bridge, 13.4 miles south of the Carmel Valley Road junction and 2.0 miles south of the Palo Colorado Road junction. The south end of Coast Road leaves Highway 1 opposite the entrance to Andrew Molera State Park, 21.6 miles south of the Carmel Valley Road junction and 4.5 miles north of the Pfeiffer Big Sur State Park entrance road.

Introduction This route provides a shorter route—one that also involves less climbing—to idyllic Pico Blanco Camp. However, there's a catch: at least in 1987, about 3.5 miles of the trail were in fairly poor condition. Along this stretch, brush often crowded along the trail, and in about a dozen or so places there were exposed (though not likely fatal) trail washouts. Unless it's greatly reworked, this is definitely a footpath—horses can't make it. With sturdy boots and long pants, you won't find the walk along this generally well-graded, well-planned trail all that bad. From oak-shaded Pico Blanco Camp, a short footpath leads down to a redwood-shaded grotto complete with waterfall and chilly swimming hole.

Description From the trailhead (elev. 290′) you drop for several minutes to the Little Sur River's South Fork, which in all times but severe storms is a docile creek. You hike through a verdant, linear oasis, one shaded by redwoods, bay trees and tanbark oaks, which sharply contrasts with the chaparral on south-facing slopes you'll be traversing all too soon. The first leg of the Little Sur Trail is across private land that has signs of campsites. The last one (315-1.0) is at the end of a 40-yard-long spur trail that branches left across a flat. We curve right, crossing a minor ridge, and soon reach the unmarked Los Padres National Forest boundary (440-0.5). We now traverse across a parcel of private land, Section 3 on the map, which lies within the national forest. After a few minutes of shady hiking, we come to a junction with a private trail, climbing right, and from it descend a moment to a well-used camp beside the South Fork (425-0.3).

We cross the creek and switchback quickly up out of the forest and onto chamise-clad slopes. Small stretches of trail ahead are washed out, and one has to be careful there. Unless the trail is revamped, these washouts will become increasingly treacherous with time. Rather than rework this chaparral stretch of trail, which is constantly being encroached upon by brush, the Forest Service should reroute it from the South Fork crossing upstream for ½ mile, from where the route should then continue upstream on Andrew Molera State Park land. Our goal, Pico Blanco Camp, lies in Ventana Wilderness just ½ mile upstream from the park's border.

But for now, you'll have to scrape past brush. Chamise is abundant, so in the rainy season, check often for ticks. I hiked it four times in summer and got nary a one. Fortunately, poison oak is minimal. You can take comfort in the brush, at least during summer, in that it supports very few flies, unlike the upcoming oak woodlands. As you progress eastward, views up and down the South Fork canyon become increasingly attractive. On many days, particularly June through October, the canyon can be foggy, but chances are that even on a foggy day you'll climb into sunshine.

Your first stretch of chaparral ends with entry into a small grove of redwoods, harboring a seeping spring, from which you go but

45 yards to a switchback in a private, well-maintained road (760-0.4). In the next ⅔ mile the trail first parallels the climbing leg of the road, ducks in and out of two shady gullies, and then reaches a switchback. Now you face your only major climb, unless you plan to continue up-canyon all the way to the Mt. Manuel Trail junction, 1¼ miles beyond the junction with the trail to Pico Blanco Camp. You first climb north, then switchback, and midway along the southeast-trending leg enter Ventana Wilderness. After rubbing shoulders with chaparral slopes and perhaps resting your heels in shady retreats, you reach a strategically located grassy ridge (1580-2.2), which has fine views to the west, south and east. The change in vegetation—to pervasive grasses and scattered yuccas—is due to your arrival on the lower flank of Pico Blanco, which is the largest mass of high-quality marble in the central Coast Ranges. Fortunately, this marble's remote location keeps it from being quarried. Because water tends to sink into the marble, rather than run off, the mountain has an "ecological desert" despite rainfall upward of 60 inches per year.

You now make an ascending traverse across a broad, grassy bowl, top out on an oak-clad ridge (1840-0.4), descend mostly grassy slopes, and then duck into a shady gully with a trail junction (1630-0.5). From it a horse trail, constructed in 1987, climbs up the gully and out of it to the end of a nearby spur road, which in turn leads up to the main road you've undoubtedly noticed many times along your trek.

Our Little Sur Trail crosses the gully and two others, then makes a traversing descent across a grassy slope to reach oak shade and, a minute later, a junction (1385-0.6) with a **trail to Pico Blanco Camp.** The camp actually has three separate, official sites, and we pass the first in about a minute. From it the trail splits, and you can take either fork across a grassy slope to a site in **Pico Blanco Camp** proper (1300-0.1). Both sites are located along a forested brink of a minor gorge, and from the down-canyon site a footpath descends up-

Waterfall and pool near Pico Blanco Camp

canyon. It is quickly joined by a steep footpath from the other site, and after a minute's walk, you drop (or fall, if you're not careful) to a swimming hole in a grotto at the base of a waterfall. The pool is certainly wide enough and deep enough for swimming, but with temperatures warming to the high 50s at best, your swim will be a short one. This redwood-shaded grotto, along South Fork Little Sur River, is unquestionably one of the most beautiful spots in the wilderness.

You probably won't want to continue up-canyon beyond Pico Blanco Camp, since all the desirable destinations there are better reached by starting from Bottchers Gap. See the preceding route description for the continuation of the Little Sur Trail and for the northern part of the Mt. Manuel Trail.

Chapter 4: Los Padres Dam

LP-1

Los Padres Dam to Bluff, Carmel River, Sulphur Springs, Buckskin Flat, Hiding and Round Rock Camps via Carmel River Trail

Distances
1.5 miles to junction with horse trail
1.8 miles to junction with Big Pines Trail
4.1 miles to Bluff Camp
4.8 miles to junction with Miller Canyon Trail
4.9 miles to Carmel River Camp
5.8 miles to Sulphur Springs Camp
7.4 miles to Buckskin Flat Camp
9.2 miles to Hiding Camp and junction with Puerto Suelo Way
    2.6 miles along trail to Puerto Suelo and junction with Ventana Trail
        3.7 miles along trail to Ventana Double Cone
0.4 mile up Carmel River to waterfall
9.6 miles to junction with Round Rock Camp Trail
    0.6 mile along trail to Round Rock Camp

Maps 6, 10 and 9

Trailhead In Salinas, leave U.S. Highway 101 at the signed MONTEREY PENINSULA exit. Drive south on South Sanborn Road, which curves west and becomes East Blanco Road. About 2.4 miles from 101, you reach State Highway 68. Turn left and follow it 8.5 miles to Laureles Grade Road (County Road G20). This junction appears suddenly, and if you miss it, you'll reach Laguna Seca Recreation Area in ⅓ mile. On steep, curvy Laureles Grade—a heavily used, paved road—you climb and descend in 5.9 miles to a junction with Carmel Valley Road (County Road G16).

If you don't like steep, curvy roads (my car always protested the grade), you can avoid Laureles Grade Road by continuing west on 68 to Monterey (or by driving south on State Highway 1 to this city). On Highway 1, you then drive 5.2 miles to Carmel, and take Carmel Valley Road 9.5 miles east to the Roads G16/G20 junction.

Eastbound on G16, you reach the heart of Carmel Valley Village in about 2.2 miles. This is your last real opportunity for gas, meals and supplies. Continue another 4.3 miles to a junction with the north end of Cachagua Road. Take this narrow, paved, sometimes steep road 5.9 miles, first over Tularcitos Ridge and then up the Cachagua Creek valley to a junction with Nason Road. If you continue 0.6 mile on Cachagua Road, you'll reach a pack station that has a small store and "cafe" (mainly beer), and a campground. On Nason Road you drive but 0.6 mile up to a large parking area immediately before a gate across the road. Along this short road, you'll pass Prince's Camp, a trailer park that also serves beer.

If you're driving from the central Salinas Valley or from southern California, your most direct route to the trailhead is to leave U.S. Highway 101 in Greenfield, and take Elm Avenue (County Road G16) 5.8 miles southwest to Arroyo Seco Road (County Road G17). (See Chapter 6's Route AS-2 for details.) The two roads coincide for the next 6.5 miles, then split. You keep right, on G16, which is now Carmel Valley Road. After 17.0 miles you reach the south end of Cachagua

Road. Turn left, and take it 1.3 miles to a junction with Tassajara Road (the route for Chapter 5's trailheads), then 4.5 miles farther to Nason Road.

Introduction Most of this popular route is along the bottomlands of the Carmel River canyon. Such a route location has its advantages and disadvantages, depending largely on the season. If you go all the way to Hiding Camp or Round Rock Camp, you'll have to cross the Carmel River 26 times!

From May through October, when the canyon's bottomlands can get into the 80s (or even the 90s), the numerous crossings will offer abundant chances for a drink of water plus a few chances for splashing about in some cool pools. During this prime period, the river is usually low enough that you can boulder-hop most or all of the crossings. The only drawback, besides possible crowds on weekends, is flies, which will swarm about your face if you're sweaty.

From November through March the river is higher, and you'll likely have to make a number of wet fords through numbing water. You'll certainly want to avoid this route during stormy weather, for then some of the fords are deep enough and the river swift enough to sweep you off your feet. In fact, your very first ford can be up to 5' deep, and an attempt to cross the river there would be suicidal. This ford is immediately past Bluff Camp, 4.1 miles into the route, which is as far as you can safely go in stormy weather. During the storm season, check the weather first if you plan to hike up this river canyon. The last major storms usually come in mid- or late March, and April brings a transition to summer conditions. Days can warm to the 70s and 80s, and most crossings are boulderhops, though you may have to search both up- and downstream to find a series of boulders that save you from a wet ford. In early spring the canyon is verdant with new growth. Flowers abound and the grasses stay green through April or May, then the colors begin to fade. However, with the demise of grasses comes the demise of ticks, which can be a problem during the wet season. Fortunately, this trail is usually kept in good condition, so the tick problem isn't a major one. Another problem is poison oak, but the plants, while present, aren't all that numerous.

Description Since the road is blocked by a locked gate (elev. 980'), we use an adjacent gate, put there for the benefit of hikers, equestrians and fishermen (nonmotorized rafts—*not air mattresses or boats*—are allowed on the reservoir). We start southwest, passing through an open grove of valley oaks. These lose their leaves in winter, and then the stark branches are conspicuously clothed with a droopy, wispy, gray-green lichen, known appropriately as old man's beard. The road soon turns southeast for a short climb across steep granitic slopes, and live oaks put in an appearance.

They will be the dominant vegetation you'll see along your hike, and the granite will certainly be the dominant rock. The road soon starts a short but moderate descent, and along it you're likely to find a half-barrel fed by spring water. For those coming out of the wilderness, especially along the dry Big Pines Trail, this barrel of water could be extremely tempting. However, don't forget that horses, dogs, deer and other animals also drink from it. Perhaps it's best to pass it up for the 0.4-mile trek to your vehicle, then a short drive to Prince's Camp for a thirst-quencher.

Ahead, the road turns southwest, crossing a broad river terrace, and we ignore roads branching first left, then right. We cross the dam's spillway, walk briefly northwest along the dam, continue in that direction up to a crossing of a steep-walled gully, and then turn south. Over ⅓ mile we climb and then descend into a second prominent gully, and then in 150 yards reach a steep, narrow road, which today is largely used as a **horse trail** (1090-1.5). Those bound for Danish Creek Camp (Route LP-2), won't save any distance by taking this road, but those bound for Big Pines Camp or beyond (Route LP-3), will save 0.7 mile. Also, to its advantage this 1.2-mile horse trail to the Big Pines Trail has a spring-fed water trough 0.8 mile up it, and the trail is relatively free of poison oak and tick-laden shrubs and grasses. To its disadvantage, the horse trail has an average gradient of 17.3%, versus 14.7% for the Big Pines Trail. While that difference may not seem like much, in reality it's quite noticeable, for most hikers labor when the gradient exceeds 15%.

From the horse-trail junction, we immediately bend to the right to drop into and climb out of a smaller gully. After a minute or two's walk across gentle slopes, we meet a road, branching left, which gives rise to three shore-access roads before looping back to ours. Because this reservoir is a source of domestic drinking water, *no swimming* is permitted. On our road we walk but a minute or two farther, to a road fork, where we veer right onto a road that quickly narrows to become the Carmel River Trail. On trail tread we make an easy climb about 120 yards to the start of the **Big Pines Trail** (1170-0.3). Those bound for Danish Creek (Route LP-2) or Big Pines/Pat Spring (Route LP-3) branch right here.

Onward, we quickly emerge from live-oak cover for a brushy traverse high above the south half of Los Padres Reservoir, passing a *de facto* trail down to it along our way. Near the south end of the reservoir, we descend a bit, then switchback down to a crossing of Danish Creek (1050-1.0) immediately west of where it meets the bank of the reservoir. California-American Water Company, which owns the dam, reservoir and adjacent lands, forbids camping by this perennial creek. In some future year, the dam may be raised, and the trail then will cross higher up. In wet months Danish Creek can be a wet ford. A minute past it we jump cross a smaller perennial creek that has a minor waterfall.

Next we contour, staying low in the Carmel River canyon, first heading southeast across shady slopes with oaks, buckeyes, maples and sycamores, then south across open ones with chamise, sage and manzanita (some chance of ticks here). Below, we view oak-shaded riverside flats—tempting, but still on private land.

Next, from a broad, maple-shaded gully with a seasonal creek, we make a short, moderate climb east to a low point on a minor ridge, from which we have a fine view up-canyon. Southward, we begin a short descent, crossing some precariously steep slopes before reaching a junction. The older route plunges straight ahead, while the recommended newer one (branching left) jogs a few paces west before descending to meet the older one in **Bluff Camp** (1150-1.3). This is the only legal camp on the private land we've been hiking across—and soon will leave. The main campsite is on a shady, spacious bench immediately before our first Carmel River crossing. One of this site's pluses is an adjacent, waist-deep Carmel River "lap pool." Crossing the river during summer and fall is usually done by boulder hopping just downriver, unless a fortuitous log is available. In winter and early spring you can expect a wet ford, perhaps knee-to-thigh deep. During or just after a rainstorm, a crossing could be a waist-to-head deep ford across a rampaging river, which would likely be suicidal. Bear this in mind if there's a chance of bad weather.

From the opposite bank we climb past two more of Bluff Camp's sites—one on each side of the trail—then climb moderately up brushy slopes to a minor ridge, where we enter Ventana

The Carmel River Trail (left) high above Los Padres Reservoir

A pool by Bluff Camp

Wilderness (1430-0.3). Then we make a mirror-image descent, entering shady confines just before we meet the **Miller Canyon Trail** (1220-0.4), this junction being the end of Chapter 5's Route CC-1. Heading up this trail, whose lower half is quite scenic, you'd reach China Camp in 10.2 miles.

From the junction we must cross the adjacent Miller Fork Carmel River, which can be a problem in the wet months. If necessary, try boulder-hopping the creek on large, granitic boulders immediately upstream, which sure beats a wet ford. Ahead, our trail enters the confines of **Carmel River Camp** (1220-0.1), with two small northern sites and a mid-size south site, which is under spreading live oaks just above a "lap pool." These sites are separated from the main site by the trail's rapid

double crossing of the Carmel River. However, for most of the year, you don't have to cross. Rather, staying only a foot or so above the river, traverse along the base of a bedrock cliff. It's easier than it looks, unless you've got a heavy pack. You'll end your traverse in the main site of Carmel River Camp, complete with table and stove.

Not far south of the main camp you make a third crossing, then quickly bend west, only to make two more crossings before reaching **Sulphur Springs Camp** (1350-0.9). This is the smallest and least attractive of the official camps, having room for only two tents. The camp derives its name from one or more nearby springs that are rich in hydrogen sulfide, which give them a rotten-egg smell. One easily found spring emanates from the base of a large,

A Bluff Camp site just above a Carmel River ford

mossy boulder that sits between trail and river some 90 yards east of the camp. Your nose will help you locate it.

Westward, you soon cross a permanent creek that originates on the east slope of Elephant Mountain, then you curve south and in a few minutes make your sixth crossing since the Miller Canyon Trail. Ahead, you generally bear southwest, hugging the riverbank. About 130 yards beyond the seventh crossing, you meet a small, pleasant campsite (1430-0.6), shaded by maples and sycamores. Upriver, you face more crossings, and will have counted off a full dozen since the Miller Canyon Trail before you enter spreading **Buckskin Flat Camp** (1580-1.0). Note that the first site you come to is merely a northern outlier of the larger, main site.

Leaving the grassy-floored flat, we pass among poison oaks and blackberries (a frequent combination), and among some chain ferns, which are easily the largest kind of fern growing in the wilderness. We then encounter our first tanbark oaks as we make a brief climb to a shallow notch in a granitic ridge, around which the Carmel River is forced to meander. From the ridge we quickly descend, then have a leisurely ⅓-mile stroll before encountering the first of our second set of a dozen Carmel River crossings. These boulderhops or fords (depending on the season) are closer spaced than the preceding set, the distance from first to last being just under one mile.

Between crossings four and five, you'll spot the river canyon's first ponderosa pines. Then, as you head southwest from crossing 10 to 11, you'll view the mouth of a major side canyon, which I call Uncle Sam Creek canyon, after the major peak above it. This northwest-trending canyon is the surface expression of a part of the Church Creek Fault, which is one of the wilderness' largest. This fault begins at the east-west Willow Creek canyon, runs northwest up lower Tassajara Creek, then up Church Creek, down Pine Valley and part of Hiding Canyon, up Uncle Sam Creek canyon, and beyond it many miles to Kaslar Point, where it continues offshore.

The short stretch between crossings 11 and 12 sees us around a resistant granitic knob, which on both U.S.G.S. and U.S.F.S. maps is inaccurately shown to be the site of Hiding Camp. Actually, the camp lies 0.2 mile southeast upstream, and when the river is high, you're likely to get your feet wet along this water-level stretch of trail. From where the trail abruptly begins to climb away from the bank,

Hiding Camp

look across the river—**Hiding Camp** (1740-1.8) lies on the long, narrow terrace above the opposite bank. Reaching the camp requires another crossing, the 26th since the trailhead. About 100 yards long, this pleasant, misnamed camp (it's not in Hiding Canyon) is a wonderful spot to just loll about, and it makes an ideal base camp for two side trips: up Puerto Suelo Way to Ventana Double Cone and up the Carmel River to a waterfall.

Puerto Suelo Way to Ventana Double Cone

Ventana Double Cone, which is one of the prime summits in the wilderness, is usually reached from the Bottchers Gap trailhead (Chapter 3's Routes BG-1 and BG-2). That trailhead is at an elevation of 2080', versus 980' for ours, and the trail's length is 14.7 miles, versus 15.5 via Puerto Suelo Way. But in actuality, both routes are equally difficult. What advantage the Bottchers Gap route has with its significantly higher trailhead, it totally loses in the approximately 2000' of elevation loss along various downhill stretches between Skinner Ridge and Puerto Suelo saddle. And for the most part, the Bottchers Gap route is *very dry*. Thus, it has an advantage over your Carmel River route only in the wet months, when the river crossings are bound to be a problem, or only if you like lots of crest views.

With that said, look for the start of Puerto Suelo Way at the *downstream* end of Hiding Camp. With an average gradient of 13%—a bit on the steep side—the trail begins by climbing about 80 yards west up a minor gully and crossing its usually reliable stream. It then winds in and out of usually dry gullies before switchbacking up a brushy slope to a saddle (2110-0.5) on a resistant ridge that guards the mouth of Uncle Sam Creek canyon. Onward, we traverse past shady bay trees and tanbark oaks before reaching a channel of Uncle Sam Creek. This we cross and quickly recross, then soon cross the main channel (2160-0.5). This is your last reliable water. Over the next 0.9 mile, the trail is often densely lined with green-stemmed ceanothus, which can be a problem if the trail hasn't been maintained for a number of years. Then, from where you can glimpse southeast down-canyon, your ascent switches from mostly moderate to fairly steep. The last 0.3 mile is up short, steep switchbacks, which you'll want to avoid on a hot summer afternoon. Just 270 yards from the top is the upper of two closely spaced springs, both *usually* reliable from about November through May. Then, take a well-deserved rest when you arrive at an oak-and-madrone-shaded saddle, **Puerto Suelo** (3530-1.6). Ahead, follow the brushy, though highly scenic, final 3.7 miles of Chapter 3's Route BG-2 south up to **Ventana Double Cone**.

Ventana Mesa Creek Fall

You can start along either side of the Carmel River, but invariably you'll have to make at least one crossing, if not several. In all times except when the river is at its lowest, you're likely to get your feet wet. Just beyond Hiding Camp's limits you pass southeast through a small but impressive sandstone-walled gorge, then the river canyon widens and soon turns south. You enter a second gorge and soon arrive at the confluence of Ventana Mesa Creek with the Carmel River. As you'll see, farther progress up the river would be very difficult indeed. A few yards from the confluence the

Ventana Mesa Creek Fall

creek plunges into an oversized "spa," which is a suitable goal in itself. However, 70 yards above it is a pool large enough for swimming, complete with its own **waterfall** (1880-0.4). During winter and early spring the creek may be too full for you to reach the pool. But then, the water would be too cold for a dip. Even in summer it is usually brisk.

To conclude the main route—up to Round Creek Camp—take the trail, which climbs moderately southeast up to the **Round Rock Camp Trail** (2030-0.4). Chapter 5's Route CC-2, originating at China Camp, heads west through Pine Valley and down Hiding Canyon to this spot. From the junction you have a good view of the river gorge below you, but to see Ventana Mesa Creek Fall, which was mentioned above, you'll have to walk a few steps toward the gorge.

Onward, you go straight ahead, gaining just several feet in elevation as you skirt the brink of a sandstone cliff. You then drop fairly steeply 250 yards to the Carmel River, which here is more of a creek than a river. Immediately downstream from the crossing the river starts a cascading chorus down through a scenic, steep-to-overhanging-walled gorge.

Once across the river, which is usually an easy task, you're on a small flat with an inviting, medium-size campsite. Rather than head 160 yards southeast up to the river's junction with Hiding Canyon creek, the trail starts from the camp's west side, climbs first up and then across slopes of green-stemmed ceanothus, descends south to a minor creek, and shortly reaches the Carmel River. This you cross at a gigantic boulder—perhaps Round Rock—by whose base the river has excavated a pleasant swimming hole. In about 80 yards your route ends on a spacious, partly shaded river terrace, which is large enough to hold a dozen backpacker tents. Perhaps because of its open, grassy meadow, this site, **Round Rock Camp** (1910-0.6), is popular with equestrians. At the south side of the camp is an even larger boulder, which is moss-covered and is perhaps too angular to be the official Round Rock.

From May through October, when the trail up the Carmel River is so inviting, one wishes it would continue an additional 2.9 miles upriver to the pool of upper Pine Fall (see Route CC-2). Currently, this stretch is rugged cross-country, for the Carmel River Trail leaves its namesake for a drier, fault-line route up Hiding Canyon to Pine Valley.

LP-2

Los Padres Dam to Danish Creek and Environs via Big Pines Trail and Alternate Routes

Distances
3.7 miles to Danish Creek Camp via Big Pines Trail and Danish Creek Trail
3.7 miles to Danish Creek Camp via east-side road (horse trail) and Danish Creek Trail
3.7 miles to Danish Creek Camp via east-side road and west-side road (both horse trails)
4.4 miles to Danish Creek Camp via Big Pines Trail and west-side road (horse trail)

Maps 6 and 5

Trailhead Same as the Route LP-1 trailhead

Introduction The most easily reached camp from the Los Padres Dam trailhead is Danish Creek Camp, which is 0.4 mile closer to the trailhead than is the Carmel River Trail's Bluff Camp. Danish Creek Camp is also larger—broad enough to hold a troop of Scouts. Furthermore, the camp can be enjoyed every month of the year, for the creek flows even in the driest summer months and the camp, located at the base of south-facing slopes, gets a fair amount of winter sun.

On the negative side, the Big Pines Trail up to a ridge has quite a bit of poison oak along it, while the Danish Creek Trail down to the camp has a dense growth of chamise along it, these shrubs often being laden with ticks, especially during the wet months. Then, you may have to pick off 100 or more of these slow-moving blood suckers. You can avoid most of the ticks in two ways: 1) wear either a poncho or rain pants, since ticks slide right off them, or 2) take the east-side and west-side roads, which have minimal tick and poison-oak problems. You'll note from the above distances that three out of four possible routes to the camp are the same length.

Equestrians should definitely take the roads, since the tread of the lower Big Pines Trail is easily damaged by horses' hooves, and the horses have no protection from the 100–200 ticks they're likely to glean along the Danish Creek Trail.

Description See the first three paragraphs of the previous route description (LP-1) for directions to the start of the **horse trail** (1090-1.5). If you're on horseback, take this route. If you're on foot, you'll probably find it too steep, even with just a daypack. Instead, follow the fourth paragraph of the previous route description to the start of the **Big Pines Trail** (1170-0.3). The trail's tread and sign are usually obvious, but if you miss them, you'll immediately traverse a small, steeply dropping gully. The trail's route up to a secondary ridge was well thought out, though at an average gradient of 14.7% some backpackers will find it on the steep side.

As you ascend the well-graded, switch-backing course, you may see examples of where horses have obliterated the often-narrow tread. Poison oak commonly grows along the trail's side, but it is a real problem only along the last 160 yards before you reach a chamise-cloaked ridge (1920-1.0). With the bulk of the climbing behind you, now make a moderate ascent up the brushy ridge to a junction (2050-

0.2) with the **Danish Creek Trail,** which is immediately before and below a minor summit (BM 2058 on the map).

Ahead, an old trail tops the summit, while the correct, sometimes obscured route of the Big Pines Trail angles right, through some bushes, winding from saddle to ridge saddle before reaching the alternate horse route in ⅓ mile. Those who've ascended the east-side road (horse trail) to the ridge have a choice of descending ⅓ mile to our junction or ascending 220 yards up to a junction with the steeply dropping (22.5%!) west-side road (horse trail). You can descend it, and from its terminus about 30 yards downstream from a cabin, continue 0.3 mile downstream to Danish Creek Camp.

On foot we begin west on the Danish Creek Trail, starting on a gentle descent that gives way to a moderately steep one after we round a ridge. We pass through chamise, switchback, and head south down a gully with a usually dry waterfall, then curve west into a second gully. This we steeply descend, soon pass above a usually dry bed of a cascading creeklet, then cross a minor ridge. In about 2 minutes from it we're at **Danish Creek Camp** (1430-0.7). Most of the tent sites are out in the open, which is particularly desirable during the cold winter months of short days. Beneath a fairly large live oak, whose trunk is slowly growing over a granitic boulder, you're likely to find a table and a cooking grate.

This spot serves as a base camp for further exploration. From the camp's west end, one can follow a lightly used trail upstream. In about 300 yards, where you turn north and are forced by bedrock to cross and immediately recross the stream, you'll meet the lower end of Rattlesnake Creek. I didn't check out a cross-country route up it, but such a route can't be any worse than the abandoned trail to the creek.

To reach that trail, one continues up Danish Creek about 230 yards to a junction with the lower end of the west-side road. In 30 yards you reach a cabin—on private land—and then cross Danish Creek to enter a spacious, half-moon meadow. Head about 100 yards west across it to a minor ridge, up which you'll see pieces of metal, nailed to tree trunks, marking the very steep ascent route up the ridge. From the top of the minor ridge you climb south steeply up the main ridge. The unmaintained route quickly becomes brushy, and I didn't pursue it any farther.

One can also follow an unmaintained trail up Danish Creek. It goes about 0.3 mile, passing the mouth of a prominent side canyon before you cross Danish Creek. Over the next 0.4 mile you make four more crossings, and then, just within Section 18, the trail becomes quite brushy, and I mapped it no farther.

A last possibility, which I didn't explore, is a cross-country romp from Danish Creek Camp downstream to the Carmel River Trail, which crosses the creek near the south tip of Los Padres Reservoir. Such a hike could be quite demanding physically and mentally, with brush and other obstacles to circumvent.

A fairly large live oak offers shade at Danish Creek Camp

LP-3

Los Padres Dam to Big Pines Camp and Pat Spring Camp via Big Pines Trail

Distances

    3.0 miles to junction with Danish Creek Trail

    5.0 miles to wilderness boundary

    8.8 miles to junction with trail to Big Pines Camp

        0.1 mile along trail to Big Pines Camp

    8.9 miles to junction with trail to Pat Spring and Pat Spring Camp

        0.5 mile along trail to junction with Ventana Trail

            0.3 mile along trail to Pat Spring and Pat Spring Camp

    9.1 miles to junction with start of Ventana Trail

Maps 6, 5 and 4

Trailhead Same as the Route LP-1 trailhead

Introduction This route, which is mostly on the westbound Big Pines Trail, is a longer way in to Big Pines and Pat Spring camps than is the route east from Bottchers Gap (Chapter 3's Route BG-1). That route also starts 1100' higher, making it look even more attractive. However, the round-trip Bottchers Gap route gives you about 1000' of extra climbing to do, thanks to its vaulting of Skinner Ridge and Devils Peak and its descent to the two camps. The Big Pines Trail certainly has an easier gradient, which is something all backpackers will appreciate. The Bottchers Gap route is taxing even for day hikers.

    The Big Pines Trail is one of the few wilderness trails that can be enjoyed year round—with some reservations. During the wet months, ticks can be locally abundant. During the dry months, flies abound, particularly among oaks and madrones. Carry enough water to last to camp, for this route is usually waterless except during and just after storms. During the summer there's always a chance that the two water sources—upper Danish Creek and Pat Spring—could go dry, so check in advance, if possible, or carry an extra quart of water to get you back to the trailhead.

Description As with the previous route, read LP-1's first three paragraphs of route description, which get you to the start of the horse trail (1090-1.5). Then, read LP-2's first two paragraphs of route description, which get you up the Big Pines Trail (1170-0.3) to a junction with the **Danish Creek Trail** (2050-1.2). Along the last 0.2 mile to this junction you'll get your first of many ridge views. The third paragraph of route description gets you to a junction with the upper end of a west-climbing road, which is part of a horse-trail route up to the Big Pines Trail. If you've opted to take this steep, 1.2-mile-long road, you'll cut 0.7 mile off your total one-way distance. Onward, the Big Pines Trail is a road, and you go but 220 yards to where a second road/horse trail branches left (2240-0.5), and it immediately crosses the adjacent crest for a 0.7-mile very steep descent to a cabin on private land that is 0.3 mile upstream from Danish Creek Camp.

    Ignoring this horse route, we continue up the ridge road. In a couple of minutes we note a shortcut trail, which climbs directly up the ridge, while the road makes an easier climb up to it. In another couple of minutes, we come to a second junction, this time the trail being on our right. Both routes ahead are equally long. The trail is shadier and cooler, but it does have some poison oak. It climbs moderately northwest to Blue Rock Ridge, then follows an old road southwest 100 yards up to the ridge road.

    From the union of the two routes (2620-0.5) along the northwest side of a shady knoll, our road gently undulates along Blue Rock Ridge for ½ mile before narrowing, at a saddle, to a trail. Westward, we make a short, moderate, unnecessary gain, almost topping a 2778' ridge summit before using short switchbacks to drop to a barren outcrop of pale-green serpentine, which is an anomaly in our otherwise granitic route. We skirt this outcrop and after a momentary climb reach the **Ventana Wilderness boundary** (2720-1.0). Almost immediately we leave the crest, and make a madrone-and-black-oak-shaded descent west to a ridge, then a steeper descent south around a bowl and southwest to a saddle (2270-0.8). If you're short on water, this spot is perhaps the only reasonable opportunity to leave the trail and get water. With luck you'll reach, in under 300 yards of northwestward descent, a perhaps-hopefully *flowing* tributary of Pine Creek. During the driest months, you may have to

View east down the Danish Creek canyon

descend all the way to Pine Creek, which is 830 vertical feet below the trail and about 1.0 mile away.

Westward our trail climbs ¼ mile, skirting across the north slopes of a 2525′ ridge summit to a chamise-cloaked saddle. The dense brush prevents easy access to seasonally flowing Danish Creek, to the south and barely 200′ below us. Now we confront the second largest climb of our route, a 700′ ascent. It begins steeply, along a brushy ridge, then climbs moderately through a forest of mature madrones (and unfortunately, some poison oak), then switchbacks to the brushy ridge. Chamise dominates, but also present are manzanita, yerba santa, golden fleece and pungent, warty-leaved ceanothus. The last species, with narrow, sawtooth leaves, can make hiking unpleasant if the trail hasn't been maintained. With vegetation like this, one may feel he or she is hiking in southern California's Angeles National Forest.

The ascent ends when we top a 3097′ ridge summit, and just west of it, on a similar point (3090-1.4), we have fine views in all directions. Unfortunately, the route drops 200′ over the next ¼ mile, the last part of this brushy descent being quite steep. From a saddle you once again have an opportunity to drop, in pursuit of water, several hundred yards northwest to a seasonal tributary of Pine Creek.

Onward, we have a gentle ascent for ⅓ mile along the ridge, then leave it at a minor saddle (2980-0.6), which is immediately beyond two shady live oaks. Now we make a traversing ascent southwest up varying slopes. After ⅓ mile we spot the route's first ponderosa pines, which alert us that Big Pines Camp can't be too far ahead. About ¼ mile later we cross a minor ridge with tall pines, these urging us onward. We contour to a nearby gully, climb across a pine-clad slope, cross a grassy swale and in 50 yards reach a junction (3350-1.0) with a **trail to Big Pines Camp.** This junction, beside a 2′ broad stump, can be easily missed if the junction lacks a sign, in which case you'll probably go another 220 yards, ascending a minor ridge, to a more conspicuous junction. The spur trail drops rather steeply southeast 120 yards to a one-tent campsite, which is pleasant enough, but not far below it is the real **Big Pines Camp** (3290-0.1), with room for two tents. A short stretch of Danish Creek beside this camp usually flows year-round, unlike stretches just upstream and downstream, which are often dry in summer and early fall.

If you want more-spacious campsites, continue onward past the Big Pines Camp spur trail to the aforementioned junction (3370-0.1). To the right, the lesser used Big Pines Trail climbs briefly west, then traverses in that direction to a crossing ot the seasonal headwaters of Danish Creek, which once was the site of Spaghetti Camp (3440-0.4). The trail, briefly indistinct, first heads northwest upstream about 50 yards, then west through brush about 90 yards. An obvious route then makes short switchbacks up to a broad saddle, on which you meet the start of the southbound **Ventana Trail** (3620-0.3). Bottchers Gap Campground and trailhead is 6.3 trail miles to the west (via Chapter 3's Route BG-1).

Back at the junction just past the Big Pines Camp spur trail, most folks opt for the Pat Spring environs, and they head left, descending 250 yards to often flowing, alder-lined Danish Creek. The trail now follows the creek's diminishing south branch upstream, crossing it about 35 yards before a junction with the **Ventana Trail** (3560-0.5). See the last paragraph of Route BG-1 for the short conclusion of your trek to **Pat Spring** (3740-0.3) and environs, which include the spring, a nearby camp and two outlying camps.

Chapter 5: China Camp

CC-1

China Camp to Miller Canyon Camp, Clover Basin Camp and Carmel River Trail via Miller Canyon Trail

Distances

    1.8 miles to Tamarack homes' pond
    4.3 miles to Nason Cabin site
    6.4 miles to junction with Hennickson Trail
         2.0 miles along trail to Tin House site
    7.1 miles to Miller Canyon Camp
    7.7 miles to Clover Basin Camp
    10.2 miles to junction with Carmel River Trail
    10.9 miles to Bluff Camp
    13.2 miles to junction with Big Pines Trail
    15.0 miles to Los Padres Dam trailhead

Maps   11 and 6

Trailhead   If you're driving from the Monterey-Salinas area or points north, you'll drive first to Carmel Valley Village, and then southeast 6.5 miles to a junction with the north end of Cachagua Road. See the trailhead directions in Chapter 4's Route LP-1 for details. Stay on Carmel Valley Road (County Road G16) for another 7.3 miles to reach a junction with Tassajara Road.

If you're driving from the central Salinas Valley or from southern California, reach this junction by following directions given in Chapter 6's Route AS-2 trailhead description.

On Tassajara Road you go 1.3 miles to a junction with Cachagua Road. (If you were to follow it 4.5 miles, you'd reach a junction with Nason Road—the approach to Chapter 4's routes.) Stay on Tassajara Road, whose pavement ends in 1.8 miles. Ahead, the road might be briefly closed at times after severe storms, primarily due to fallen trees. You make a pro-

tracted climb 4.8 miles to White Oaks Campground, climb another 1.3 miles to Chews Ridge, and then descend 1.5 miles to the entrance to China Camp, 10.7 miles from the Carmel Valley Road junction. Both Forest Service campgrounds are fairly small and, in my opinion, equally attractive.

Introduction   The Miller Canyon Trail is a smaller-scale version of the Carmel River Trail (next route). As with that route, the first few miles are usually dry, then one begins a canyon-bottom hike with many stream crossings. However, the Miller Fork Carmel River is considerably smaller than the Carmel River proper, so the fork's 20 crossings are usually quite easy except during and just after storms. This route offers good boulder-hopping practice for tackling the Carmel River's more difficult 24 crossings that lie between the Miller Canyon Trail junction and Hiding Camp. So if you want to make a loop trip out of China Camp, first descend the Miller Canyon Trail, then follow the last part of Chapter 4's Route LP-1 up the Carmel River Trail from Carmel River Camp to the junction with the Round Rock Camp Trail. Complete your 24.2-mile loop trip by following Route CC-2 in reverse.

Some people prefer to go from the China Camp trailhead down to the Los Padres trailhead, making a 15.8-mile car shuttle via Tassajara, Cachagua and Nason roads. Such a hike, via the Miller Canyon Trail, is 15.0 miles, versus 18.8 miles via the Carmel River Trail (Route CC-2 and Chapter 4's Route LP-1). The latter is certainly more scenic and offers more camping opportunities, but the former is better if you're not proficient at boulder-hopping 10-yard-wide streams. If you're on horseback, you'll have to take the latter, for a short section of the Miller Canyon Trail beyond the Nason Cabin site is often, if not always, impassable for stock.

The Miller Canyon Trail has highly variable seasonal attributes. In winter its trail camps can be cool and damp. Below the Hennickson Trail junction, stream crossings can be a problem during and after rains. Spring is your best season, though between the Tanbark homes and the Hennickson Trail junction, ticks can be locally abundant in grassy and brushy sections. With the arrival of summer, canyon hiking and camping below the Hennickson Trail junction are pleasant, though it can get quite warm. Fortunately, the stream is nearby, but unfortunately it lacks swimming holes. Above the trail junction the route is often unpleasantly hot and flies abound. In fall the route to the Hennickson Trail junction can be warm and quite fly-prone as late as mid-November. Usually from mid-October onward, at least several streams flow along this stretch. Fall colors are best below the trail junction, particularly in November, which offers some potentially wonderful camping.

Description The China Camp road traverses 0.1 mile northwest to a junction with gated Jeffery Road, from which the main road drops south to the campground proper. If you're hiking overnight, don't park at any of the cramped campground's 10 sites. Rather, park near the gate across Jeffery Road, taking care not to block traffic. From the gate (elev. 4270') you start a descent that is mostly shady, thanks to mature live oaks, tanbark oaks, madrones and, to a much lesser extent, Coulter pines. The gradient, once steep, is now merely moderate, thanks to a regrading and lengthening of Jeffery Road. After a mile we come beside Miller Fork Carmel River, this stretch of stream usually flowing from mid-October through May.

In ¼ mile we reach a sign stating that we're entering private property of the Tanoak association, which is comprised of a number of homes. After several minutes we pass a road branching left to the first home, then over the next few minutes pass roads branching both left and right to homes. The only spot you're likely to take the wrong road is at a junction immediately past a usually dry creek (the only creek in the vicinity). Two roads diverge, the right one climbing more steeply than the left one, up to some homes. Take the left road. In a couple of minutes you'll pass by the **Tamarack**

homes' pond (3420-1.8), then after 120 yards you'll reach a gate.

Now you enter Ventana Wilderness but unfortunately don't leave the private inholdings among U.S.F.S. land. After 130 yards the road turns sharply right for a steep, brief climb east. Leave it here at the turn, taking a nearly level trail for 125 yards northwest to a junction with a road from the steeply climbing road. On the road you go down-canyon barely 20 yards before it divides, only to rejoin in about 70 yards. The left fork is a bit more prominent and direct, and from the rejoining point the road ends in about 40 yards (3360-0.2).

The Miller Canyon Trail branches right from it, reaches a gate in 50 yards, and then weaves in and out of gullies as it descends northwest, basically paralleling a nearby straight canyon, which in turn parallels the unseen floor of Miller Canyon proper. The minor though very obvious canyon is running along part of the Miller Canyon Fault, which continues from southeast of the China Camp saddle northwest down its namesake to at least where the Miller Fork veers west.

The trail stays above the minor canyon's usually dry creek and, at the canyon's mouth, comes to within 150 yards of Miller Fork before starting a 0.3-mile traverse north to an unnamed creek (2880-1.0), which is just within Section 36. It's obvious that people have camped along the sloping lands bordering this alder-lined creek, despite the fact that it's not an official campsite and, furthermore, it's on private land. Far better potential camping lies about 230 yards down this seasonal creek, where it joins the Miller Fork, and the camping zone extends continuously ¼ mile downstream. This zone, too, is on private land, as is all of the southern quarter of Section 36. The Forest Service would do well to acquire this unused land, or at least rights to it, since the camping potential is superb and the Miller Canyon Trail could use additional camps.

From the creek, which is usually flowing at least from late October through May, we climb a bit to the first of several saddles (2980-0.5). Only 10 yards before it you'll note a use trail, which quickly deteriorates into a number of deer paths that steeply descend to the nearby Miller Fork, with its potential camping on private land. After several minutes' progress, we cross a second shallow saddle, this one with a use trail that goes 100 yards west along a crest to a precipitous view down into Miller Canyon's inner gorge. Onward, we pass a seasonal creek midway to a higher third saddle, which is more prominent than the previous two. We then have a short ¼ mile descent to the crossing of a three-season creek near the **Nason Cabin site** (3090-0.8). As at the previous three-season creek, the gently sloping lands bordering this creek show considerable signs of camp use, although it is not an official site. It could stand some development.

Note that unless the trail is reworked ahead, *only those on foot can expect to get through to Miller Canyon Camp,* and even then, a spot or two over the next mile could be quite intimidating. In late 1986 a few yards of trail across a precipitous gully had barely a trace of tread. While this piece of trail is likely to be repaired, I noted other pieces of trail that were likely to slough off in future, heavy rains. However, on foot one should be able to climb above and around such washouts. Parts of this trail are bordered with California sagebrush, whose dull-green leaves, cleft into hairlike filaments, can abound with ticks in spring.

With this warning in mind, leave the three-season creek and climb west above a bit of debris that marks the Nason Cabin site, then round a nearby ridge with a fine view up-canyon. Next, traverse briefly, then make a short, steep climb to a fourth saddle (3070-0.6), one with oak-filtered views to the north and south. Now the route ahead is downhill virtually every foot of the way to Miller Canyon Camp.

Continuing down-canyon, we wind past two gullies to a broad, fifth saddle, and cross just east of and above it. Four more gullies intervene on our way to another broad saddle, our sixth (2620-1.2). Continuing northwest, we make a moderate-to-steep descent down a gully that is probably being eroded along the Miller Canyon Fault. In 0.2 mile the trail jogs right for an immediate crossing of the gully's ephemeral creeklet, while an abandoned stretch of trail—the old route—continues straight ahead. In a minute or two, barely 50 yards beyond the crossing of a minor gully, we arrive at a junction with the **Hennickson Trail** (2420-0.3).

Hennickson Trail

This trail is not shown on the U.S.F.S. *Ventana Wilderness* map, and I wouldn't mention it were it not so blatantly obvious. No hiker in his or her right mind would take this often brushy, usually waterless, overly steep trail 2.0 miles up to the bone-dry Tin House site. It appears to me that most of the trail's users are equestrians ascending from private lands, who are bound for the Miller Fork Carmel River.

This trail first traverses in and out of two deeply cleft gullies before reaching, after ⅓ mile of route, a third, with a three-season creek, which is your only hope for water. Next, you face a grueling 460′ brushy climb, which can be fairly tick-prone in spring. From a saddle (2820-0.7), you can almost see your goal, which lies immediately to the right and out of sight of the highest point you see along Chews Ridge, to the northeast.

You start a traverse in that direction, and in 110 yards leave the chamise and other shrubs for live oak and madrone. After crossing three gullies, the last one significant, you enter the usually dry streambed of a Miller Fork tributary and advance about 50–60 yards up it, to where I hope you'll spy the continuation of your trail (2760-0.7). A vague use path upstream leads to nowhere.

You start very steeply north, then the tread becomes obvious as you start to climb steeply west up chamise-clad slopes. The gradient eases to moderate by the time the trail turns northwest, and you can now enjoy the views to the west, the canyons dominated by Uncle Sam Mountain. You reach a gate atop a minor saddle along Chews Ridge and a well-used jeep road immediately beyond it. Supposedly the **Tin House** (3100-0.6) once lay about 100 yards east along the road, but you won't find a trace of it. A bit farther, one reaches some cypresses at a gully. By descending north far enough, the thirsty hiker may reach water. Please note that the road and its offshoots all enter private property, no matter what course you take.

Beyond the Hennickson Trail junction, you descend moderately northwest, staying just above a straight gully that is being eroded along the Miller Canyon Fault. Perhaps of more interest is the fairly dense stand of Santa Lucia firs that thrive in this gully. Soon you veer east into an adjacent, shallower gully, then make a short, rather steep descent to a three-season tributary (2190-0.4) of Miller Fork. When the tributary is flowing, you'll hear it before you see it, due to the songful splashing of a 20′ high waterfall just upstream. You'll also note a use trail, which climbs steeply up-canyon to the Hennickson Trail.

Downstream, your route is a delightful hike as you parallel the charming, cascading creek through a narrow, steep-walled canyon. Anyone attempting to take stock through it will find that even one downed tree can stop their progress. Furthermore, the footpath, often less

A 20′ high waterfall

than a foot in width, is across unstable soil, which easily supports hikers but can give way under horses. Near the canyon's end you cross the creek a second time, this spot supporting a cluster of hoary nettles, which can grow to more than head height. Get to know and avoid this alien plant, which has clusters of small, drab flowers arising from the bases of the opposite-paired, stinging-haired leaves. You'll encounter more of them downstream.

Hoary (stinging) nettle

In about a minute's time you reach the Miller Fork and make your first of 20 creek crossings. This one gets you to **Miller Canyon Camp** (2000-0.3), perched on a creekside bench. The main campsite is at the east end of the bench, by the trail ford, but you'll find a smaller site at its west end, 70 yards away, and

all the space between them is also suitable for camping.

Onward to the Carmel River your hike will be just as wonderful and rewarding as the delightful stretch from the Hennickson Trail down to Miller Canyon Camp. From above the west-end site on what seems to be an old roadbed, you go 0.1 mile west to your second crossing, which is at a major bend in the Miller Fork. You negotiate three more crossings, and then your trail, for a few yards, almost plows down the creek just before reaching **Clover Basin Camp** (1870-0.6). This site is certainly pleasant enough, with its sycamores, alders, bays and madrones, but it's not spacious enough to hold a Scout troop, unlike upstream Miller Canyon Camp or downstream Carmel River Camp.

Bound for the Carmel River, we make six crossings as we proceed north, and then a seventh crossing (1690-0.7) directs us west. For a spell we don't have to think about crossings, since we make only one in the next mile, after ⅓ mile. From the south bank we gradually veer away from the Miller Fork and soon can see below us spacious benches that would be fine sites for a developed camp. The route could certainly use an additional site or two. The trail climbs gradually, rising almost 200′ above the North Fork as it turns a steeply dropping ridge. Then, in three switchback legs, it descends to your 14th ford of the Miller Fork (1450-1.0).

Crossings are once again frequent, with two closely spaced ones just before a conspicuous, recent rockfall at the base of a steep, undercut granitic ridge. You then breeze past a dry, yucca-speckled cliff, pass beneath a large, mossy cliff, and soon commence four rapid-fire crossings before terminating at a junction with the **Carmel River Trail** (1220-0.8). Spacious Carmel River Camp lies 250 yards upstream, just one immediate (21st) Miller Fork crossing and two Carmel River crossings away. Before the two river crossings, you'll find two outlying Carmel River campsites, each with a fire grate.

If you're heading down-river toward the **Los Padres Dam trailhead,** see the first part of Route LP-1, and follow its description in the reverse direction. If you're heading upriver back to China Camp, follow the second half of that route in the described direction, then follow in reverse the description of Route CC-2. Either way, you certainly can't get lost, since the Carmel River Trail usually stays close to the river and is quite obvious where it occasionally veers away from it.

CC-2

China Camp to Pine Valley, Round Rock Camp and Hiding Camp via Pine Ridge and Carmel River Trails

Distances

   3.6 miles to Church Creek Divide

   5.3 miles to Pine Valley Camp

      0.7 mile along use-trail/cross-country route to upper Pine Fall's pool

      1.5 miles along Pine Valley-Pine Ridge Trail to junction with Pine Ridge Trail

   9.2 miles to junction with Round Rock Camp Trail

      0.6 mile along trail to Round Rock Camp

   9.6 miles to Hiding Camp

  11.4 miles to Buckskin Flat Camp

  13.0 miles to Sulphur Springs Camp

  13.9 miles to Carmel River Camp

  14.0 miles to junction with Miller Canyon Trail

  14.7 miles to Bluff Camp

  17.0 miles to junction with Big Pines Trail

  18.8 miles to Los Padres Dam trailhead

Maps   11 and 10

Trailhead   Same as the Route CC-1 trailhead

Introduction   This route offers at least three possibilities: 1) stop at Pine Valley and return, 2) descend all the way along the Carmel River to the Los Padres Dam trailhead, or 3) descend part-way along the river and ascend the Miller Canyon Trail back to your trailhead.

Pine Valley, lying about 5.3 miles from the trailhead, is actually within day-hike range. Allow about 4 hours for the complete round trip. From late spring through summer, this gives you plenty of time to lounge about the valley or to climb a few routes on its abundant sandstone cliffs (bring ropes). While the valley does get some day hikers, it probably gets more backpackers, particularly on weekends, for the valley is an ideal year-round two-day hike. Between winter storms the valley, which is about 3150' in elevation, is well above the cold, damp canyons, and temperatures can get into the 60s, even if the morning starts around freezing. During the summer, temperatures can get into the 90s, but there is plenty of shade, and the creek is always reliable. Furthermore, one can cautiously descend to upper Pine Fall's pool for a brisk, refreshing swim. Spring and fall are probably best, as temperatures are then ideal and storms aren't very frequent.

The 18.8-mile one-way hike down to the Los Padres Dam trailhead is relatively easy, energy-wise, but can be rather difficult and time-consuming if you're not adept at hopping boulders. You'll face 25 Carmel River crossings; two more if you visit Round Rock and Hiding camps. Odds are that you'll get your feet wet at least once while crossing; assume all boulders are loose until proven otherwise. This hike is a fine one except during winter, when the river will be higher and many crossings might be cold, wet fords. During or just after a storm, some crossings can be dangerous enough to be life-threatening. Spring and fall are best, temperature-wise, but summer's heat warms the river to sufficient temperatures for dipping in its pools.

If you can't arrange a 15.8-mile car shuttle between the China Camp and Los Padres Dam trailheads, you still can see the best scenery the Carmel River has to offer. Make a 24.2-mile loop trip, utilizing the Carmel River and Miller Canyon trails. The route, too, is suitable in spring, summer and fall. For three reasons I suggest you descend the Miller Canyon Trail (previous route), then ascend the Carmel River Trail, instead of the other way around. First, at the start, when your pack is heaviest, you begin downhill. Second, should you want to spend a few days along the trail, you can spend your last night at Pine Valley Camp and then face about a 2000' climb 5.3 miles out to your trailhead. Ascending the Miller Canyon Trail, your last night would be at Miller Canyon Camp, and you'd face about a 3000' climb 7.1 miles out to your trailhead. Finally, Miller Canyon's creek has 21 crossings, most or all of them easier than the 24 along Carmel River proper. So by descending Miller Canyon, you'll get plenty of practice for the harder crossings ahead.

Description   The Pine Ridge trailhead (elev. 4350'), which may be unmarked, is on the saddle immediately above China Camp, and is just 90 yards south of the campground's entrance road. Only 15 yards north of the trailhead, you'll spot a trail that drops 70 yards west through brush to conclude at the campground's upper east end.

The first 1.2 miles of trail could have been better routed, for it climbs 400' in elevation,

Backpackers' tents at ponderosa-pine-shaded Pine Valley Camp

only to drop an equal amount to the west end of a long saddle. When you top out in a tanbark-oak stand (4750-0.6), at least you have the satisfaction of reaching one of the higher spots in the Santa Lucia Range with relatively little effort. You next traverse briefly southwest past snags and brush, crossing an ill-defined crest, then make a brushy, open, sometimes steep descent to the west end of the aforementioned saddle (4350-0.6). Along this descent you have panoramic views to the south and west, and can identify, roughly along a 165° bearing, 5155' Cone Peak, 17 miles distant, which is a point atop the farthest ridge. Despite its almost mile-high elevation, it stands only 3.2 miles from the Pacific Ocean. The Santa Lucia Range is indeed youthful and rugged.

Even higher 5862' Junipero Serra Peak comes into full view as we climb west. This peak, on the southeast skyline about 13½ miles distant, rises over a mile above the unseen Salinas Valley. Now oaks give way to grasses, and we come to within several feet of topping the ridge at a minor saddle. In two minutes we do top the ridge—at a prominent saddle—then climb moderately southwest to a switchback. Views temporarily disappear as we climb north to our second highest point (4740-0.9); note that you've just climbed a total of about 800' along your "descent" to Pine Valley. But now it's all downhill, and views soon reappear as we

gently descend through a ghost forest of tanbark-oak snags. After a ½-mile westward descent, one with views to the south down at sandstone formations in upper Church Creek canyon, the trail abruptly bends southwest and the gradient steepens. Overall, it maintains a moderate-to-steep gradient of 13.2% as we lose 850' of elevation on a switchbacking, generally open course down to **Church Creek Divide** (3651-1.5). With pines, oaks and madrones, it provides a shady haven, particularly during summer, when your ascent back up this stretch can be a real scorcher—start early.

Church Creek Divide is a deep cleft that lies between and roughly 1000' below two west-trending ridges. Why this prominent mountain saddle? The divide lies along the path of the wilderness' longest fault, the Church Creek Fault. Starting from the wilderness' only major east-west fault, this fault heads northwest up its namesake, Church Creek, crosses the divide, then quite closely follows our route down to Hiding Camp. It then quite closely follows Puerto Suelo Way up to Puerto Suelo, which is Spanish for deeply cleft mountain saddle. Eventually, after about 29 miles from its start, it goes offshore, entering the Pacific near Kaslar Point.

Church Creek Divide is the crossroads of several different trails. We've been on the Pine

Ridge Trail, and from the divide it climbs westward, reaching Divide Camp in 0.5 mile and Pine Ridge Camp in 4.2 miles. See Route CC-3 for details. The fault-hugging Church Creek Trail descends 2.1 miles to the wilderness boundary, from which a road continues downcanyon. This canyon route goes past the wonderful sandstone cliffs you saw en route to Church Creek Divide. See Route CC-4 for details.

Our route is to the northwest, down the Carmel River Trail. For the first ¼ mile we descend moderately, crossing the usually dry headwaters of the Carmel River several times. The gradient then slackens over the next ¼ mile and then the trail becomes essentially level. We now have a seasonal "river" on our left and sandstone outcrops on our right. The outcrops may whet some climbers' appetites, and far better exposures lie ahead. However, the climbing in this area is not as good as it may first appear. You reach the first of these cliffs about a mile from the divide, immediately after you step across a southflowing seasonal creek that has excavated a rather respectable side canyon. Welcome to Pine Valley.

As we head northwest, Santa Lucia firs momentarily distract the botanically inclined, but it's the ponderosa pines that ultimately garner our attention—along with the cliffs. These get up to about 150′ high, as do the increasingly numerous pines, by the time we reach a junction in central Pine Valley. Here you'll find a trail that immediately crosses a year-round flowing stretch of the Carmel River. Just beyond the opposite bank lies spacious, level **Pine Valley Camp** (3140-1.7), amid an open stand of mature ponderosa pines. As if the river weren't fit for drinking, a pipe spring has been developed along the camp's south border, just right of the ascending lateral trail to the Pine Ridge Trail.

Pine Valley-Pine Ridge Trail

If you're heading from China Camp to Redwood Creek Camp, Rainbow Camp or beyond, the shortest route is via the Pine Ridge Trail. However, some folks prefer a longer route via Pine Valley Camp. They then take the Pine Valley-Pine Ridge trail to get back on route. The price one pays for this more scenic alternate route is an extra 500′ of climbing over a 1.0-mile longer distance. But an evening at Pine Valley Camp usually makes this toll worth it.

From the camp's upper end this connecting trail climbs rather steeply, averaging 16.0% gradient. Most of the climb is shaded by live oaks (flies in warm weather), and is often bordered with green-stemmed ceanothus (slight chance of ticks in winter or spring). The trail stays close to an ascending ridge, crossing it several times. Near its south end, the ridge becomes almost level, and the trail comes to within a few feet of topping it. Here, it's worth the minor effort to walk a few yards west for views that include rather-flat-topped Uncle Sam Mountain, Puerto Suelo (a deep saddle at the mountain's left base), and a long ridge leading left from the saddle up to the two minor summits of Ventana Double Cone.

Just beyond these views you reach a shallow saddle where your south-ascending ridge intersects a southeast-ascending ridge (3950-1.0). From it an abandoned trail descends into Bear Basin. This trail becomes increasingly hard to follow, and all but disappears by the time one reaches Bear Basin. In it one finds a good camp about 100 yards west of the trail, just above the southwest bank of usually flowing Bear Basin Creek, which is roughly 0.8 mile from the junction. If you manage to follow the trail 0.3 mile farther, you'll reach the old Bear Basin Camp, which has nearby spring-fed

Sandstone cliffs in Pine Valley

water that is usually reliable for most of the year. Don't attempt to go any farther. The climb south, by whichever route you choose, is overly steep, and the bushwhacking near the top is horrendous.

From the trail junction at the ridge intersection, the main trail climbs southeast, usually at a gentle-to-moderate grade, mostly through dense stands of green-stemmed ceanothus, which has multiplied better than any other species in the wake of the Marble-Cone fire. Your trail's grade steepens just before you meet the **Pine Ridge Trail** (4230-0.5).

If there's overcrowding at Pine Valley Camp, which is possible on fair-weather weekends, you do have recourse to two small "overflow" sites, each with a fireplace grate. From the junction by the camp don't cross the Carmel River, but rather follow it briefly downstream to the base of a sandstone outcrop—the first site. Exploration of the outcrop will reveal mortar holes, which Indians created—likely with granitic boulders—and then used the holes to grind locally picked acorns into flour. What a heavenly summer camp they must have had.

Onward, you round the outcrop and find the second campsite just 35 yards before crossing the seasonal, south-flowing stream that drains the western part of Pine Valley. About 100 yards beyond it your use trail in effect dies out. It's just as easy to go cross-country about ½ mile down to upper Pine Fall as it is to follow vestiges of trail.

Pine Falls

There are two Pine Falls, the upper one about 100 yards before the Carmel River bends south, the lower one just after the bend. The upper one is about 50′ high and it falls partly free. The lower one is of similar height, but is more of a steep water chute than a true fall. However, the prize of this side trip is not the upper fall but the pool at its base, which is one of the largest and deepest in the wilderness. From two spots you can dive right into it, then swim laps or head over to the fall for a splashing shower. Generally, frolicking in the pool is warm enough only from about July through September. June and October are quite brisk.

Heading cross-country down to the brink of the upper fall is a relatively simple matter; you'll encounter only a few relatively minor obstacles. However, getting from the slippery, water-polished slabs just above the brink down

to the pool involves some risky, exposed climbing. There is little room for error, and a slip could be serious or fatal. While most people, including me, don't use a rope for the descent, rope is not a bad idea if you're unsure about exposed, crumbly rock. Enough said.

Perhaps a handful of hearty souls have descended along the Carmel River an additional 2.9 miles to Round Rock Camp (see Chapter 4's Route LP-1). Getting from the pool to the brink of the lower fall requires some effort, as does the descent to that fall's base, but the route is relatively safe. The river's gradient stays steep for 0.6 mile, until Bear Basin Creek, from which you have an "easy" cross-country route downriver. With all the boulder-hopping and clambering you'll have to do, allow a half day to reach Round Rock Camp.

Most folks prefer the easier route down-canyon: follow the Church Creek Fault. This is what the Carmel River Trail does, leaving the junction by Pine Valley Camp for a northwest climb to a fault-controlled saddle. You start by passing through a gate by the junction, entering private land and reaching, in 120 yards, a private cabin. Ahead, your route is very open, and you have abundant views of the valley's sandstone cliffs and surrounding slopes. Some of the pines in the valley's west end were torched by the Marble-Cone fire, and the decaying snags continue to fall, sometimes obscuring the trail. Just continue northwest toward the previously mentioned saddle. Forest shade begins to return as you leave the valley floor for a 200′ elevation gain up a gradually steepening ½-mile segment of trail to the saddle (3414-0.9).

Pass through a gate and start a moderate-to-steep descent. Quickly you'll meet a couple of trailside ponderosa pines, each with a trunk that is riddled with *thousands* of holes, drilled by industrious acorn woodpeckers, who insert a tightly fitting acorn into each hole. Were they not tight, then omnivorous Steller's jays would steal them. Acorns left on the ground are likely to be harvested by gray squirrels and, surprisingly, by band-tailed pigeons that, despite their relatively small mouths, swallow the acorns whole. That's like you swallowing an apple.

The descent takes us in and out of a number of shallow gullies, then we enter a noticeable one, soon switchback, and quickly cross the seasonal headwaters of Hiding Canyon creek (2950-0.5). You'll note that this vicinity more or less marks the western extent of the 1977 Marble-Cone fire. Down-canyon, there is little evidence of burned snags or fire-associated brush. The south-facing slopes are quite dry and brushy, but fortunately the trail usually hugs the canyon's creek, which is shaded by oaks, sycamores, bays and alders. In addition to the initial, headwaters crossing, you'll cross Hiding Canyon's creek eight more times. By the time you reach the last crossing (2140-1.4), you can expect the creek to be flowing, even in summer or early fall.

Now you make a switchbacking, winding climb up chamise-clad slopes, reaching a viewpoint in ⅓ mile. You then contour to a gully, which is probably eroding along a fault, then

meander in and out of minor gullies as you progress westward across additional chamise-clad slopes. From late winter to early summer you can expect quite a tick problem along this stretch, so check yourself every few minutes.

Eventually you leave Hiding Canyon's views where you cross a minor ridge. You quickly switchback, and along a 250-yard-long descent southwest get some views northwest, spying a pair of Puerto Suelo Way's switchbacks before you reach a junction with the **Round Rock Camp Trail** (2030-1.1). The last part of Route LP-1 describes the 0.6-mile trail over to **Round Rock Camp.** To descend to the **Los Padres Dam trailhead,** follow in reverse that route's trail description.

CC-3

China Camp to Divide Camp, Pine Ridge Camp, Cienaga Camp, Rainbow Camp and Redwood Camp via Pine Ridge and Big Sur Trails

Distances

3.6 miles to Church Creek Divide
4.1 miles to junction with trail to Divide Camp
    80 yards along trail to Divide Camp
5.8 miles to junction with Pine Valley-Pine Ridge Trail
7.3 miles to Pine Ridge
7.7 miles to junction with trail to Pine Ridge Camp
    240 yards along trail to Pine Ridge Camp
10.3 miles to junction with Big Sur Trail
    0.9 mile along trail to Cienaga Camp
    4.3 miles along trail to Rainbow Camp
11.2 miles to junction with trail to Redwood Camp
    0.1 mile along trail to Redwood Camp
13.5 miles to Sykes Camp
    0.4 mile along use trail to Sykes Hot Springs
16.4 miles to junction with trail to Barlow Flat Camp
    0.2 mile along trail to Barlow Flat Camp
17.8 miles to Terrace Creek Camp and junction with Terrace Creek Trail
    1.6 miles along trail to junction with Coast Ridge Road
        4.2 miles along road to trailhead by Highway 1

19.2 miles to junction with Ventana Camp Trail
    1.2 miles along trail to Ventana Camp
23.1 miles to Big Sur Station trailhead

Maps 11, 10 and 14

Trailhead Same as the Route CC-1 trailhead

Introduction There are three good routes providing an east-west transect of Ventana Wilderness: 1) the Big Pines and Skinner Ridge trails, 2) the Pine Ridge Trail, and 3) the Marble Peak, South Fork and Big Sur trails combined with the Coast Ridge Road. Of these, the Pine Ridge Trail takes you across the most diverse terrain and vegetation. From the trailhead near China Camp you start at 4350′ elevation, climby eventually to 4750′, then make a rollercoaster trek westward that ultimately ends at a lowly elevation of 370′, just outside Pfeiffer Big Sur State Park. Dominant vegetation ranges from tanbark oak and green-stemmed ceanothus to live oak, ponderosa pine, chamise and redwood. Parts of the route have sweeping views over much of the wilderness; others are viewless, being deep within forested canyons. In any season, temperatures can vary considerably along different parts of the trail.

Most users of the Pine Ridge Trail start at Big Sur and rarely go farther east than Redwood Camp. Certainly, few would want to continue onward—a 2800' climb—mostly up sunny, south-facing slopes to Pine Ridge. Therefore, this western half of the Pine Ridge Trail is described as a separate west-east hike, Chapter 8's Route BS-2. Hikers intent on making an entire east-west traverse from China Camp should consult that route's description (albeit in the opposite direction) after first consulting the following route description. For your convenience, mileages are listed for the entire Pine Ridge Trail and trails that branch from it. Along the China-Camp-to-Redwood-Camp stretch, which is the part described here, there are no significant problems, though ticks *may* be a real problem in spring along parts of the trail between Pine Ridge and Redwood or Rainbow Camps.

Description The first part of the previous route describes the first part of our trail, from the Pine Ridge trailhead (elev. 4350') west to **Church Creek Divide** (3651-3.6). From the saddle the trail continues westward, climbing gently up a well-graded route that weaves through two prominent gullies not shown on the U.S.G.S. topo map. The stretch is shady, having lots of madrones, black oaks and ponderosa pines. Green-stemmed ceanothus and charred snags attest to the passage through here of the 1977 Marble-Cone fire. We round a minor, descending ridge, and in about 35 yards reach a junction (3810-0.5) with a **trail to Divide Camp.** This descends a mere 80 yards to **Divide Camp** (elev. 3790'). Situated in a cozy cove with pines, oaks and alders, the camp is pleasant enough when water is present. During summer and early fall, the spring-fed water may be reduced to just a seep. Although the cove could be developed to hold quite a large party, at present the small camp holds only about two tents.

The Pine Ridge Trail climbs gently from the junction, curving around the cove just above the obvious camp. You'll cross the spring-fed creeklet that descends to the nearby camp, and since horses use the trail, the water may not be as fresh as one would desire. However, better water lies ahead, after we leave the cove and climb gently southwest across shady slopes to a tanbark-oak-lined creeklet (4000-0.6), which is the habitat of the miniscule winter wren. We then traverse first west, then north, crossing three usually dry gullies before arriving at a bend with fair views north toward the slopes above Pine Valley. Our route next climbs gently southwest along an increasingly snaggy stretch of trail, with a number of fair views. Snags stay with us as we head northwest for a few minutes

to a ridge, then just 110 yards southwest from it we come to a junction with the **Pine Valley-Pine Ridge trail** (4230-1.1). This trail is described in considerable detail in the previous route. Essentially, it drops in about 0.5 mile roughly 280' as it generally follows a northwest-descending ridge to a saddle. There you'll find a junction with an abandoned trail south to Bear Basin. Your well-maintained trail turns north and drops quite steeply 810' over the course of almost 1.0 mile to Pine Valley Camp.

Like the Pine Valley-Pine Ridge connecting trail, our main Pine Ridge Trail has a stretch of trail-hugging green-stemmed ceanothus. These tall, pliable shrubs possibly harbor ticks in spring, though I have yet to pick up a tick from this plant species. We quickly reach a minor ridge, duck into a gully, reach a second minor ridge, and have our first good views of features to the west and the northwest. Ventana Cone (4727') breaks the skyline about 2½ miles west of us, as does Ventana Double Cone (4853'), about 5 miles away. The "double cones" are merely high points at the south end of a ridge, from which slopes drop precipitously 3000' down to unseen Ventana Creek. You can trace the ridge northward to a prominent cleft, Puerto Suelo, from which arises nearly flat-topped Uncle Sam Mountain (4766').

Ahead lies a brush-and-oak gentle ascent south, a bit of the brush being chamise (tick habitat). In a relatively short time we come to a saddle (4410-0.7), from which we have a view southeast down Tassajara Creek canyon to the highest point in the Santa Lucia Range, Junipero Serra Peak (5862'). Now tacking southwest, we continue our gentle ascent, albeit one shaded with live and tanbark oaks. Our ascent tops out as we pass a few Santa Lucia firs, and then we enter confining green-stemmed-ceanothus brush as we make a minor drop to nearby **Pine Ridge** (4550-0.8). Along this broad ridge, which abounds with brush and ponderosa-pine snags, you may spy a post marking the south end of the very abandoned trail down to Bear Basin. Trying to follow it is an exercise in futility.

What the wilderness could use is a good west-east trail connecting Ventana Double Cone to Ventana Cone to Pine Ridge. But, since the Forest Service doesn't have enough funds and volunteers to maintain its existing trails, such a trail must remain my pipe dream. There's a similar ridge trail extending southeast from Pine Ridge, and it's known as the Black Cone Trail. Until late in 1987, the brush was so dense that one couldn't even locate it, but then some volunteers came in and brushed out about 2 miles—roughly one-fourth—of the route. You won't want to hike this once fine route until it is thoroughly reworked, so check with the King City Ranger Station (phone: 408-385-5434) before attempting it. Once it's ready for use, you'll be able to reach Strawberry Camp (Chapter 6's Route AS-2), and put together loop trips either west along the South Fork Trail or east along the Marble Peak Trail. Unfortunately, the Black Cone Trail was not brushed out in time to be included in this book.

Before leaving Pine Ridge, note its incense-cedars, which are common at similar elevations in the Sierra Nevada but are rare in Ventana Wilderness. This tree is identified by its scale-like leaves that are arranged in flat, fanlike sprays. Then, just a few minutes of moderate descent from the ridge, after you get a view southeast at the Black Cone Trail, you veer west and duck into three minor gullies. You then make a second, equally short descent to an important junction (4260-0.4)—a **trail to Pine Ridge Camp.** This trail descends moderately 240 yards to a small ridge flat with a view. **Pine Ridge Camp** (elev. 4170'), situated on the flat, is dominated by two mature, touching madrones; or is it one two-trunked madrone?— you decide. You'll find a dependable spring (in all but the driest summers) some 75 yards northwest of the camp. A use trail beyond the spring quickly dies out at some overflow campsites, which aren't very desirable. The camp proper has space for about four tents, and it is salvation to any backpacker who's unfortunately decided to climb east up the Pine Ridge Trail.

Ahead, we face a 2230' descent to a junction, the gradient averaging about 12.2%,

which is a bit more than moderate, but not steep enough to give us sore knees. At first the trail rambles, its tread being rather makeshift past debris and brush brought about by the 1977 fire. After a ½-mile descent, you're back on original tread and among unscathed chaparral, most of it being chamise (possible ticks), warty-leaved ceanothus, manzanita, sticky monkey flower and, sporadically, yucca. As you descend along a ridge you'll have views west to the Pacific Ocean—when it isn't fogbound.

Soon the trail veers southeast from the ridge, only to angle west back to it and descend to a long saddle (3420-1.2). Now you leave the ridge for good and have a crop of views northwest, the highest point in that direction being 4727' Ventana Cone, which rises about 2500' above Redwood Creek, seen below. Ventana Wilderness is indeed a wild and rugged landscape. After a while, your well-crafted trail bends from southwest to south, and the brush becomes overwhelmingly chamise—watch for ticks. Then we make a diversionary switchback west and spy the trail's first black sages, the odor of their leaves stirring up fond memories for those of us who were raised in the mountains of southern California.

If you're bound for Redwood Camp, you can sort of guess where it is. Below, you see a conspicuous stretch of the Pine Ridge Trail contouring southwest away from the creekside Redwood Camp environs. If you're bound for Cienaga and Rainbow camps, you'll see the first saddle you'll have to vault, which is rapidly growing nearer. The second saddle is the conspicuous notch in the ridge beyond the first saddle, and the climb to it is quite intimidating. In a relatively short time we're in a gully just below the first saddle, where we find a junction with the **Big Sur Trail** (2320-1.4).

Fire-ravaged stand of ponderosa pines below South Ventana Cone

Big Sur Trail

The stretch of trail from here to Rainbow Camp is lightly used. Certainly, it is easily more strenuous and less maintained than the Pine Ridge Trail. The terrain it crosses suffered badly in the 1977 fire, as you may have observed on your descent. One consequence of the fire is the thick growth of green-stemmed ceanothus, which you quickly confront. It can be a real nuisance for stock. The second consequence is that the trail has been relocated between here and Cienaga Camp, and the tread is quite irregular. You'll note this as you struggle up to a nearby saddle (2470-0.2), most of the ascent being at about a 20% gradient.

First you momentarily walk through chamise/warty-leaved ceanothus chaparral then descend into a grassy bowl with live oaks and ponderosa pines. The tread here may be faint, but the post-1977 trail, unlike the original switchbacking trail, maintains a rather constant southeast orientation as it diagonals down and across slopes. However, near the first, rather small trailside redwood, the trail alters its course and character, becoming a sequence of short, haphazard zigzags more or less downslope in an east-northeast direction. The grassy oak woodland gives way to green-stemmed ceanothus, and several false paths may lead you astray. In one or two places the actual route is as illogical and overgrown as the false paths, but these are very short and you probably won't go more than a few yards off route. (In the opposite direction the trail is quite easily followed.)

After about 0.2 mile of random hiking you'll approach but not see audible Cienaga Creek. Among fairly tall redwoods and dense brush you parallel the creek downstream about 0.1 mile to its boulderhop crossing, where you enter diminutive **Cienaga Camp** (1800-0.7). Nestled between the creek and steep slopes, this shady redwood spot barely has room for two tents. It also lacks a table. Furthermore, if you have need for an outhouse—good luck; you'll have to use the camp or the creekside. For this last reason in particular I suggest that Cienaga Camp be used for emergency bivouacs only. Spacious Rainbow Camp, with table and porta-potty, is far more desirable. (Note: Trail signs plus U.S.F.S. and U.S.G.S. maps misspell *Cienaga* Creek and Camp. Cienaga is Spanish for marsh, and the pre-1977 trail passed by one. Given the soil and vegetation changes caused by the 1977 fire, the marsh may not exist today. Certainly you don't see one along the post-1977 trail.)

From Cienaga Camp the trail contours south, while redwood-bordered Cienaga Creek gradually drops below us. On a generally good tread we brush past green-stemmed ceanothus to a minor saddle (1750-0.5), then descend moderately southeast to a boulderhop crossing of North Fork Big Sur River (1570-0.2). One wishes a camp were located here, among the redwoods, alders, willows, spikenards and chain ferns. One also wishes the trail ahead went around the ridge, instead of over it, to Rainbow Camp.

Instead we face over two dozen switchbacks up a route with a fairly steep gradient of 16.5%. Fortunately, the switchbacks are highly variable in length and orientation, which helps to relieve the monotony of the route. Unfortunately, the vegetation is monotonous, almost entirely green-stemmed ceanothus, with smatterings of redwood-tree "families." Before the 1977 fire this route must have been quite attractive, having many tanbark oaks, more redwoods and less brush. On your waterless ascent, you may find that the saddle looks quite close, but this is just an illusion. You'll know you're finally approaching it when you skirt along the base of a prominent cliff. Upon reaching the saddle (2700-1.3), you view two contrasting types of vegetation. Just to the north, a lone, narrow redwood rears its top above the saddle. Just to the south, live oaks share the sunny, dry slopes with yuccas and manzanitas.

The descent to Rainbow Camp is a tad longer and less steep than the ascent you've just completed. Since it's usually a sunny, dry route down generally south-facing slopes, you can be thankful you're not ascending it. It too has over two dozen switchbacks, but because of the way the route is laid out, their numbers aren't as apparent. Also, the vegetation is more diverse, as are the slopes, which makes the stretch more interesting. About 300' above unseen Big Sur River, you pass a small grove of redwoods by a seasonal creek, then in a couple of minutes cross a minor, dry ridge draped with chamise, warty-leaved ceanothus, manzanita and sticky monkey flower. What a sudden change in vegetation!

You then descend rather steeply in spots and enter the creekside vegetation of South Fork Big Sur River. After a boulder hop, which may be tricky when the river is high, you climb a few paces up to a narrow, 100-yard-long river terrace, **Rainbow Camp** (1560-1.4). While it, like other river camps, may be cool and damp in winter, this camp is a pleasure the rest of the year. In case you don't want to drink from the Big Sur, you'll find a seeping spring in mid-camp at the base of a slope. A creeklet flows down a gully just west of the camp, ending as two side-by-side, moss-draped falls that splash into an attractive South Fork pool. This is long enough and just deep enough to do some short, brisk laps, should you be so tempted in summer. Surprisingly, there aren't any red-woods in this vicinity, even though it has an environment almost identical to that of the North Fork. Instead you find riverside alders and sycamores, plus live oaks and tanbark oaks in camp.

To continue along the Big Sur Trail to Mocho Camp and the Coast Ridge Road, see Chapter 8's Route BS-3, which is described in the opposite direction. To head upstream along the South Fork, see the South Fork Trail section in Chapter 6's Route AS-2, also described in the opposite direction.

Most hikers won't go to Cienaga and Rainbow camps, but rather from the Big Sur Trail junction will continue down the Pine Ridge Trail. After 0.3 mile chamise and other

brush finally give way to trees, but we lose our views in the process. Live oaks and madrones now offer shade, but trailside green-stemmed ceanothus and poison oak adulterate the vegetation. Between two quickly passed side gullies, we hail the first redwoods, switchback, and momentarily drop to perennial Redwood Creek to quench our thirst. There's a small campsite by its west bank, but more space lies ahead. Just 150 yards beyond the creek you'll meet a **trail to Redwood Camp** (1780-0.9). This goes a stone's throw southeast to a better campsite, though this isn't the real camp. Here, cross the creek and follow a trail southeast 65 yards to a bench holding the *real* **Redwood Camp** (1810-0.1), complete with table and stove—I hope. You can put about a half-dozen tents on this site, and there is overflow space on gentle slopes just to the north.

You'll probably not descend all the way to here just to savor the pristine water under the shade of stately redwoods. Rather than retrace your steps, you'll likely continue 11.9 miles along the Pine Ridge Trail to its western terminus at the **Big Sur Station trailhead.** This stretch is described in the eastward direction in Chapter 8's Route BS-2.

CC-4

Tassajara Road to Pine Ridge Trail via Church Creek Trail

Distances
   1.1 miles to Wildcat Camp
   3.4 miles to Church Ranch Road
   6.8 miles to junction with Pine Ridge Trail
   at Church Creek Divide

Maps 16, 12 and 11

Trailhead First see the Route CC-1 trail-head for directions to China Camp. From the entrance to this campground, you continue on Tassajara Road, climbing almost 0.9 mile to a 4498' saddle with fine views on both sides. From here, a closed road to Church Ranch offers you an alternate route into the wilder-ness, making a 3.4-mile descent that drops 1770' to the halfway point of the Church Creek Trail. Keeping to the main road, you now descend 4¼ miles to the start of the Horse Pasture Trail (Route CC-5). This spot, with parking for several vehicles, is about 250 yards past the road's tight curve through a con-spicuous gully. For the Church Creek Trail, continue ¼ mile down the road to a sharp bend left. Here, there is barely space for one vehicle.

Walk 50' back up the road to a creek crossing, then another 50' to the trailhead. If you were to continue down the road, you'd reach a parking area in almost 1.1 miles. There, 17.2 miles from the Carmel Valley Road junction, a gated road enters a Zen Buddhist monastery that contains Tassajara Hot Springs.

Introduction You may see a greater number of interesting rock outcrops along this rela-tively short route than perhaps on all of the other Ventana Wilderness trails combined. This is because, overall, the wilderness' vegetation is so pervasive that sizable trailside outcrops are in short supply, greatly frustrating those trying to decipher the area's geology. Along the Church Creek Trail, outcrops of massive sand-stone beds rise up for all to see, inspect or climb. The trail more or less follows its name-sake, Church Creek, which in turn is more or less cutting down along one of the major faults in the Santa Lucia Range, the Church Creek Fault—another geological attribute.

But this lightly traveled trail is not likely to be used by geologists and rock climbers. More likely, it is used by those who are making a grand tour of the wilderness and need to get from Willow Creek up to Church Creek Divide. Due to its remote trailhead, the route is not a popular one for casual hikers, and its severity, coupled with a lot of brush and a bit of poison oak, does not make for pleasurable hiking. Ticks could be quite a problem in the wet season.

Description Leaving the Tassajara Road (elev. 2180′), the Church Creek Trail immediately crosses a transitory stream and enters Ventana Wilderness in the process, then ⅓ mile later recrosses the stream. Over the next ½ mile, the brushy, ascending trail writhes across minor ridges and gullies to arrive at the first of seven divides. Here, atop a sandstone ridge, you're only about 100 yards below the very evident Tassajara Road. It's also very evident that the dense chamise along the ridge makes a short cross-country jaunt to the road almost impossible.

You have a noteworthy view of massive, dipping beds of sandstone, and you'll see that routing a trail to them was not an easy task. The Church Creek Trail first contorts along sandstone beds of the first ridge and then makes a short descent to delightful **Wildcat Camp** (2770-1.1). This one-tent site has a table, and is located on the bank of a perennially flowing creek. If you're making a grand loop of the wilderness, you might plan spending the night here, since it is the only suitable site between Willow Creek and Pine Valley.

Onward, your trail squirms ¼ mile up to a second divide, which offers an enticing view of the third. That one's reached in about ⅓ mile, after a convoluted drop to, and climb from, a three-season creeklet. On both sides of the third divide (3240-0.6) rise the best rocks for scrambling. Bring along a rope if you're going to try any serious climbing.

Your trail continues by first traversing along a contact between two sandstone layers, then it winds down brushy slopes to a sizable gully (2760-0.5), which has a year-round creeklet. Over the next 0.2 mile, you drop 200′ to arrive at a large, bouldery wash that drains an impressive side canyon. Unfortunately, the wash is usually dry except during the wet season. From it you snake onward, climbing about 200′ up to the fourth divide (2790-0.5). This one's broad and grassy, and from it you see the fifth divide and the Church Ranch Road (my name for it), which descends along it. The road is your goal, so study the intervening terrain. In 1987 the last ⅓ mile of trail was in disarray, and deer

Sandstone outcrops tempt rock climbers

paths complicated route-finding problems. If you're heading in the opposite direction, be sure to study the terrain from the road, and identify the broad, grassy divide.

You start on a contour from the broad divide, drop a bit to a gully with a generally flowing (or seeping) creeklet, round an adjacent ridge, and then reach another one. Ahead, the trail is vague, and if it gets reworked, it may differ slightly from that shown on the map. In its 1987 condition you could easily lose the proper tread, but finding the **Church Ranch Road** (2730-0.7) is easy. The southern part of the Church Creek Trail meets this road immediately before it begins to curve around the gently descending ridge, the fifth divide, which on the map is called *The Mesa*.

Church Ranch Road

The first 3.4 miles of this road, the stretch down to the Church Creek Trail junction, is across Forest Service lands except for a section roughly between mile points 2.2 and 2.8. If you take it, you'll have plenty of views, for the roadside vegetation is mostly shadeless brush. (You wouldn't want to ascend the road on a hot afternoon, even though its gradient is a very reasonable, moderate 10%.) Your only reliable water along this descent is in a shady gully, which the road crosses at mile point 2.8 and then again at point 3.0.

The southern edge of the road is part of the Ventana Wilderness boundary, and by stepping on the road, we temporarily leave the wilderness. We curve around The Mesa and descend to the trail's best stream, which the road bridges (2580-0.3). Next it traverses west, then north, and nearly touches sycamore-lined Church Creek immediately before reaching a gate (2580-0.5). Here we enter the Bruce Church Ranch, and you must stay on the road. You go about 340 yards to a fenced-in part of the ranch, and continue onward about 70 yards to where a spur road branches across the creek to a residence near a sandstone outcrop known as The Caves which, unfortunately, is off limits. After another 150 yards, the main road becomes an old, little-used road. This stays fairly close to Church Creek, continuing up-canyon 350 yards before dying out at an often-dry creek bed (2610-0.5). Welcome back to the wilderness.

Now on the north segment of the Church Creek Trail, we stay close to Church Creek for about ¼ mile, then climb a grass-and-oak ridge to a minor divide, our sixth (3130-0.7). From

it, and from much of the trail over the next ½ mile, you have striking views of major sandstone outcrops just across the creek—a mouth-watering sight for rock climbers. Others can water their mouths at a usually reliable creeklet just past the divide or, around a nearby ridge, at another one (3340-0.6).

Tree cover predominates as we make the last stretch. We cross several usually dry gullies, and then the adjacent live oaks and black oaks are joined by madrones, whose berries attract flocks of pigeons in the fall. The final part is along the generally waterless head-waters of Church Creek, and we pass a few ponderosa pines just before reaching our final divide, **Church Creek Divide** (3651-0.8), where we meet the Pine Ridge and Carmel River trails. See Routes CC-2 and CC-3 to continue onward.

CC-5

Tassajara Road to Marble Peak Trail and Tassajara Creek via Horse Pasture Trail and Tassajara Cutoff

Distances
    1.4 miles to Horse Pasture Camp
    2.3 miles to junction with Tassajara Cutoff Trail
        1.0 mile along trail to junction with Tassajara Creek Trail
            0.2 mile along trail to its end
    5.1 miles to junction with Marble Peak Trail

Map 16

Trailhead See the Routes CC-1 and CC-4 trailheads

Introduction Like the previous route, this lightly traveled one probably gets the most use from those folks trying to get from Willow Creek to Church Creek Divide. Like it, the trail has a lot of brush, including local populations of poison oak. Unlike the Church Creek Trail, this trail is not very scenic, despite traversing mostly through the wilderness' 1992 addition. However, it does have one notable attraction: by taking the Tassajara Cutoff, you can reach some fine pools along Tassajara Creek. Unfortunately, climbing back from the pools will probably get you quite hot and sweaty, which is counterproductive to visiting the pools. These are much more easily reached from nearby Tassajara Hot Springs, which lie on the grounds of the Zen Mountain Center, a Buddhist mon-

astery. The Buddhists do take in guests from May 1st through early September, but do not accept drop-in visitors, since this disrupts the ambience of the setting. They lack the facilities to handle a crowd, and you may not even find available parking space outside the gate. If you're seriously interested in staying at the monastery (whose lodging is usually booked months in advance), contact the Zen Center in San Francisco at (415) 863-3136.

Description From the Tassajara Road (elev. 2320') the Horse Pasture Trail makes an easy climb, first across gullied, grassy slopes, then across brushy ones to the wilderness boundary by a saddle (2650-0.7) on a long ridge. Now with eastern views we switchback down to a seasonal creek, cross its adjacent tributary, and there find defunct **Horse Pasture Camp** (2140-0.7). Pasturage, like water and camp space, is essentially nonexistent, and you should camp here only in an emergency.

Traversing down-canyon, we reach in ¼ mile a shady gully, blessed with chain ferns and, almost always, water. In another ¼ mile we come to an open ridge with mildly inspiring views, then circle around a bowl to reach a near-crest junction with a trail, the **Tassajara Cutoff** (2200-0.9). Unlike the trail ahead, this one is meritorious.

Tassajara Cutoff

This trail has a moderate-to-steep average gradient of about 13.7%, which you'll certainly feel when climbing back up it. Downward, it's a joy. You descend into a fairly dramatic side canyon, crossing its bouldery, seasonal stream in ½ mile. This you parallel briefly, leaving it just before a waterfall. The trail switchbacks once, descends to the fall's base, and then quickly arrives at a junction with the **Tassajara Creek Trail** (1440-1.0), this point lying 35 yards downstream from the side canyon's creek. On this informal but generally well-built trail, you can walk momentarily downstream to a large, usually dammed, pool—a goal of many Tassajara Hot Springs visitors. The trail continues along bedrock just above the pool, and since the rock is very water-worn, be careful. It then **ends** (1420-0.2) by small pools near the creek's union with a

A Tassajara Creek pool

tributary. *What is needed is a continuation of the trail 2¼ miles down Tassajara Creek to Willow Creek where, on an adjacent bank, one would find Tassajara Camp.* At present, the user can get from Tassajara Road to the Marble Peak Trail, along Willow Creek, only by the Horse Pasture Trail or the Tony Trail—neither desirable.

Upstream from the Tassajara Cutoff trail, the Tassajara Creek trail reaches the Tassajara Hot Springs monastic grounds in about ½ mile. This trail to the grounds and out to the end of the Tassajara Road is a public right-of-way, but I discourage all but the monastery's visitors from using it.

On the Horse Pasture Trail you climb about 100 yards to a ridge, take a few steps up it, then make a ⅔ mile, viewful traverse across a broad bowl to another ridge. About midway along it, you'll cross a spring that is reduced to just a seep in the dry months. From the second ridge, you head south, staying just east of and below its crest, then wind down to a creek crossing (1810-1.2). Over the next 0.4 mile you cross it six more times, and even in the dry season may find just a small pool or two of stagnant water—not very desirable. This stretch has more than its share of poison oak. The trail then continues about ¼ mile downstream before making a brief climb to a saddle (1500-0.7) by a massive, scenic, sandstone outcrop.

With the Willow Creek/Tassajara Creek canyon in sight, you next wind down chamise-covered slopes of a gulch, and cross its creek bed just before reaching a crossing of the main creek's bed (1180-0.5). This junction is by a 20' high sandstone boulder, and just downstream you reach a twin boulder. Just past it, the trail splits, and the unofficial fork, along the creek, may look like the main trail. You take the uphill fork, which quickly reaches a bench and traverses south along it, then makes a short drop to Tassajara Creek, which is easily boulder-hopped. Momentarily you find yourself at a junction with the **Marble Peak Trail** (1070-0.4), which is described in Chapter 6's Route AS-2.

Chapter 6: Arroyo Seco

AS-1

Arroyo Seco to Rocky Creek Camp via Rocky Creek Trail

Distance
2.5 miles to Rocky Creek Camp

Map 16

Trailhead See the Route AS-2 trailhead

Introduction Rocky Creek Camp, located on land added to Ventana Wilderness in 1992, is just as nice as most camps within the older part of the wilderness except for one problem: it may be waterless from as long as mid-May through mid-November. Fortunately, you can get water from Rocky Creek before you reach the camp. There is also a problem with the trailhead: you won't find any roadside parking anywhere near it. The only place you can leave a vehicle is in Arroyo Seco Campground, about ½ mile up the road, but doing so usurps a campsite that could be used by others. If you are just on a day hike, you can park in nearby Arroyo Seco Picnic Ground, but then you won't want to go all the way to the camp, but just to Rocky Creek. Unlike Arroyo Seco, it is too small to support swimming holes.

Description From the east side of the bridge over pool-blessed Arroyo Seco, a driveway (elev. 790') climbs northeast to a fenced-in U.S.F.S. building. You go up the driveway to the fence, then take an obvious trail, which immediately crosses a minor wash and parallels it north. Quickly, you'll pass a trail branching right, down to the usually dry wash, and just beyond it you'll reach a saddle. Here you have a revealing view of local sedimentary rocks as well as one of spacious Arroyo Seco Picnic Ground. On warm summer days, you're likely to see swimmers frolicking in a large pool by the picnic ground as well as in a string of pools

extending ½ mile up beyond the picnic ground. As you climb a bit westward, you have a view of the northern of two artificial lakes—off limits to swimming.

The trail turns southwest and gives rise to misleading spur trails as it contours to, and then across, a broad bench. From a brink at its end, you traverse across chamise-clad slopes that likely harbor abundant ticks in the spring. Fortunately, this trail is *usually* well maintained, so you don't have push through brush. Near the west end of your traverse, you can look directly across the canyon and see, high on Arroyo Seco canyon's opposite wall, some impressive river sediments—atop which lies Arroyo Seco Campground.

About one mile into the route, good views fade as you turn northwest and traverse up Rocky Creek canyon. Chamise gets joined by other vegetation, from drought-loving yerba santas to water-loving sycamores. After a ½-mile stroll past interesting bedrock outcrops and two small, usually dry, waterfalls, the trail cuts through a man-made gap in a minor ridge, and then quickly reaches lush, shady streamside vegetation, including some poison oak. Here you make the first easy crossing of Rocky Creek, and over the next 0.4 mile make seven more crossings.

In dry months you'll want to get water at one of these crossings. Just beyond the last one, you'll find a small flat, where folks have obviously camped, and with good reason, for above it, the creek may be dry. A minute past the camp, you round a rocky ridge and then soon leave the creek for a climb across grassy, brushy slopes. The climb is short-lived, and you descend toward the creek, then curve right, north, into a dry wash. You could lose the trail here, for it goes a few yards upstream before starting west. All in a couple of minutes, you first cross seasonal Rocky Creek, cross its seasonal western tributary, and then arrive at **Rocky Creek Camp.** The camp itself is relatively small, hardly larger than the tight cluster of several buckeyes that seasonally shade it. Still, on minor flats here and there, you can pitch several tents. Westward, a use trail goes about 100 yards before dying out. Northward, the bulk of Rocky Creek canyon lies ahead of you, but without a trail through the brush, few people will want to explore it.

Right: Rocky Creek Camp

AS-2

Arroyo Seco to Tassajara Camp, Willow Springs Camp, Strawberry Camp, South Fork Camp, Rainbow Camp, Tan Oak Camp, Indian Valley Camp, Upper Higgins Camp, Marble Peak and Coast Ridge Road via Marble Peak, South Fork and Lost Valley Trails

Distances
    0.3 mile to bridge across Arroyo Seco
    1.2 miles to junction with Horse Pasture Trail
    2.3 miles to Tassajara Camp
    4.1 miles to junction with Tony Trail
    4.5 miles to Willow Springs Camp
    5.8 miles to saddle at head of Willow Creek canyon
    9.4 miles to junction with South Fork Trail
        0.3 mile along trail to Strawberry Camp
        3.2 miles along trail to South Fork Camp
        5.2 miles along trail to Rainbow Camp
    9.8 miles to Tan Oak Camp
    11.1 miles to saddle above Tan Oak Creek canyon
    12.5 miles to junction with Lost Valley Trail in Indian Valley
        0.7 mile along trail to junction with Indian Valley Camp Trail
            0.2 mile along trail to Indian Valley Camp
        1.4 miles along trail to Upper Higgins Camp

    13.8 miles to fork in Marble Peak Trail
    the 0.1-mile-long west fork to Coast Ridge Road is a private trail—*no trespassing*
    0.3 mile along south fork to junction with Coast Ridge Road

Maps 16, 15 and 14

Trailhead If you're coming from the north, drive to Salinas, and from the Monterey Peninsula exit drive almost 26 miles south on U.S. Highway 101 to the Arroyo Seco Road/Mission La Soledad exit. This is the first exit past the town of Soledad, and it is about 0.4 mile beyond a long bridge across the Salinas River. Head 1.1 miles west on Arroyo Seco Road to a sharp bend left, where you'll meet Fort Romie Road (County Road G17), which goes northwest to the nearby mission. From this junction, Arroyo Seco Road is County Road G17 for 8.5 miles south, to a junction with Elm Avenue (County Road G16).

    If you want to get supplies in Greenfield, you can take a different approach. Continue south on 101, driving about 7 miles past the Arroyo Seco exit, and take Greenfield's Walnut Avenue exit. Head about ⅓ mile west to a stoplight, passing a shopping center, on the right, along the way. Turn left onto El Camino Real and drive ½ mile south through the small town to Oak Avenue, then ¼ mile beyond it to Elm Avenue. (Unlike 101's Walnut Avenue exit, which has only offramps, the Oak Avenue exit has offramps *and* onramps for both north- and southbound 101 traffic.) Turn right on Elm Avenue, and drive 5.8 miles southwest to a junction with Arroyo Seco Road, bridging Arroyo Seco—a small river—and then immediately veering *left* just before the junction.

If you're coming from southern California, King City will be the last major town before you leave Highway 101. About 11 miles past its last exit—Broadway (gas, food, lodging)—you'll reach Greenfield's southernmost exit—Route 101 Business. Take it and reach Elm Avenue in about ½ mile. If you don't need supplies, turn left and drive, as mentioned above, 5.8 miles southwest to a junction with Arroyo Seco Road.

Over the next stretch, Arroyo Seco Road coincides with Carmel Valley Road and is signed as County Road G16. After 6.5 miles west, the two roads split. *If you're bound for the China Camp environs, continue 17.0 miles northwest on Carmel Valley Road to a junction with Tassajara Road, then consult the trailhead directions for Chapter 5's Route CC-1.*

For Chapter 6's routes, take Arroyo Seco Road, which goes 5.0 scenic miles to its official ending immediately before the self-service pay station at spacious, live-oak-shaded Arroyo Seco Campground. Some points of interest along this stretch are: Millers Lodge (on the left, mile 0.5—cabins, cafe, bar, groceries, gas, laundry, campground, firewood, bait, river swimming), Robbies Store (on the right, mile 0.8—minimal supplies), Arroyo Seco Guard Station (on the left, mile 4.4—information and phone), bridge over Arroyo Seco *(start of Route AS-1),* then Arroyo Seco Picnic Ground (on the right, mile 4.5).

About 0.4 mile beyond the campground's entrance, you reach a gate and here the pavement ends. Ahead is a narrow, winding, sometimes climbing, but not too bad, 16½-mile-long dirt Arroyo Seco-Indians Road (also known as Indians Road). Fortunately, you need to drive only 2.4 miles along it, to a conspicuous parking area holding about a dozen vehicles, which is immediately beyond the start of the Marble Peak Trail. Be aware that the road is typically closed from November or December through April or May.

Introduction The Marble Peak Trail, by itself or combined with other trails, offers you the southernmost of three lengthy east-west routes across the wilderness. However, you may not want to go past Willow Springs Camp, 4.5 miles along the trail, since it is one of the nicer camps in the wilderness and is reached with a minimum of effort. To reach the South Fork Trail, you'll have to expend a moderate amount of effort, but along it you can descend to the very pleasant South Fork and Rainbow camps, which are among the most isolated camps in the wilderness. These two can be reached via the Big Sur Trail, which branches off the Pine Ridge Trail (Chapter 5) and the Coast Ridge Road (Chapter 8), but these two approaches involve several thousand feet of elevation change, which is not desirable if you're on foot with a heavy pack. Before the 1977 Marble-Cone fire, Indian Valley was a delightful pine-and-oak woodland, but now it is all too shrubby and, perhaps because of the fire, its creeks dry up sooner than they used to, creating problems for the dry-season visitor.

This trail is best taken in late winter or early spring, when flowers are at their best, or in fall, when leaves are changing color. Unfortunately, during these times, Indians Road is likely to be closed. Parking near the gate by Arroyo Seco Campground, you'll have about 2½ additional miles to hike to reach the trailhead, but you'll can console yourself that, due to this inconvenience, you won't have much company.

Description The Marble Peak Trail begins (elev. 1340') as a broad, well-used path, which drops at an average gradient of 23%—you'll certainly notice this steepness on your return trip. Just after ¼ mile, it reaches a junction with a well-used, unofficial path, which heads south about 200 yards to some shallow pools of Arroyo Seco (Spanish: *Dry Creek*). A cross-country trek south up along Arroyo Seco will yield more pools and in itself is a worthy excursion. The Marble Peak Trail drops a bit more to quickly span Arroyo Seco on a sturdy **bridge** (960-0.3). This is about as far as many, if not most, summer visitors get, for beneath the bridge is a fine swimming hole. About 120 yards north, downstream, Arroyo Seco is joined by east-flowing Tassajara Creek. From this juncture, you'll find additional, desirable pools just west up Tassajara Creek and just east down Arroyo Seco.

From the bridge, the Marble Peak Trail starts as an old road, which quickly branches left into oblivion, and we continue straight ahead, west, on a broad path. Within Ventana Wilderness since spanning Arroyo Seco, we pass first manzanitas, then live oaks and poison oak, and soon arrive at a steep bluff overlooking Arroyo Seco. From this bluff, the trail immediately crosses a steep, unstable slope, where future trail washouts could occur and possibly stop exposure-conscious hikers.

Continuing up our straight canyon, which is cut along the wilderness' only major east-west fault, our oak-shaded trail ducks in and out of two gullies, and then soon reaches a junction with the **Horse Pasture Trail** (1070-0.9).

Horse Pasture Trail

This 5.1-mile trail passes through mostly brushy, rather mediocre terrain, and a hike along it can be a miserable experience if the trail hasn't been maintained for several years. Even when it's in prime shape, this well-graded, mostly waterless trail offers you little other than a route over to Tassajara Road. On that road you can descend ¼ mile southwest, then take the scenic Church Creek Trail up to Church Creek Divide. The Church Creek and Horse Pasture trails are described in the previous chapter as Routes CC-4 and CC-5.

Just 200 yards beyond the trail junction, we reach another, and a spur trail goes 45 yards to a two-tent campsite that in 1987 had a fire ring and grate, but no table. From the site, a use trail headed downstream, passing a one-tent campsite and quickly dying out by the Tassajara Creek ford of the Horse Pasture Trail.

Onward, the trail is routed essentially along an abandoned jeep road. This makes an initial climb and then traverses fairly high above the creek, ducking in and out of gullies and passing two reliable springs along the way. Just a few minutes after we weave in and out of a side canyon vegetated with maple, alder, madrone, spikenard and the all too common poison oak, we arrive at **Tassajara Camp** (1150-1.1). As with the previous campsite, this one has space for about two tents near alder-lined Willow Creek (willows are present, as are maples and sycamores, but alders dominate this misnamed creek). A pit toilet is just south of the trail. The ground in this area is fairly level, offering possible campsites for about a 200-yard stretch south of the camp proper. In this vicinity you can find the union of Tassajara Creek with Willow Creek. The wilderness definitely could use a trail ascending 2½ miles up scenic Tassajara Creek canyon to a junction with the Tassajara Cutoff trail. If it is built, then the undesirable Horse Pasture and Tony trails could be abandoned. For now, the route up the canyon is straight-forward cross-country, not very difficult, but tedious, and often giving one the chance to slip while boulder-hopping.

Just 100 yards beyond Tassajara Camp we make our first of 17 boulderhops of Willow Creek. You can expect all to be quite easy except during or just after heavy rains. The first 11 occur in fairly rapid succession over a verdant ⅔-mile stretch. The 12th occurs 0.2 mile later, the 13th 0.4 mile after that, and the 14th 0.5 mile farther. Just 60 yards past it, you're likely to see a junction with the **Tony Trail** (1800-1.8).

Tony Trail

If you're eastbound on the Marble Peak Trail and want to get to the Church Creek Trail, this is a shortcut route to it—only 4.6 miles versus 8.1 via the Horse Pasture route. Still, I don't recommend it, for the trail ends on the grounds of a Zen Buddhist monastery in the Tassajara Hot Springs vicinity. The public does have a legal right-of-way across the grounds to the Tassajara Road, but the monks would prefer to have as few unannounced guests as possible. The Forest Service's 1987 Ventana Wilderness topographic map depicts this brushy, essentially waterless trail as abandoned, yet just months after the map was published, the trail was thoroughly reworked and resigned. So, one is left with mixed signals about whether or not to take the trail. Certainly you shouldn't take it to get help at the monastery; heading east on the Marble Peak Trail toward Arroyo Seco Guard Station involves much less effort.

With the above said, I'll describe the trail for those who feel they need to take it. It quickly crosses Willow Creek and then an adjacent, side-canyon creeklet—your only sources of water. It then climbs a bit before traversing rather precariously along steep slopes above Willow Creek. Ahead, your route is brushy—a problem when the trail's not maintained. Via more than a dozen switchbacks along a ridge, it gains about 400' of elevation over the next ½ mile, then climbs along slopes and past gullies, generally through chamise (the winter tick's favorite bush), up to a saddle (2930-1.6). The view received is not worth the energy expended.

Ahead, the route is worse. It starts out nicely enough with a scenic traverse, followed by a moderate descent, but then from a gully

(2700-0.6) it makes a plunge (24% gradient!) past tall brush to Tassajara Creek (1550-0.9). In this direction the trail is obvious; in the reverse its start is not, for there are several other trails by the creek. However, the Tony Trail is the only one that climbs from the creek.

Considering the extensive drainage of Tassajara Creek and its principal tributary, Church Creek, you'd expect the creek crossing to be difficult. But in summer and early fall the creek's broad bed can be entirely dry! The creek bed swings around a prominent east-dropping ridge, and by the north side of its snout you'll find a road. Follow it for about ⅓ mile as it parallels the creek in an arc past monastery buildings to a junction. From here you take a north-climbing road 160 yards up a canyon to a gate by the end of the Tassajara Road (1570-0.4). Continue up the road, perhaps getting water midway along the route where the road crosses the creek. On shadier slopes, you continue up the road to a sharp bend, immediately recross the creek, and then immediately reach the south end of the Church Creek Trail (Chapter 5's Route CC-4).

From the Tony Trail junction the Marble Peak Trail makes three rapid crossings of now much diminished Willow Creek, then it crosses a trickling tributary before arriving at a second one, within the confines of spacious, live-oak-shaded **Willow Springs Camp** (1970-0.4). This camp is probably the most desirable one along the Marble Peak Trail, its only detraction being slightly sloping ground. If you just want a pleasant campsite, you needn't go any farther.

Ahead, you face an 800' climb. The first ⅓ mile is an easy, shady climb, but then you duck in and out of a gully, switchback up over to a ridge, then climb up it, exchanging oaks for chamise, manzanita and warty-leaved ceanothus. The tradeoff does have one redeeming feature: as you climb to a saddle, you have a number of good views east down the Willow Creek canyon. The gradient eases when the trail turns south. Here, toyon and yerba santa line part of the easing trail, while oaks provide some shade. Soon you reach a **saddle at the head of Willow Creek canyon** (2770-1.3), and now you have views to the south and west as well as ones to the east. From the saddle or just west of it, a trail once descended less than a mile to Zigzag Camp. In 1987 there wasn't a trace of the trail, but given the zeal of volunteer trail crews, it's possible that in a future

year the trail will be re-opened. If so, I hope the camp will be relocated to a more reliable stretch of creek.

From the saddle, the South Fork Trail junction lies about 1.5 miles due west, out of sight. Lamentably, your trail will take about 3.6 miles to reach it. This stretch has to be hiked to be believed. The highly contorted, though amazingly level, trail winds in and out of two major side canyons plus myriad gullies. On your traverse west you see miles and miles of chaparral. At one time there was a considerable forest of oaks and madrones below you, but the 1977 Marble-Cone fire ravaged this area, and dense brush, mostly green-stemmed ceanothus, has replaced the trees.

After much winding, we make a gradual descent into a side canyon and cross refreshing Camp Creek (2760-0.9). An easy climb out of the canyon gets us to a minor saddle, from which we snake into another side canyon, this one harboring diminutive, but usually reliable, Shovel Handle Creek (2720-0.7). Westward, we ramble past more brush, climbing more than 200' to cross one ridge, then contouring over to a second, passing a fairly reliable spring midway. From the second saddle we leave the chaparral landscape behind as we drop just over ¼ mile to a junction with the **South Fork Trail** (2750-2.0).

South Fork Trail

This 5.2-mile trail offers superior camping to that along the Marble Peak Trail, though you wouldn't conclude it from viewing the first site, **Strawberry Camp** (2840-0.3), which is small and is on sloping ground. Still, you could cram four tents into the vicinity. This camp is located to the northwest, up Strawberry Valley, and is reached after two crossings of the valley's creek. From about June through October you can expect the creek to be dry—another negative feature. Before the 1977 fire, the Black Cone Trail started north up a gully, but then the route became throughly overgrown with blackberries. In fall 1987 volunteers began brushing out the trail from the north end southward, and by spring 1988 the entire trail may be followable. Unfortunately, the resurrection of this trail happened too late to be mapped and included in this current edition. Before planning a trek along this trail, first check with the King City Ranger Station (phone: 408-385-5434) to verify its condition.

Onward, you climb moderately west up a gully to a brushy saddle (2940-0.2), and have your first view of a long ridge traversed by the

Coast Ridge Road. On a hot summer day, it's hard to believe that a cool fog bank lies just a mile or two down the other side of the ridge. Now you make a switchbacking descent, leaving chamise, manzanita and warty-leaved ceanothus for live oak, green-stemmed ceanothus and a few Coulter pines. Where you first cross the canyon's creek (2550-0.6), you can expect water to be absent during the dry months. Onward, you cross generally shady slopes before switchbacking to a second creek crossing (2280-0.4). You can almost always expect to find water here. If not, it's likely to be in small pools between this crossing and the next one, about 240 yards downstream. The quality of the possibly standing water may leave something to be desired, but it may be the only water you'll find in the canyon.

Past the third crossing we make three more, these usually dry in summer and early fall. Now we stay on the canyon's lower north slopes, paralleling the seasonal creek westward. What's labeled on U.S. Forest Service and U.S. Geological Survey maps as the South Fork Big Sur River, joining our creek from the south, is also seasonal, and very likely you'll not even see it. The *real* South Fork joins our creek about ½ mile down-canyon, and we spy its spirited water just moments after crossing a reliable, trickling creeklet. The trail drops to the South Fork juncture, and folks have camped here, perhaps not realizing that just 90 yards down-canyon lies moderately large **South Fork Camp** (1800-1.7). Live oaks, alders, maples and sycamores provide welcome shade on a warm summer day. In winter, all but the oaks lose their leaves, so the camp isn't as shady as one would imagine. A shallow, adja-

cent South Fork pool provides a refreshing dip on a hot day.

The route ahead is now quite shady, and water problems are over, unless you're hiking the South Fork Trail during or just after a storm. Then, the five downstream boulder-hops, which are usually easy, may be replaced with cold, wet fords. From the fifth crossing, the trail climbs fairly high to skirt just above steep slopes, then it methodically descends, ending with a series of short switchbacks immediately before entering **Rainbow Camp** (1560-2.0), which stretches west along a 100-yard-long terrace. While it, like other river camps, may be cool and damp in winter, this camp is a pleasure the rest of the year. In case you don't want to drink from the Big Sur, you'll find a seeping spring in mid-camp at the base of a slope. A creeklet flows down a gully just west of the camp, ending as two side-by-side, moss-draped falls that splash into an attractive South Fork pool.

By the camp's east end, you meet the Big Sur Trail. North, it drops to immediately cross sizable South Fork Big Sur River, then this poorly laid-out route makes an intimidating climbing/descending track across two major ridges to reach the Pine Ridge Trail. See the last part of Chapter 5's Route CC-3 for a description of this 4.3-mile-long ordeal. West, the Big Sur Trail is equally intimidating, despite the route being laid out fairly well. It first traverses 0.7 mile over to Mocho Camp, then makes a major, two-tiered climb to Logwood Ridge. For a detailed account of the 5.0-mile stretch from Rainbow Camp to Cold Spring Camp, follow the last part of Chapter 8's Route BS-3.

South Fork Camp is shady in summer but fairly sunny in winter

From the junction with the east end of the South Fork Trail, the Marble Peak Trail immediately crosses Strawberry Valley's seasonal creek, and then in 120 yards passes a small, open campsite with a fire ring. The trail makes two more crossings, the second one just below a short, usually permanent stretch of creek, though in summer and early fall, the essentially standing water could be unsafe to drink. A minute past this crossing, you enter **Tan Oak Camp** (2680-0.4), which is not located on Tan Oak Creek and is *not* shaded by tanbark oaks (it's shaded by stately bays, madrones, and white alders). The linear camp, with room for two or three tents, occupies gently sloping ground beside a *blackberry*-lined stretch of *Strawberry* Valley's creek. Should you find the creek dry, don't worry. Head 40 yards south down along the trail to where it curves right, away from the creek, and then continue along the creek 35 additional yards to lilting Tan Oak Creek.

Beyond the camp the Marble Peak Trail quickly turns southwest to climb up Tan Oak Creek canyon. The trail soon comes alongside the creek for a brief spell, and this is your last chance to easily obtain water—*ahead, for about half of the year, the Marble Peak Trail is likely to be entirely waterless.* The trail continues to parallel the creek, though dense brush and steep slopes make creek access more difficult. About ¼ mile past the camp, the creek often dries up in the dry season, then, ¼ mile later, we leave the creek altogether. Ahead, the tread is generally quite broad, which is fortunate, for otherwise the pervasive brush would impinge against us. On a climbing ½-mile

Tan Oak Camp

ascent, we weave in and out of several gullies, reach a scenic saddle and, just above it, reach an even more scenic one. You get a view northwest down the South Fork Big Sur canyon, and can identify 4853' Ventana Double Cone among many horizon summits. It stands just east of the canyon, and the ridge descending west from it has a noticeable cleft—a barrier to mountaineers trying to reach the summit's western outlier.

Onward, the very broad trail makes a moderate-to-steep ascent through a dense stand of youthful oaks, which someday will shade this stretch, but in doing so will block the views. After a ¼-mile effort, we reach a **saddle above Tan Oak Creek canyon** (3537-1.3), and have manifest views in all compass points other than west and east. If you look southwest down the trail, you'll see a minor summit on a long ridge. This is overstated 4031' Marble Peak, our trail's namesake, and it rises a mere 200' above two minor saddles that bracket it.

You now enter chaparral lands of chamise, manzanita and warty-leaved ceanothus. However, if you're observant, you should see a few knobcone pines, which are uncommon in the wilderness. This low, scraggly pine does best in fire-prone chaparral communities, and it differs from youthful, more common Coulter pines in that it has clusters of small cones clinging to the tree's main branches. Along this first stretch, a trail once branched downslope to Higgins Camp, but after the Marble-Cone fire it was thoroughly overwhelmed by brush. Still, there's a slight possibility that the trail may be resurrected by volunteer trail crews.

About ½ mile from the saddle the scenery makes a dramatic change. You may have noticed some outcrops of sedimentary rocks over the last mile or so, but now you are walking completely among such rocks. You leave shale behind as you cross a sandstone ridge, then wind southwest down to an adjacent ridge that has large sandstone boulders (tempting to rock climbers) just south of the trail. Shale predominates as we wind westward, crossing a major gully and a minor saddle, but soon we turn southwest and see an interesting assortment of sandstone boulders plus some fine views of rapidly approaching Indian Valley, with its ghost woodland of roasted oak snags. The Marble-Cone fire was intense here, and you'll see abundant evidence of it. Also note Anderson Peak—a minor summit to the right of Marble Peak—identified by a white tower atop it.

In Indian Valley we reach a junction with the **Lost Valley Trail** (2805-1.4). Formerly, if you'd follow often dry Higgins Creek about 200 yards up the grassy valley, you'd reach a camp. Not today. Since fewer snags abound, the upper reaches of this valley would be nice for camping, were it not for a lack of water from about May through early November. To find a suitable camp, you'll have to descend along the Lost Valley Trail.

Lost Valley Trail

This parallels the seasonal creek 0.4 mile southeast downstream, crosses it, and soon becomes brush-lined. The trail keeps close to the creek, and where both bend south, they cross a resistant, massive sandstone layer. When the creek's dry, you can miss the layer, but when it's flowing, a small, chorusing waterfall calls your attention to it. Barely a minute's walk south past the fall, you come to a junction with the **Indian Valley Camp Trail** (2700-0.7).

This side trip on a minor trail climbs west rather steeply past brush to a wisp of a saddle, from which you'll see, about 80 yards away, three tall black oaks and several ponderosa-pine snags. That is the site of **Indian Valley Camp** (2810-0.2). Crossing a grassy flat toward it, the trail dies out. Like the former Indian Valley Camp, this newer one lacks a year-round water supply. The adjacent creek is likely to be dry from about June through October. If you were to continue cross-country a fairly level ¼ mile northwest, you'd reach a grassy meadow shaded by ponderosa pines—an admirable setting for a camp. However, unless a well were dug, seasonal lack of water would still be a problem. The wilderness could use a stretch of trail to this meadow, and then one just beyond it up dense-chaparral slopes to the nearby Marble Peak Trail.

From the Indian Valley Camp Trail junction, the Lost Valley Trail immediately heads east across a gully then quickly rejoins Higgins Creek for a short arc from southeast to south. Rather than continue down along the seasonal creek, the trail crosses it, climbs northeast to a low saddle, and then descends moderately along oak-shaded, somewhat brushy slopes. On open slopes you negotiate several short switch-backs to quickly arrive at **Upper Higgins Camp** (2315-0.7), immediately past a seasonal Higgins Creek tributary. Fortunately, you can find water by continuing 80 yards east to a second tributary. The water barely flows late in summer and in the driest years, so if you want water of better quality, continue about 250 yards along the trail, to where you see Higgins Creek flowing among trees below you. To continue southeast along the Lost Valley Trail, consult Chapter 7's Route IR-1, which is described in the opposite direction.

In Indian Valley, we step across seasonal Higgins Creek just southwest of the Lost Valley Trail junction, continue southwest up a minor gully, and then veer east to a minor ridge. This we briefly ascend southwest to a larger, west-trending ridge, and from it we can gaze southeast down at a grassy flat with stately ponderosa pines. This flat would make a very pleasant camp, at least in the wet months, when the flat's creek is flowing, and indeed, a trail once descended about 250 yards to it. Today, however, an essentially impenetrable barrier of chamise, manzanita and warty-leaved ceanothus bars access. Hikers could use a new trail to the flat.

Onward, the Marble Peak Trail climbs up the ridge toward its namesake, veers southeast over to a minor, almost level ridge with a fine view of the drainage area, then makes a generally viewless, switchbacking ascent to a fork in the **Marble Peak Trail** (3790-1.3). The right fork is a private trail—absolutely no trespassing—and it goes west over to a saddle and down to the nearby **Coast Ridge Road**. From the junction with the two forks, follow the left fork southeast across marble outcrops, getting great views east that include Junipero Serra Peak—the highest in the area—and Bear Mountain and Pinyon Peak, just north of it and slightly farther away. The left fork reaches the ridge, *descends slightly along it and passes a misleading, former tread,* then leaves the ridge for a 90-yard traverse to the **Coast Ridge Road** (3770-0.3). Regardless of which way you head along the Coast Ridge Road, you'll consult Chapter 8's Route BS-4, which describes a stretch of the road from the Cold Spring Road junction southeast to road's end.

Chapter 7: Indians Road

IR-1

Escondido Campground to Fish Camp, Coast Ridge Trail, Lost Valley Camp, Pelon Camp, Upper Higgins Camp, Indian Valley Camp and Marble Peak Trail via Lost Valley Trail and Lost Valley Connector

Distances
    4.0 miles to Fish Camp
    4.9 miles to junction with Lost Valley Connector
        1.6 miles along trail to Coast Ridge Trail
    5.8 miles to Lost Valley Camp
    8.9 miles to Pelon Camp
    10.0 miles to Upper Higgins Camp
    10.7 miles to junction with Indian Valley Camp Trail
        0.2 mile along trail to Indian Valley Camp
    11.4 miles to junction with Marble Peak Trail

Maps 20, 19, 18 and 15

Trailhead The trailhead is at the west end of Escondido Campground, which in turn lies along Arroyo Seco-Indians Road ("Indians Road," for short, and on the topo map). You can reach the campground from either end of the road. From the north end, first read Chapter 6's Route AS-2 directions to the start of the Marble Peak Trail. From that trailhead Indians Road climbs 3.6 miles to the second of two saddles, where you'll find, at its south end, the start of the Santa Lucia Trail. This descends southeast to South Fork Santa Lucia Creek, then climbs a long, dry distance to a saddle junction with a trail to Junipero Serra Peak. In 1987 the trail was unsigned, though in fairly good shape. Because the Forest Service has

designated it an unmaintained, historic trail, I've not included it in the book. Still, a few avid hikers may want to take this brush-lined, virtually dry route.

From the saddle Indians Road winds gently upward for 3.3 miles, but then more or less traverses for 3.1 miles, passing sandstone outcrops that will tempt climbers. It passes more sandstone as it tops a ridge to start a 1.4-mile descent to Escondido Campground's entrance, reached after 16½ dusty miles. Most folks will want to reach the campground by starting from the south end of Indians Road. Along it, you drive 2.6 winding miles up to the campground's entrance. For this approach see Route IR-2's trailhead directions.

Introduction This route takes you to some lands greatly affected by the 1977 Marble-Cone fire, and it is only marginally appealing. Fortunately, the pines around Lost Valley Camp were spared destruction, and for those who like isolated camping, this is a very desirable goal. From mid-February through mid-April, when flowers and grasses are at their best, Indians Road will very likely be closed, and from its south-end gate you'll have a 2.6-mile walk up the road to the campground, then a 0.2-mile stroll through it to the trailhead. However, when the road is closed, from about mid-fall through mid-spring, few others will take the route, so you can have it all or mostly to yourself.

71

Description Leaving the oak-shaded campground (elev. 2125'), you quickly encounter chaparral, which will be your nearly constant companion most of the way to Lost Valley Camp. From November through June, watch for ticks. Just several minutes into your journey, you hear Arroyo Seco, and after passing a seasonal waterfall, you soon start a descent to the creek. As you approach it, you'll see a shady, spacious bench on the creek's far side which offers tempting though unofficial sites for camping. About 60 yards after crossing wide, bouldery Arroyo Seco and entering Ventana Wilderness, you cross an east-flowing tributary (1640-1.0), and from it a use trail heads 45 yards down Arroyo Seco to a camp with a fire ring, perched on a long, grassy bench. Like other sites upstream, this one is also unofficial.

Ahead, you first meander along the tributary, passing live oaks, maples and bays, then start a major climb that will take you more than 1000' higher. Beyond encroaching brush you ascend a steep tread averaging 18.5% in gradient, tough enough to warrant several stops. If you take them at the right places, you'll be treated to views down-canyon to Indians Road and Junipero Serra Peak. You top out at a minor saddle (2852-1.3), only to find that the *real* saddle (2900-0.2) lies beyond. Midway between them, you'll spot a solitary knobcone pine. Others lie ahead, but this pine species occurs only in sparse numbers in the wilderness.

Exchanging views of spreading Junipero Serra Peak for canyon lands below the Coast Ridge, we start a gentler, albeit equally brushy, descent. Wandering down the Lost Valley Creek canyon, we cross two closely spaced tributaries, typically flowing only during and just after rains. Between them, on a ridge opposite a prominent south-wall sandstone cliff, is a one-tent campsite, which I don't recommend, due to its location, small size, and seasonal abundance of ticks. Sandstone and shale yield to granite, and ⅓ mile past the second tributary we reach a use trail (2280-1.2) which drops very steeply a few steps to an alluring pothole. About 12' across and 5 deep, this pool, located at the base of a small waterfall, is particularly inviting in late spring, when the seasonal creek is still flowing and is warm enough to relax in.

Brush soon gives way to shade as we descend to often-dry Lost Valley Creek. We cross it and immediately boulder-hop its adjacent, reliable southern tributary, then find ourselves in **Fish Camp** (2040-0.3). In and around this relatively small, lackluster camp, you can find room for several tents. Looking for better camping, we continue onward, wandering in and out of numerous shady gullies, cut into shale, a few with seasonally seeping springs. After spying a minor though noticeable ridge whose south slope is peppered with yuccas, we quickly arrive at a junction with the **Lost Valley Connector** (2276-0.9).

Lost Valley Connector

This is a route you won't want to ascend. Descending it from the Coast Ridge (Chapter 9's Route CP-1) is bad enough. A trail, averaging 23.4% in gradient (very steep!), climbs a manzanita-covered sandstone ridge to a firebreak (2680-0.3). The ridge-hugging firebreak averages 17.2%, but it contains two nearly level short stretches between three very steep, longer ones. From where the firebreak, after climbing the third very steep stretch, almost levels off as it turns from south to southeast, pace off 50 yards to find a junction that is obscure if not signed (3610-1.0). Take a slightly descending trail across two gullies to a junction with the **Coast Ridge Trail** (3540-0.3). The last few yards of route, to the base of a steeply ascending ridge, were cross-country in 1987. I hope the tread will be rebuilt, for the trail is invisible to those starting in the downhill direction.

From the Lost Valley Connector, the Lost Valley Trail descends steeply at first, but takes on a more reasonable gradient as it winds down to a boulder-hop of Lost Valley Creek (1795-0.6). This we parallel downstream, and in 100 yards you may see a use trail branching south, immediately crossing the creek. This you ignore, but too often eastbound hikers mistake it for the real Lost Valley Trail. You can also ignore a trail just above yours, on your right, which is an abandoned segment of the Lost Valley Trail. It briefly descends to reunite with the new segment in **Lost Valley Camp** (1750-0.3). You'll find several campsites in this spacious camp, which is nestled in a conspicuous grove of Coulter pines. In my opinion, this ranks as one of the wilderness' three best *year-round* camps, the other two being Vicente Flat and Pine Valley. Lost Valley Camp gets plenty of sun in the winter, yet has sufficient shade in the summer. Unlike the two other camps, this one is isolated, so its use is light, a definite plus. There is virtually no use when Indians Road is closed.

Lost Valley, seen from the junction with the Lost Valley Connector

About 100 yards beyond the camp's confines, you cross multibranched Lost Valley Creek and an adjacent southern tributary. Dense willows hamper your efforts, particularly if there have been recent heavy rains. Eastbound hikers can lose the tread in this crossing, though once through the willows, they'll easily identify the grove of Coulter pines harboring Lost Valley Camp.

Coulter pines shade Lost Valley Camp

Just beyond the creek your westbound trail gives rise to a misleading northbound trail. This goes about 200 yards before fading quickly. One could use it as a start of a cross-country creekside loop, first north through a 600' deep cut, then east past Zigzag Creek's mouth to Arroyo Seco, and finally up it back to the Lost Valley Trail. I haven't done this route, but being very familiar with the wilderness' geography, I'd expect no problems along it.

Beyond the junction, the Lost Valley Trail climbs up a low ridge, traverses a snag-and-chamise flat, then quickly reaches a shaley, minor divide (1820-0.2), which separates Higgins Creek drainage from that of Lost Valley Creek. You are now in the center of Lost Valley. This differs from a typical mountain valley, which has a stream flowing through it. Rather, two streams, flowing in opposite directions, converge in the valley, then flow north out its *side*—through the 600' deep cut.

From the divide we descend shortly northwest through a gully, reach a minor divide with a fence, and from it drop to nearby Higgins Creek (1700-0.4). In times of high water you may have to look up- or downstream for a dry crossing of this vigorous creek. This site, or a spot near it, could use a developed camp, since upcoming Pelon Camp leaves much to be desired. Now we walk over ½ mile through the linear west arm of Long Valley, passing through two very minor gaps in the process.

We leave the valley and its grassy slopes by climbing briefly northwest to a broad, somewhat minor divide, from which we descend briefly southwest down a brushy gully to quickly arrive at the banks of Higgins Creek.

Along it we walk about ¼ mile, then cross to the southwest bank, walk a shorter distance, and recross. Just within Section 25, we first head briefly west-southwest, passing an unofficial campsite near horsetails, then bend north-northwest. Soon we turn west-southwest once again and momentarily cross an often flowing creeklet. Paralleling Higgins Creek, the trail goes about 300 yards in this direction, rounds a low-but-prominent ridge and then starts north-northeast before dying out. You, however, look for a junction (1850-1.5), which is difficult to find if it's not signed. *This is about 100 yards before the prominent ridge.*

Note that if you continue about ¼ mile beyond the ridge via relatively easy cross-country hiking, you'll reach one of the wilderness' better swimming pools, complete with a splashing waterfall. Smaller, shallower pools lie just downstream from the main pool. Regardless of whether you reach these pools by accident or by intent, they are worth the minor effort.

A pool complete with a splashing waterfall

From the junction you immediately hop across Higgins Creek, and find the route ahead very obvious. It climbs first south, then makes an ascending traverse northwest across brushy slopes. Past a minor ridge, it levels off, then soon descends slightly to a second one. In this vicinity you'll see the previously mentioned pools and waterfall, and from this ridge you could make a short, steep, brushy, rocky descent to them. The trail, however, drops west to an adjacent creeklet, then starts another ascending, brushy traverse. You leave down-canyon views behind when you top a descending ridge, from which you switchback down to a double boulder-crossing of a creek and adjacent Higgins Creek. Just a few yards up from the latter, you reach undesirable **Pelon Camp** (2000-1.0). It's barely large enough for one tent and a fire ring, and when I visited it, the site lacked a table. However, sandstone boulders partly compensated for this inconvenience. The site is tightly confined by dense brush, with ticks likely from December through May.

Onward, you parallel Higgins Creek up-canyon, generally staying within a stone's throw of the creek. Along the way you cross two usually dry creeklets before crossing a third, which you meet 80 yards before arriving at **Upper Higgins Camp** (2315-1.1). This third creeklet flows year-round, even in most dry years, which is a blessing, since the creeklet beside the camp is definitely seasonal. If you were to go about 0.7 mile cross-country up the camp-side creeklet (not recommended), you'd reach the site of former Higgins Camp, which is hundreds of feet higher than *Upper* Higgins Camp. Interesting. Upper Higgins is not much larger than Pelon, but the surroundings are nicer and, if necessary, you could camp in the general vicinity.

Up-canyon, there are plenty of potential spots for camping, but none with a permanent source of water. The remaining 1.4 miles of trail are described in the reverse direction near the end of Chapter 6's Route AS-2. Basically, the Lost Valley Trail climbs over a gap in a divide, drops to a seasonal stretch of Higgins Creek, crosses it, and follows it about 230 yards to a junction with the **Indian Valley Camp Trail** (2700-0.7). This trail climbs up toward, but dies out before reaching, **Indian Valley Camp** (2810-0.2). The Lost Valley Trail then continues up along usually dry Higgins Creek, crossing it midway en route to an Indian Valley junction with the **Marble Peak Trail** (2805-0.7).

IR-2

Memorial Park Campground to Forks Camp, Madrone Camp and Coast Ridge Trail via Arroyo Seco Trail

Distances
1.7 miles to Forks Camp
1.9 miles to junction with firebreak (Rodeo Flat Trail)
   2.8 miles along firebreak to Coast Ridge Trail
3.0 miles to Madrone Camp
5.0 miles to junction with Coast Ridge Trail

Maps 20 and 19

Trailhead First, you'll have to get to Mission Road. If you're driving south through the Salinas Valley on U.S. Highway 101, take the Jolon Road exit. This is a full 10 miles south of the last Greenfield exit. If you were to continue 0.8 mile farther, crossing the Salinas River in the process, you'd reach the first of three King City exits: Broadway. That gives you access to gas, food, lodging and downtown King City. Take the second exit, Canal Street, if you want to reach the Los Padres National Forest's King City Ranger Station. The third exit is used for those heading to the east side of Pinnacles National Monument. On Jolon Road (County Road G14), drive 17.8 miles south to a junction with Mission Road. Here you'll find a well-equipped general store, complete with gas pumps, a laundromat, and an adjacent "restaurant" (more a bar than anything else).

If you're driving north through the Salinas Valley, take the Jolon Road exit, which is about 1¼ miles past the Bradley exit (no services), and about 30 miles south of King City. If you need major supplies, get them in Paso Robles, which is about 20 miles south of the Jolon exit. Jolon Road begins as County Road G18, and it goes 8.9 miles to a junction with a road to the east shore of Lake San Antonio. Just past the junction is a small store with gas and limited supplies. After 6.2 more miles, County Road G18 ends at a junction. Here too is a small store with gas and limited supplies. To the left, County Road G14 heads south to provide west-shore access to the artificial lake. Continue straight ahead on Jolon Road, now G14, reaching the Mission Road junction in 6.0 miles. The store here is definitely better equipped than the other two along the way, for it caters to personnel at adjacent Hunter Liggett Military Reservation.

On Mission Road you reach the reservation's gate in 0.2 mile, and usually a guard asks to see your driver's license and vehicle registration slip. In 2.9 miles you reach an important junction, which unfortunately is easy to miss along this high-speed road if you're driving in the dark. *Branching left is paved Nacimiento-Fergusson Road, which provides east-side access to the Cone Peak area (Chapter 9).* This road winds 17.9 miles to a crest intersection with Coast Ridge Road. You'll find fairly large, complete Ponderosa Campground 11.5 miles along this route, and small, rather primitive Nacimiento Campground 2.6 miles farther. Just 300 yards before South Coast Ridge Road is the U.S. Forest Service's Nacimiento Station. Northbound, the Coast Ridge Road is signed as the Central Coast Ridge Road. It's more often called Cone Peak Road, which is a better name. From the intersection Nacimiento-Fergusson Road drops 7.3 very winding miles to State Highway 1, the Cabrillo Highway. (See Chapter 9's Route CP-1 trailhead directions for west-side approach to the Cone Peak area.)

Still on Mission Road, those driving to Chapter 7's trailheads continue 1.8 miles past Nacimiento-Fergusson Road to a major intersection, 4.9 miles past the Mission Road/ Jolon Road junction. Branching right would take you up to a nearby hill capped with Mission San Antonio de Padua and other structures. You branch left, on Del Ventura Road, and keep right in 0.8 mile where a paved road branches left. Del Ventura Road eventually becomes Milpitas Road at an unspecified spot, and 12.0 miles from the intersection you cross Rattlesnake Creek, exchanging military land for national-forest land. You soon pass some interesting sandstone outcrops—an attraction for rock climbers—and in 1.9 miles pass a road, one of several branching left, this one signed for the San Antonio Trail. The eastern part of this trail is defunct; see Chapter 9's Route CP-3 for a description of the viable western part.

In 1.1 miles you bridge a creek, then climb and descend along The Rocks—a fantastic scrambling area if you like sandstone outcrops—and in 2.0 miles reach a spur road right, which goes 80 yards to a gate, the trailhead for Route IR-3: Junipero Serra Peak. Just 0.1 mile

The Rocks is a geologic formation made up of thick layers of sandstone

past this spur, you pass another one, on the left, leading to the Forest Service's Indian Station, which is often unmanned. Then, just 0.1 mile past it, you reach Memorial Park Campground, on the right, 17.2 miles from the intersection where you left Mission Road. Here, the pavement ends, and in a final 0.1 mile, at a fork, Milpitas Road also ends. To the right, Indians Road, with a gate, immediately crosses a creek for a 2.6-mile climb to Escondido Campground and beyond (Route IR-1). A road to the left immediately forks. The fork straight ahead momentarily crosses Arroyo Seco, doubles back, and quickly dies. The left fork goes a few yards to a gate. For Route IR-2, the Arroyo Seco Trail, park nearby, but don't block the gate.

Introduction The Arroyo Seco Trail takes you up the headwaters of Arroyo Seco, which in Spanish means *Dry Creek*. In and about Ventana Wilderness, Arroyo Seco is anything but dry. The trail is a very pleasing one, first taking you through a scenic canyon to Forks Camp, then up a shady side canyon to Madrone Camp, and finally up scrubby slopes with ranging vistas. Although you can use this trail to connect to the Coast Ridge Trail and thereby put together one or more loops, Arroyo Seco Trail is a delightful reward in itself.

Description From the gate (elev. 1960'), you walk 200 yards along a nearly level road to the grounds of the Southern Monterey County Sportsmen's Association, and just past the main building you'll find the start of the Arroyo Seco Trail and the boundary of Ventana Wilderness. After a shady 0.3-mile traverse beneath looming faces of The Rocks sandstone formation, you cross Arroyo Seco. The next 0.4 mile stays close to the creek, which has many miniature cascades and pools. You then veer right, away from the creek, climb into a gully with yerba santa, curve left around a chamise/scrub-oak ridge, and enter a larger gully. From here you have the trail's only problem—several hundred yards of bad tread. This stretch of sandstone terrain is landslide-prone, and future, minor slides are likely. Just beyond this stretch, you skirt above a small flat that supports a few rare, endangered Santa Lucia firs.

Beyond the firs you round a ridge with Coulter pines, and have your first good view up-canyon. In the next gully, which harbors the first trailside yuccas, you may see an unofficial campsite on sloping ground below you. Bypass it in favor of upcoming Forks Camp. About ¼ mile past the site, the trail reaches a notable ridge and turns from southwest to west.

Here you have excellent views up and down the canyon. Junipero Serra Peak occupies the eastern skyline, The Rocks the southern skyline, and Coast Ridge the western skyline.

In 115 yards you descend a bit to a junction with a steeply climbing road, on the right, which is more of a firebreak than anything else. It's not worth taking, unless you want better views of this part of the wilderness. Just 45 yards past it you reach level, live-oak-shaded **Forks Camp** (2440-1.7), which has room for about three tents. Onward, you climb a bit to a broad saddle that has a knoll, with manzanitas and Coulter pines, just south of it. In a minute, you'll reach a junction with a **firebreak** (2480-0.2).

Rodeo Flat Trail

On the Forest Service's map, this is identified as the Rodeo Flat Trail, and indeed, it does start as a trail. After going about 60 yards up-canyon to a ford of a seasonal creek, the trail widens to a jeep road, which soon becomes an excessively steep, ridge-hugging firebreak. This averages about 20% gradient for the first 0.8 mile, to a tight curve on a ridge with excellent views, and is almost as steep over the next 0.7 mile. It then stays on south-facing slopes, passing a spur road to a nearby summit just before descending south to the **Coast Ridge Trail** where it crosses a broad saddle, presumably Rodeo Flat (4485-2.8). Since this firebreak route is essentially shadeless, definitely waterless, and perspiringly steep, no one would want to ascend it, and I'm not too sure anyone would want to slip-slide down it either.

But it is a viable shortcut to the Coast Ridge Trail.

From the junction, the Arroyo Seco Trail forks left, immediately crosses the seasonal creek, and passes a small campsite midway to a crossing of Arroyo Seco (2480-0.1). You climb shady slopes and, just before turning southeast into a shallow gully, see a shady bench below you, with large mossy boulders. This bench, if developed, would probably make the best camp along this entire route. The shallow gully quickly dissipates, yielding to a shady flat carpeted with bracken ferns. This flat, too, could be developed into a nice camp. In this vicinity, the trail makes its last crossing of Arroyo Seco (2645-0.3), and makes an easy climb up a shady, verdant canyon. In about 0.4 mile, the canyon forks, and we ascend the smaller, western side canyon. The west fork of Arroyo Seco is quite small, and one would expect it to be fishless. Nevertheless, I spotted a belted kingfisher plying its waters. Climbing moderately to steeply, we soon reach the vicinity of **Madrone Camp** (3020-0.7). The camp actually lies just below the trail, on sloping ground next to the west fork. It's too small for medium and large groups, and too damp and shady for half the year—definitely inferior to the potential campsites I've just mentioned.

About 200 yards past the camp, the Arroyo Seco Trail switchbacks, and it quickly climbs north out of forest shade onto manzanita slopes. From here almost to trail's end, you're treated with numerous views east of The Rocks

The otherwise undesirable Rodeo Flat Trail offers fine views of The Rocks

and more-distant Junipero Serra Peak, which looks more like a ridge than a peak. Fire damage is very obvious along this scenic, moderate-to-steep ascent, and you'll spot many charred knobcone pines, which, like the legendary phoenix, find new life in a firey death. Indeed, without periodic fires, which open the pine's cones to allow seed dispersal, this short-lived pine would go extinct. To a lesser degree, manzanita, chamise, yerba santa and most other shrubs along this stretch also rely on fire to maintain their numbers against various species of trees. These include live oaks and tanbark oaks, which dominate the last part of the trail. Along this last part, you're bound to see remnants of an old telegraph line.

A pair of shady, viewless switchbacks concludes the route, which ends at a saddle junction with the **Coast Ridge Trail** (4430-2.0). Views aren't good here, but they improve greatly after a short climb to the northwest. To follow the Coast Ridge Trail in that direction, consult Chapter 9's Route CP-1.

Left: Fire-charred knobcone pines

IR-3

Memorial Park Campground to Junipero Serra Peak via Santa Lucia Trail

Distances
   1.6 miles to junction with southbound trail
   3.7 miles to saddle
   6.2 miles to lookout tower

Maps   20 and 21

Trailhead   See the Route IR-2 trailhead

Introduction   The summit area of Junipero Serra Peak offers farther-ranging views than those obtained from any other peak mentioned in this book. Despite it being the easternmost peak you can reach by trail, it offers you a wider panorama of ocean than any western peak. It's also the only peak high enough to offer you a view of the very distant High Sierra. For several reasons this route is best done during the rainy season, which lasts from about mid-November through late March. First, the route is mostly shadeless, and is too hot for most folks for most of the year. Second, the route is waterless for most of the year. Right after storms, you may find some water, but you can't count on it. In the cooler, wet months,

you won't perspire as much, and can get by with just a quart of water (two, if you're a liberal drinker). Finally, you can see farthest in winter. During the dry months an extensive fog bank often hides the Pacific Ocean, and polluted air often obscures eastern lands. But during wet months, particularly for a day or two after a storm, the air is clear and the High Sierra is visible. During this time of year, its peaks are snow-covered, which aids in their identification. Bring binoculars, particularly if you're familiar with the High Sierra; you just might recognize some of the peaks.

Description   From your trailhead (elev. 2090'), at a gate by a turnaround spot that can hold up to a dozen vehicles, you can see your objective—a lookout tower atop the peak (if you don't have eagle eyes, look through binoculars). Your broad trail heads in that direction, quickly entering an extensive grassland, Santa Lucia Memorial Park. On its far side, you climb up beside the east end of a sandstone cliff, which offers rock climbers moderate to difficult Class 5 routes, then you climb up to a ridge and climb briefly northeast to a minor gap. Ahead, the trail, like an arrow, points to the summit. Northeast, you traverse a grassland with scattered live oaks, and climbers will be tempted to veer right from the trail up to two sandstone cliffs.

You'll notice, on the left, some incongruous vegetation: prickly pear cacti. These plants are not a native species, but rather one brought up from Mexico by Spanish missionaries. You can see this species, appropriately called mission cactus, at many of California's 21 missions, including the southernmost one, San Diego de Alcala, and the northernmost one, San Francisco Solano. The cluster of cacti you see here likely owe their origin from plantings coming from San Antonio de Padua, located today on Hunter Liggett land. Despite its fairly northern location, this mission was the third one to be founded, in July 1771, two years after the founding of San Diego de Alcala, and 21 years before founding the last, San Francisco Solano.

Next you climb briefly up another ridge, which offers rewarding views for those just out for a short stroll, and then you traverse east to a saddle (2350-1.0). Your eastern route is now an obvious, abandoned road, which differentiates it from cattle paths. You meander down to a usually dry wash (2260-0.3), lined with willows and sycamores, and then climb moderately for two minutes to an abandoned tractor, which will probably be around for quite some time. Your route is now again a trail, and it climbs at an easier grade to a junction with a lightly used, **southbound trail** (2430-0.3). Remember this spot, which is in a dense stand of drab manzanita bushes and silvery-green leaved woolly yerba santas. It's possible, though not likely, that on your way back you could miss the junction. This vegetation is your trailside companion as you start what will be a grueling climb. From here to the summit, most of the trail is graded at about 15%. While this is only marginally steep, it will nevertheless tire you out, since the ascent has very few letups. You'll almost certainly want to take a number of rest stops.

You head up a true arroyo, which is a steep-walled canyon having a flat-floored bed incised with a seasonal stream. You soon cross the stream, then quickly recross it. Note the many granitic boulders 2 to 6′ in diameter. These require quite a wall of water to be transported. Fortunately, such gargantuan floods don't occur that often, perhaps on the order of about

once every 100 years. But when they do, they can transport colossal amounts of boulders and sediments, and a new stream channel can form on the arroyo floor. Judging by the size of the live oaks, this event hasn't happened in some time.

The trail, constrained between two parallel washes, squiggles up a bouldery route before finally crossing the west wash (3170-1.0). From it you climb briefly up through a dense stand of blackberries and bracken, which after initial autumn rains magically spawn myriad ladybugs. Immediately beyond the lush vegetation you enter a small, sloping grassy area, which may still have a sign telling you how far it is to the top. As you climb higher, live oaks stubbornly yield to chamise, and after considerable effort, you reach a second sloping grassy area. Near its upper end, the trail fortunately starts to switchback, saving you from what would be a very steep climb. Across the grass you have a fine view down-canyon, but better ones lie ahead. You conclude your switchbacking ascent among chamise, arriving at a notable **saddle** (4170-1.1). From it, the Santa Lucia Trail traverses brushy slopes to another saddle before disappearing from view. In 1987 this trail was in fairly good condition, but since it was unsigned and listed as abandoned by the Forest Service, I didn't map it. For those who love brush and abhor water, this route is for them. The vegetation, mostly chamise, is prime tick habitat, though surprisingly I got nary a tick when mapping this country in tick season.

Your saddle is just over halfway up to the summit—very little consolation for those who are tiring out, but the lookout tower is noticeably closer, and it urges you onward. You'll note traces of a trail northeast, straight up a ridge—the wilderness' boundary—but fortunately a newer, switchbacking tread was built. Views improve with almost every switchback, urging you onward. After ¾ mile the trail skirts a nearly level part of the ridge, then it climbs briefly but very steeply up it. Next, it veers left, away from the crest, and climbs at a more reasonable grade through the charred remains of a live-oak forest that is beginning to make a comeback. This vegetation yields to manzanita as you climb to a windswept saddle (5440-1.6). For some folks the views from this vicinity, or from the open ridge just north of it, would suffice.

The trail now turns east, traversing past scrubby oaks, and you may see a post marking a junction with a long-abandoned trail that once

Pinyon Peak

plunged down to a camp. Soon, oaks are joined by Coulter and sugar pines. Both have large cones, the Coulter's up to the size of a football, the sugar's sometimes longer but quite narrow. The trail quickly reaches a saddle that separates a ridge from Junipero Serra Peak proper. The lookout tower is now alluringly close.

Unfortunately, at least in 1987, the next stretch was overgrown with dense brush, and progress was hampered by spiny gooseberries and downed logs. I hope a trail crew will have tidied up this stretch before you hike it. It begins by skirting just below the saddle, then traversing ¼ mile over to a minor ridge. Just beyond it the trail turns south and makes a short, steep climb to gentler slopes. Here, all brush problems end, but unless the tread is revamped it will remain faint and possibly hard to follow. If you're on track, you'll wind up on the west brink of the summit area and will curve momentarily over to the south side of the peak's 40' high, abandoned **lookout tower** (5910-0.9). I climbed its steep ladder on a very blustery winter day, and found it quite intimidating.

From the tower you have a commanding view over most of Ventana Wilderness. To the northwest you see two distant drainages descending toward you. These are the Tassajara Creek (left) and Church Creek canyons, and behind them rises 4766' Uncle Sam Mountain. Left of it, is 4853' Ventana Double Cone, from which a ridge drops to the horizon over the Pacific Ocean. Except where Cone Peak barely

scratches the horizon, the ocean extends uninterrupted all the way south to the vicinity of 3594' Pine Mountain, to the south-southeast, a 60-mile stretch of coast. Of course, the Coast Ridge hides the coast; you see the distant ocean, or on a bad day, a fog bank.

Pines block views to the north and east, so for these, walk over to Junipero Serra Peak's conspicuous east summit and perhaps east just below it to a granitic outcrop. The view to the southeast encompasses virtually all the lowlands making up Hunter Liggett Military Reservation—and well beyond. Most of what you see was once part of the vast Hearst Ranch, whose northern part became, in 1940, the military reservation. The Hearst Ranch extended south to San Simeon, then up and down the coast. To the east, Salinas Valley is largely hidden by a high ridge, which is capped by 5264' Pinyon Peak. South of it, between two gaps in the Diablo Range, which rises above the far side of Salinas Valley and is about 35 miles away, you may see two slivers of the High Sierra. These are mostly part of the Sierra crest along the east edge of Kings Canyon National Park, about 165 miles away.

From the east side of your peak, an abandoned, ridge-hugging road runs many miles east, eventually leading to roads that will take you to the Del Ventura Road/Mission Road junction. This essentially shadeless, waterless route deserves to be left alone. Return the way you came. If you're in good shape, you can reach your trailhead in 2 hours or less.

Chapter 8: Big Sur

BS-1

Big Sur to Manuel Peak via Mt. Manuel Trail

Distances

0.6 mile along Oak Grove Trail

3.4 miles to junction with trail to seasonal spring

5.4 miles to Manuel Peak's viewpoint, summit 3379

8.7 miles to first reliable water

10.3 miles to junction with trail to Vado Camp

18.1 miles to Bottchers Gap

Maps   12 and 8

Trailheads If you are day-hiking, which I strongly recommend, then you'll start at the Oak Grove trailhead—see the first three paragraphs of Chapter 13's Oak Grove Trail.

If you are backpacking, you'll have to leave your vehicle at the parking lot for the Pine Ridge Trail. See the second paragraph of the trailhead description for the next route, BS-2, for its location and for how to walk 1.0 mile from it to the Mt. Manuel trailhead.

Campgrounds, resorts, stores and restaurants are given in the "introduction" section at the beginning of Chapter 13.

Introduction This 5.4-mile trek, with an *average* gradient of 11%, climbs about 3150' to a sometimes scenic viewpoint. The best view from the summit is toward the ocean, but on all too many days, particularly during summer and early fall, the coast is fogbound, and then you'll be disappointed with what you see. While it is, in my opinion, the best view of the Big Sur area, I don't feel it's good enough to justify the effort in reaching it. Hikers who take this generally well-graded, fairly well-maintained trail will do so mainly because they want a strenuous workout.

Most of the trail is up shadeless, chamise-clad slopes. From May through October, this can be quite a warm if not a downright hot climb. In the other months you may find water flowing from a seasonal spring part way up, but in summer carry a quart of water. If you're backpacking, carry at least two quarts, since you've got an additional, fortunately mostly downhill and shady 3.3 miles from the summit viewpoint to your first reliable water, beside which you could also camp in an emergency. To reach the first *bona fide* camp, Vado, you'll have to go an additional, 1.6 easy miles.

Because the first 3.5 miles of the north-bound Mt. Manuel Trail are up mostly brushy slopes, there may be some ticks, particularly in spring. The remaining stretches to the view-point and beyond are largely through an oak forest, which has its share of warm-weather flies. Poison oak is minimal up to the summit, but can be locally plentiful along the stretch beyond it to Vado Camp.

Description Read the first three paragraphs of the Oak Grove Trail for directions to the trailhead (elev. 230') and for the description up the first part of the **Oak Grove Trail** to where Mt. Manuel Trail branches from it (560-0.6). Here you leave the oak cover behind to start a switchbacking ascent past chamise, sage, coffeeberry, monkeyflower, poison oak and other brush. After you switchback five times, you reach the 900' elevation, this spot marked by your first view of either the ocean or a fog bank above it, depending. Better views lie ahead, after you turn the sixth switchback. For a while your attention is riveted on the Big Sur River and across its deep canyon to a landslide scar, across which the Pine Ridge Trail traverses. On your eastern climb, you veer in and out of several gullies and, like ones higher up, these offer shade from bays, live oaks, maples and sycamores, which is welcome on hot days.

After 2½ miles your trail turns north and climbs into a live-oak/madrone forest, which then yields to a tanbark-oak/redwood forest. We are now within Ventana Wilderness, and this stretch is a real delight except on hot days, when flies are exceptionally active. From a major gully you leave the shade, but after ⅓ mile dip into a smaller but more significant gully. Just 12 yards east of the gully's creek, you reach a junction (2130-2.8) with a 24-yard-long trail steeply down to a **seasonal spring.** This flows best from November through March, when you need it least. The rest of the year it may be little more than a seep.

From the gully you climb east to a bend north (2220-0.3), and here achieve your first view, to the northeast, of Ventana Double Cone and attendant summits. You're also high enough to look across yucca-dotted slopes and see the ocean over forested Pfeiffer Ridge to the southwest. Climbing north, you pass some of the first trailside specimens of yerba santa, an aromatic shrub that California Indians used

for tea and medicinal purposes. You'll also see specimens of warty-leaved ceanothus, with pungent, sawtoothed leaves. This shrub can have a sensuous aroma when it's flowering in early-and-mid spring. For the time being, you leave ocean views behind as you reach an east-dropping ridge (2520-0.4) to begin a climb west across north-facing, oak-clad slopes. Through openings you have views of Ventana Double Cone, then after ¾ mile, you top a crest and regain your ocean (or fogbank) views. You traverse briefly along the crest, switchback up a steeper part of it, and then on an easier grade make a short ascent to **Manuel Peak's view-point,** (3379-1.3). You'll identify this open summit by a large, trailside, camouflaged reflector just a few paces before the top.

The summit offers almost a 360° view, with only brushy, viewless Manuel Peak, just north of you, blotting out the horizon. Despite the panorama, the view is anticlimactic, since you've been seeing vignettes of the scenery along most of the ascent. You won't want to continue onward unless for some reason you want to reach Bottchers Gap: it's far better to hike in the opposite direction. In that southern direction Chapter 3's Route BG-3 describes the route in detail.

Hikers relaxing after a perspiring toil up to Manuel Peak's viewpoint

BS-2

Big Sur to Ventana, Terrace Creek, Barlow Flat, Sykes and Redwood Camps via Pine Ridge Trail

Distances

3.9 miles to junction with Ventana Camp Trail

1.2 miles along trail to Ventana Camp

5.3 miles to Terrace Creek Camp and junction with Terrace Creek Trail

1.6 miles along trail to junction with Coast Ridge Road

6.7 miles to junction with trail to Barlow Flat Camp

0.2 mile along trail to Barlow Flat Camp

9.6 miles to Sykes Camp

0.4 mile along use trail to Sykes Hot Springs

11.9 miles to junction with trail to Redwood Camp

0.1 mile along trail to Redwood Camp

Maps 12, 13, 9, 14 and 10

Trailhead From the junction of Carmel Valley Road (County Road G16) in Carmel, drive 26.1 miles south along State Highway 1 to the entrance to Pfeiffer Big Sur State Park, then another 0.5 mile beyond it to the entrance to Big Sur Station, a complex that serves the U.S. Forest Service, CalTrans and the California Department of Parks and Recreation. There is an obvious visitor center, at which you can get information or, if necessary, a fire permit (see "Campfires," p. 11-12). *No wilderness permits are required in Ventana Wilderness.* You will find a large, impressive trailhead parking lot, completed in October 1993, beyond the visitor center at the end of the main road. All destinations along and off the Pine Ridge Trail are now about 100 yards longer than they were from the old trailhead. However, now there should be ample parking, which was not always true in the past.

If you plan to *backpack* up the Mt. Manuel Trail, which starts in Pfeiffer Big Sur State Park, you'll have to inconveniently park your vehicle here rather than at the Oak Grove trailhead (page 130). Before the new Big Sur Station complex was constructed, one could take a route from this vicinity down to the state park's campground road. Hopefully a trail will be constructed so that backpackers and equestrians from the Pine Ridge trailhead can go down across the campground's road to the seasonal crossing of the Big Sur River and thence north to the Oak Grove trailhead.

Until such a trail is built, backpackers should head out to Highway 1 and then down it about ⅓ mile to just past the bridge across the Big Sur River. Leave the highway and cross in front of the Big Sur Lodge over to the nearby park road. Eastward, this quickly splits, the right branch crossing the river. Take the left branch and walk 0.7 mile along it to a road branching right, into a huge picnic area. The picnic-area road immediately forks, and you veer left and continue just a few yards to the base of the closed, climbing road—the Oak Grove/Mt. Manuel trailhead. The total distance of this route from the Pine Ridge trailhead to this trailhead is about 1¼ miles.

Campgrounds, resorts, stores and restaurants are listed in the "introduction" section at the beginning of Chapter 13.

Introduction This route, or at least part of it, is unquestionably the most popular backpackers' trail in the wilderness. Over spring vacation, as many as 100 hikers (several Scout troops) may congregate at Barlow Flat Camp, which fortunately is the most spacious camp in the wilderness, and it can accommodate the hordes. This camp has some excellent nearby swimming holes, as does Ventana Camp. On warm days in spring and fall, these holes can range in the mid-to-high 50s by afternoon; on hot summer days, they can get into the low-to-mid 60s. Another popular attraction is the cluster of hot springs a bit downstream from Sykes Camp. In my opinion, they are over-rated.

If you like swimming, summer is the obvious season for a visit. However, if you want a floral display, take the trail in March or early April. During the wet months, and as late as June, there's a chance for a tick or two along the trail. A meeting with a rattlesnake is also possible, but not too likely. Poison oak is minimal. From November through February the canyon-bottom camps are often shady, cool and damp, but if you don't mind these conditions, you'll probably have few, if any, neighbors at the camps. The only ford of the Big Sur River is at Sykes Camp, and it can be a cold one in winter. During or just after a storm, it could be treacherous.

Maps   12, 13, 9, 14 and 10

Description From the obvious trailhead
(elev. 370'), we make a brief climb to round a
fenced-in pasture, then soon traverse steep,
redwood-shaded slopes, staying high above Big
Sur Campground. Gradually, the trail starts to
descend, and then it abruptly drops to cross
perennially flowing Post Creek (280-0.7) at a
point about 100 yards southeast of the campground's main road. If you're camping there
and want to day-hike a stretch of Pine Ridge
Trail 3E06, stroll over to campsite 147 and
head up the creek.

The trail next switchbacks to gain some
elevation above the campground, and then
switchbacks again, this time to begin a climb in
earnest. As you'll discover, the trail from camp
to river camp up the Big Sur canyon is anything but level; it vaults from camp to camp.
With elevation come views northwest through
the fault-line valley containing Pfeiffer Big Sur
State Park. The gradient soon abates, and we
have an easy, climbing traverse to a northwest-
plunging ridge (850-0.8). Now climbing east,
we exchange campground and highway cacoph-
ony for the refreshing, muted roar of the cascades of the Big Sur River (the goal of the
Gorge Trail, mentioned in Chapter 13).

In about 2 minutes we cross an active
rockslide. When I hiked across it in spring, the
exposed trail was narrow and loose, and a fall
would likely have been fatal. I hope it will be in
better shape when you cross it, but future rock-
slides are likely to repeatedly eradicate the
trail. The exposure does permit you to gaze
across the canyon to the brushy flank of
Manuel Peak and the conspicuous Mt. Manuel
Trail. Onward, we immediately enter viewless
forest, which is largely tanbark oaks on slopes
and coast redwoods in gullies. In spring this
stretch has one of the best displays of irises to
be found in the Santa Lucia Range. By a carpet
of redwood sorrel we enter Ventana Wilderness (1075-0.8), and soon turn north. On this
stretch we have several views west down-
canyon of the alternating rapids and pools of
the Big Sur River.

We essentially top out where we bend east
(1320-0.3), then make a viewless traverse before dropping abruptly to a redwood gully. This
drop is partly across an unseen 80' high vertical cliff, and a slip, though unlikely, would be
fatal. We then pass an adjacent gully, which
above the trail has a seasonal, 40' high waterfall that usually goes unnoticed. Onward, we do
some more climbing and have some views
before we again top out and then make a slight

descent to a nearby ridge having a junction with
the **Ventana Camp Trail** (1500-1.3).

Ventana Camp Trail

This trail, with a rather unrelenting
moderate-to-steep gradient of 13%, begins by
making tightly confined switchbacks north
down the ridge. It then drops east into an
increasingly shady forest and makes several
long switchbacks down to a high, slightly
sloping river terrace holding **Ventana Camp**
(660-1.2). Shaded by live oaks, tanbark oaks,
madrones and redwoods, the camp is a fine one
for hot summer days. A fairly large swimming
hole at the bend in the river is another summer
attraction. (If you're visiting in warm weather,
plan to climb back up to the Pine Ridge Trail
early in the morning, or else you'll be hot and
sweaty by the time you reach it.) The camp
proper has about a half-dozen sites, though its
western suburb, across the river, has a few
more. With luck, you can reach them by one or
more large logs, or else you'll have to make a
shallow wade just below the pool.

Just below the pool and the overflow sites,
the river turns from south to southwest, and
here passes through a miniature gorge, cut
through banded gneiss. The rock is quite resistant, and in one spot the river flows through a
restriction less than 10' wide. It then plunges
into one of Ventana's finest pools, which is up
to 20' deep, and this spot offers sunbathing and
high diving from adjacent rocks. If you continue about 150 yards downstream, you'll
reach the river's confluence with Ventana
Creek, whose canyon offers the adventurous
hiker additional exploring opportunities.

Onward, the Pine Ridge Trail makes a fairly
level, shady traverse in and out of gullies, the
first one with a cascading winter stream. Then
the trail finally reaches a ridge and makes a
short plunge south from it to jump-across
Terrace Creek. Only a few yards past it, you
reach the **Terrace Creek Trail** (1320-1.4).
From this junction you walk but a stone's throw
up to **Terrace Creek Camp** proper. In reality, a
host of small sites are scattered on both sides of
the creek crossing. Nestled among redwoods,
the camp is cool even in summer. From
November through mid-March, it may be too
cool and damp for most folks to enjoy.

Terrace Creek Trail

You can do a loop trip by ascending southwest on this trail and then take the limited-
access Coast Ridge Road west down to

Highway 1 (the reverse of the first part of the next route, BS-3). If you've left a vehicle down there, you'll avoid a 1.7-mile walk down that highway to the U.S.F.S. Big Sur Station road. The shady trail ascends along the creek's east bank for about ¼ mile, crosses it, and then continues a similar distance to where Outlaw Camp once existed. You'll find neither camp nor flat space. This is your last chance to stock up on water.

The trail now switchbacks up to warmer, oak-and-grass slopes, and then proceeds southwest up Terrace Creek's side canyon. Near its head the trail crosses its usually dry creeklet, and then climbs, in ⅓ mile, past some poison oak to a live-oak ridge saddle and meets the **Coast Ridge Road** (2590-1.6).

Beyond the Terrace Creek Trail, we climb again, rounding a ridge, ascending east across a marble slope, and then reaching two springs, spaced about a minute's walk apart. From the second, which may be seasonal, we make a traverse north through a redwood glen, climb past live oaks, and then round a ridge, getting views to the west, north and east in the process. We get another view or two as we curve east down to a second ridge, and from it we switchback down to Logwood Creek (970-1.2). In the past, folks have tried to camp beside it, perhaps not realizing that Barlow Flat Camp lay just over the hill. From the crossing you can follow the creek about ¼ mile down a moderate grade to the Big Sur River, if so inclined. Upstream, the redwood-lined creek has a gentle grade for the first ¾ mile, and may be worth pursuing for those who want to get away from the crowd. If you traversed far enough up-canyon, you'd eventually reach, near Cold Spring Camp, the Big Sur Trail.

Bound for the crowd, you first climb to a saddle (1090-0.1). From it, a use trail with a 24% gradient gains 200' as it climbs 280 yards north to a brushy 1290' summit. The 360° panorama is not spectacular, but you do have a pleasing view south up Logwood Creek canyon to Timber Top, at its head.

From the saddle you have a quick descent to a junction (1040-0.1) with a **trail to Barlow Flat Camp.** This descends quite steeply to the outskirts of **Barlow Flat Camp** (890-0.2). The camp can be divided into three parts. First, there's a cool, redwood-shaded bench that has about six sites. Next, there's a more open, riverside bench, lined with tanbark oaks, bays, maples, alders and sycamores. This has about four sites. Finally, the bulk of the camp's space

A swimming hole at Barlow Flat Camp

lies across the river, and you'll find an assortment of both large and small sites. Generally there's a log or two downed in this area, allowing you to cross the river with dry feet. If a wade is necessary, you'll find it a relatively easy one except during or just after a rainstorm.

Lots of camp space plus alluring pools attract the hordes to this camp. From the far side, a 150-yard-long use trail heads upstream to a 40-yard-long swimming hole. This one is quite shady, though it is pleasant enough on hot days. The better pools lie downstream. The first is just below the far end of the riverside-bench campsites. It's got sunny bedrock outcrops suitable for sunbathing and diving. Expect temperatures in the low 50s on warm spring afternoons, and in the low 60s on hot summer afternoons. (Be aware that the river can easily cool about 10° overnight.) Heading north, downstream, you quickly reach a large, though mostly shallow, pool. About 150 yards beyond it, the river curves west, and you quickly encounter a better pool. This Olympic-size pool is long and deep enough for swimming and diving. In fact, it's generally too deep to wade along. Climbing the pool's north-edge slopes to keep dry can be treacherous, and is best avoided. Next, you descend along rapids, pass a narrow, 80' high waterfall, and beyond it reach a deep pool with a diving rock in its center. There is no way you can progress safely downstream short of swimming, so I turned around.

Author in the best of the Sykes Hot Springs

Back on the Pine Ridge Trail, you now start another sizable climb by first skirting past redwoods growing on a treacherously steep slope—no place to daydream over the bountiful spring wildflowers. Next you climb into three increasingly larger gullies, the first with an impressive fern-cloaked cliff that is decked in the rainy season with a gossamer fall. From the third, you climb north from the redwoods and tanbark oaks onto slopes of grass and live oaks, and finally to a ridge with chaparral (1640-1.5). Chamise intermingles with green-stemmed and warty-leaved ceanothuses, these two species producing a profusion of tiny, blue, aromatic flowers in March and April. During this period, when you look across the canyon, you see countless acres of slopes painted blue with their flowers. Both species did exceptionally well in the mammoth 1977 fire, and have increased their range, even at the expense of the fire-loving chamise.

Now you descend about 200' to a redwood gully with a small, usually splashing fall. From here, you contour 0.2 mile east to diminutive Dolores Creek, then soon contour a few minutes north to the northwest-descending ridge of a small knoll. You then drop quickly to its north ridge, where you are directly above Sykes Hot Springs, unseen below some very steep slopes. Your trail descends southeast, switchbacks northwest, and then, at the end of that leg, meets a use trail that descends to the nearby river. Take this trail if you're heading over to the springs. Onward, you descend about

60 yards to the Big Sur. Ford or boulder-hop the river to arrive at linear **Sykes Camp** (1080-1.4). A 230-yard-long riverside trail runs through the camp, ending just short of a bend in the river. Unseen just beyond it is the first in a series of inviting, slab-lined pools.

Sykes Hot Springs

Sykes Hot Springs is a popular hiking destination. In the past, many couldn't find the springs, mentioned in two guidebooks, due to the poor descriptions in the books. The springs are farther downstream than one is led to believe. From the previously mentioned switchback, take the use trail north down to the adjacent riverbank and cautiously traverse across a small stretch of bedrock. Wade, if that feels safer. You'll then pass a campsite and quickly, on a northeast tack, will reach another. From it, both river and use trail angle west-northwest, and lead in that direction, and in several minutes, you'll pass a small campsite just before river and trail angle southwest. In 70 yards you'll reach the first of several small, hot seeps, perhaps one or more of them dammed each to create a small hot pool. About 20 yards past these you should reach the best of the **Sykes Hot Springs** (1080-0.4), complete with a stone-lined hot tub about 8' across and knee deep. This pool, which averages about 100°, can hold four adults. At times that is not large enough, and also, unfortunately, at times you may find a rowdy group—it's not the best place to bring your children.

From Sykes Camp, only serious hikers need continue onward. As usual, to reach the next camp, you'll have to do quite a bit of climbing, but unlike previous ascents, you won't end this one with a major drop. Also unlike the others, this one is mostly across south-facing slopes, which can be hot in spring and scorching in summer. Try to avoid the heat of the day, unless it's winter.

You first climb ¼ mile to a long, narrow saddle, then soon cross a gully with a seasonal creek. Ahead, you have lots of brush—perhaps a tick problem in the wet season. Soon you pass above a descending belt of redwoods, which contrast with drought-tolerant yuccas immediately upslope. Next, you climb south and have a view down-canyon toward hulking, fire-scarred Manuel Peak, then you switchback to climb over a south-trending ridge (1680-1.0). At the base of this ridge is the unseen union of the north and south forks of the Big Sur River, and it's a shame that trails don't go up either fork. To reach Rainbow Camp you have to vault two ridges over a 6.5-mile stretch. A river trail up the South Fork would be half as long and have only a minor elevation gain.

Wishful thinking aside, we make a largely brushy ascent north, then a similar brushy traverse southeast to another ridge. Rounding it brings music to our ears—Redwood Creek— and, momentarily, temporary relief from the overbearing sun, in the form of redwoods.

Brush returns as we cross a dry, weathered-granite slope and then round into a gully with large boulders. But soon shade returns for good—if Redwood Camp is your final destination—and in a few minutes one reaches a junction (1780-1.3) with a **trail to Redwood Camp.** If you were to continue just 150 yards up the Pine Ridge Trail to where it crosses Redwood Creek, you'd find a small campsite, which I suppose has been mistaken for the true camp.

To reach Redwood Camp, go down the side trail. In a stone's throw southeast you reach a better campsite—but even this is not the real camp. From it, cross the creek and follow a trail southeast 65 yards to a bench holding the *real* **Redwood Camp** (1810-0.1), complete, I hope, with table and stove. You can pack about a half-dozen tents into this site, and there is overflow space on gentle slopes just to the north. This camp is a fair goal for those seeking relative solitude, though the long haul in to it will be too much for many people. The camp is an ideal place to spend the night if you're continuing east on the Pine Ridge Trail, either to reach China Camp or to make a grand loop of the wilderness. From Redwood Camp you can face the 3000' climb ahead in the cool, early morning weather. (Only the Mt. Manuel Trail, out of Pfeiffer Big Sur State Park, is a longer, more strenuous climb.) To continue onward, see Chapter 5's Route CC-3, which is described from China Camp to Redwood Camp.

BS-3

Highway 1 to Cold Spring, Mocho and Rainbow Camps via Coast Ridge Road, Cold Spring Road and Big Sur Trail

Distances
1.5 miles to second locked gate
4.2 miles to junction with Terrace Creek Trail
   1.6 miles along trail to junction with Pine Ridge Trail
5.4 miles to third locked gate
8.8 miles to junction with DeAngulo Trail
   3.8 miles along trail to trailhead at Highway 1
9.5 miles to junction with Cold Spring Road
   0.6 mile along road to Cold Spring Camp and start of Big Sur Trail
      4.2 miles along trail to Mocho Camp
      4.9 miles along trail to Rainbow Camp

Maps 12, 13 and 14

Trailhead This is at a gated road beside prestigious Ventana Inn. The inn's entrance road is located along State Highway 1 just 2.2 miles south of Pfeiffer Big Sur State Park's entrance road, which in turn is 26.1 miles south of Carmel's Carmel Valley Road junction. Ventana Inn's entrance road is only 0.1 mile before Highway 1's summit, from which you start a winding descent. About 0.6 mile past the summit is Nepenthe, which serves lunches and dinners from an ocean-view terrace (they claim you can see 40 miles of coastline, but fog often prevails). Finally, 0.7 mile past Nepenthe is Deetjen's Big Sur Inn, which has lodging and serves breakfast and dinner.

You can find nearby camping at the state park or at three private campgrounds just north of the park—see Chapter 13. Ventana Inn also has a campground, a lovely, though high-priced, one with 95 sites, nestled in a grove of redwoods along Post Creek. The campground's road forks left just 50 yards from Highway 1.

Driving toward Ventana Inn proper, you continue about 260 yards east, and on your right meet a public parking area for *day use only*. Unfortunately, overnighters will have to park along one of Highway 1's nearby turnouts. From the day use parking area the paved main road continues east 0.1 mile farther, then abruptly turns left at a fork to climb past the inn's restaurant and reach the office. Straight ahead from the fork the gated Coast Ridge Road begins, and route mileage is measured from this spot.

Introduction The euphoric feeling one has along this route—mostly a high ridgecrest traverse above the Pacific Ocean—is aptly expressed in words from *Nothing but a Breeze,* a song written by Jesse Winchester and recorded by John Denver:

> I wish you would take me
>   where the grass is greener
> I couldn't really say where it
>   may be
> Oh, some place high on a mountain
>   top
> Down by the deep blue sea.

It's best to take at least the first part of this route—up to the Terrace Creek Trail—from about February through May, when poppies, lupines and other wildflowers abound, and the Pacific Ocean is usually in view. This stretch alone, having an average grade of only 7.0%, is an excellent day hike. From late spring through early fall, the ocean is too often enshrouded in fog, obscuring your views.

If you're packing in to Cold Spring Camp, any time of year is fine. High above the canyon floor, the camp is suitable for year-round use, as opposed to Mocho and Rainbow camps, which are quite shady, cool and damp in the rainy months.

The Coast Ridge Road is the *only* wilderness-access route that this guidebook covers that would be suitable for mountain bicycles. The road bed is good enough for them all the way to the Bee Camp spur trail (next route). *However, bicycling is expressly prohibited along this private road.* You may *only* hike up it or take a horse up it, and you must not veer from it onto private land.

Description The route begins at a locked gate (elev. 1040'), the first of six along closed, maintained Coast Ridge Road. You may see a PRIVATE ROAD, NO TRESPASSING sign here and at spots higher up, but these signs refer to vehicles and bicycles. For those on foot or on horseback, the road is a public right-of-way. The road first skirts around Ventana Inn, then climbs past several spur roads to residences before reaching a redwood-cloaked gully with a usually trickling creek (1420-1.0). You exit from this to enter a smaller but more interesting gully (1470-0.2). Here, immediately past a spur road up to a residence, you'll see a minor creek dropping over what appears to be a 40' high stalagmite, something you'd expect to see in a marble cave. Well, in effect it is a stalagmite, *sans* cave. Marble from a nearby formation is dissolved in water and then deposited here, building up the structure. Most of the building probably occurs in the drier months, for when the creek is flowing briskly the marble stays in solution and is carried out to sea.

Now you leave shade mostly behind, at least until you reach the Coast Ridge. Still, you'll encounter enough shady gullies on your ascent to it to find temporary respite on hot days. At the next gully you meet the **second locked gate** (1635-0.3). In ½ mile you reach a switchback with your first rewarding views. To the north you see the bulk of Manuel Peak, though the actual summit is hidden. To the northwest, a fault-line valley strikes out toward Point Sur, which in the geologically near future will become an island. To the west, you look down Sycamore Canyon to the environs near Pfeiffer Beach. The tiny creek flowing down that sizable canyon today didn't create it. In earlier times, a major creek cut through it, but today the canyon's upper part is missing, due to faulting, which caused a drainage rearrangement.

After ⅓ mile we reach a saddle and have a sneak peek into the heart of Ventana Wilderness. Ventana Double Cone is the high summit to the north-northeast, while to the left is its prominent, virtually unreachable western outlier. Ahead, you have continually changing views of canyons and ridges descending to the California coast. By one minor gully, you pass a private, gated, steeply climbing road (2100-1.2) on your left. From about this junction on, a springtime hike is particularly rewarding, for then the grasslands and chaparral slopes are

An ocean view, from the Coast Ridge Road near its Terrace Creek Trail junction

resplendent in vibrant colors and subtle fragrances. After crossing four minor ridges, the road heads out to a major one, which has a fine exposure of banded gneiss, not to mention exceptional views. You climb up it and then over to an adjacent, similar ridge, up which you head north toward a conspicuous saddle. In this general vicinity you can obtain good views of the wilderness, standing in the east, and of the grassy coast lands, descending to the west. The road, now immediately below the ridge, quickly turns east, toward the nearby saddle, and you'll meet a gated road. Just 90 yards farther, at the oak-shaded saddle, you arrive at a junction with the **Terrace Creek Trail** (2590-1.5). This 1.6-mile long trail is described in the previous route. It provides access to redwood-shaded Terrace Creek Camp, located just before the trail ends at the Pine Ridge Trail.

If you're day hiking, this junction is a good turnaround point. Alternatively, if your hiking party has left a vehicle at the Pine Ridge trailhead, you can descend the Terrace Creek Trail and then head west out to your vehicle. From late spring through summer you might first head east on the Pine Ridge Trail over to Barlow Flat Camp, which has excellent swimming holes along the Big Sur River. The total length for this semiloop trip is 19.6 miles, which is too much of a day hike for most people, but it's fine as a backpack trip. Another day-hike suggestion is to continue along the Coast Ridge Road, and then descend the moderate-to-steep, scenic DeAngulo Trail (Route BS-5), a total of 12.6 miles. A 5.7-mile car shuttle along Highway 1 completes the loop.

From the Terrace Creek Trail junction, you climb east to a ridge, and then traverse south to a minor saddle, from which a gated, private road descends left. After more near-crest walking, you soon reach a north-dropping spur ridge (2770-0.7), with a private road south up to a home. Next, our road descends south to a saddle, which has a minor, west-heading, gated road, and then we cross a second saddle before reaching a third, this one with our route's third locked gate (2740-0.5). Here too, you'll find a minor, gated road, branching right, as well as very intimidating NO TRESPASSING signs. The warnings apply to bicycles and unauthorized vehicles, not to hikers or equestrians. If you traverse the entire length of the Coast Ridge Road, you're almost certain to meet one or more vehicles, these belonging to residents, the Forest Service, or the Air Force.

Ahead, the Coast Ridge Road stays on the ridge or not far below it. The vegetation of grass and brush permits us views, and oaks, madrones and bays offer us shade. You'll see three kinds of oaks along the route: live, black and tanbark. We pass two spur roads as we progress southeast, first one left down to a residence, then one right up along a stretch of the Coast Ridge. Not far past this junction, our road turns left to round Timber Top. From its north side (3050-1.5), you have one of many views north into the wilderness which, as usual, is dominated by Ventana Double Cone. During summer months, the fog bank can advance up the Big Sur canyon, burying its river under as much as 2000' of fog. Timber Top undoubtedly owes its name to its stand of ponderosa pines, which was partly razed in the Marble-Cone fire.

After rounding Timber Top, the road rounds a similar though smaller summit area. At one time the original tread plowed straight ahead up a ridge, but it is now overgrown. The loop, though adding ¼ mile to the length of your route, compensates with a gentle grade and plenty of views. Over the next ½ mile we stay on generally shady, north-facing slopes, and then reach a saddle (3180-1.4) with an ocean view through an open stand of ponderosa pines. The view improves as you head briefly southeast along the ridge; then, on north-facing slopes, you have wilderness views. You quickly reach another stretch of crest, briefly traverse on the level, and you come to a junction with the **DeAngulo** ("day-an-GOO-low") **Trail** (3250-0.5). If it's not signed, you can easily miss it.

DeAngulo Trail

This 3.8-mile trail offers you the shortest access to Cold Spring, Mocho and Rainbow camps. It is more easily followed, and certainly more easily walked, in the downhill direction. Since it's described in detail in Route BS-5, it will be only briefly mentioned here. The trail heads over to a steep ridge and then descends steeply along it—essentially as an abandoned firebreak—to a shady saddle. There, trail tread resumes, and you leave the ridge—to avoid the first of many homesites—for a descent to an abandoned road, which the trail crosses and then soon dies out. Follow this road up to the main road, which you take down past private lands to a junction with a road branching right. Traverse northwest along it, passing a eucalyptus grove midway to a gated road. Switchback down from this road to a junction, and keep left (south), traversing beneath a homesite and shortly beyond it to a road bend. Immediately past it, you'll find the trail's resumption, and you should have no problem descending this scenic stretch to Highway 1.

From the DeAngulo Trail junction, you once again veer onto north-facing slopes, but soon

Cold Spring Camp's water tank

regain the Coast Ridge at a saddle with an excellent view south down the California coast. Then you leave the crest again, only to return to it, at saddles, two more times, the first with a tree-filtered ocean view, the second viewless. At the latter, you find a junction with gated, somewhat-maintained **Cold Spring Road** (3430-0.7). To continue on the rollercoastering, though generally ascending, Coast Ridge Road, consult the next route. However, unless you're a marathon miler, you'll probably want to spend your first night at Cold Spring Camp rather than sprint to distant Bee Camp—your only other source of water.

Cold Spring Road and Big Sur Trail

Cold Spring Road descends, mostly at a gentle grade, through a burned-over tanbark-oak forest that is now more brush and snags than mature trees. The road then levels as it reaches **Cold Spring Camp** (3260-0.6), which fortunately was spared from the Marble-Cone fire. The camp is small, and being along a roadside is hardly attractive. But it does have a filtered view through an assortment of trees and, more important, has plenty of water and camping space. You get water from a faucet by a fairly large water tank, which exists more for fire-fighting purposes than for campers' convenience. Though space is limited, at the camp, there's a large turnaround just east of it— hardly esthetic but very utilitarian. On rare occasions, you may find trucks and horsemen here.

The Big Sur Trail begins by leaving the turnaround as an abandoned road, which quickly narrows to a trail. You'll pass some poison oak early along it, and more in small amounts at various places along the trail. After rounding a ridge with a view down-canyon toward the ocean, you traverse over to the usually dry headwaters of Logwood Creek (3230-0.3) and enter Ventana Wilderness. Climbing past live oaks, some Coulter pines, and some yerba santas, coffeeberries and green-stemmed ceanothus, you almost top a stretch of nearly level ridge, but then veer from it only to reach a ridge a bit farther. This ½-mile stretch differs radically from the previous stretch of ridge. It is composed of conglomerate—the fossil form of ancient stream beds. The "soil" is hardly more than rounded cobbles. Here, summertime temperatures are often in the 90s, and for half the year hardly a trace of rain falls. It is one of the most extreme environments in the wilderness, so only the hardiest species thrive here: manzanita, warty-leaved ceanothus and chamise. For you, the traveler, this means you'll have unrestricted views. You can see much of the wilderness, including the intimidating canyon you'll have to descend, and on fog-free days you can see the ocean.

After traversing open "Conglomerate Ridge" (actually, a part of Logwood Ridge), you re-enter forest cover and soon reach a saddle (3410-1.0). From here, the larger part of your two-stage descent to Mocho Camp begins. This part is somewhat shaded by live oaks and at times encroached upon by brush. The descent is steep, and if you're climbing up it on a warm or hot day, certainly you'll want to do it early in the morning. The knee-knocking descent ends where you cross reliable Cisco Creek (2160-1.4). Several times the trail recrosses the creek, and then, among redwoods, leaves it for a traverse, first east and then northeast. Unfortunately, instead of continuing around a ridge to **Mocho Camp,** the trail switchbacks up to a ridge (2250-0.6). Now you start the second descent, taking switchbacks down to Mocho Creek, crossing it, and then continuing 75 yards farther to Mocho Camp (1580-0.9). The camp is shady, and is on gently sloping ground. You can put up two or three tents here, and more on a bench just downstream, near a pit toilet.

Rainbow Camp

For a roomier, more esthetic campsite, take an undulating segment of the Big Sur Trail east to **Rainbow Camp** (1560-0.7). This lies on a level, 100-yard-long bench just above South Fork Big Sur River, a broad stream. Like Mocho, Rainbow is cold in the winter, and damp from about November through March, but enjoyable the rest of the year. Most folks camp near the east end of the bench, by a junction with the South Fork Trail. That trail continues up-canyon, and is described in the opposite direction in Chapter 6's Route AS-2. Your Big Sur Trail immediately crosses the South Fork to start an exhausting climb to a ridge and then down to the North Fork. This segment is described in the opposite direction in Chapter 5's Route CC-3.

BS-4

Highway 1 to Anderson Peak, Marble Peak, Indian Valley and Bee Camp via Coast Ridge Road, Marble Peak Trail, Coast Ridge Trail and Bee Camp Trail

Distances
9.5 miles to junction with Cold Spring Road
11.2 miles to fourth locked gate
13.6 miles to Anderson Peak's southwest ridge
14.3 miles to fifth locked gate
14.6 miles to north fork of Marble Peak Trail (private—no trespassing)
15.0 miles to south fork of Marble Peak Trail
     1.6 miles along trail to Indian Valley
18.3 miles to sixth locked gate
18.8 miles to junction with Bee Camp Trail
     0.3 mile along trail to Bee Camp
30.6 miles to southern trailhead

Maps   12, 13, 14, 15 and 18

Trailhead   Same as the Route BS-3 trailhead

Introduction   This 9.3-mile-long central part of the Coast Ridge Road is seldom taken. Indeed, one homeowner along the road said he sees only a few people per year hiking it. But for a full appreciation of the Coast Ridge lands, you should hike (or ride on horseback) the entire stretch: from Ventana Inn to the Cone Peak environs. Note that bicycles are not allowed. This route involves quite a vehicle shuttle. From Ventana Inn's entrance, you drive 25.7 miles south on State Highway 1, then 7.3 miles up Nacimiento-Fergusson Road to a summit, and finally either 5.3 miles up Central Coast Ridge Road to the Cone Peak trailhead or 1.3 miles beyond it to road's end.

Description   From the junction with **Cold Spring Road** (3430-9.5) (see Route BS-3), you continue your major trek. The first stretch is mostly wooded, though from the north and east slopes of Michaels Hill you can see much of the distant wilderness and much of the nearby fire damage. By the far end of Michaels Hill, the road regains the crest at a saddle with the **fourth locked gate** (3620-1.7), and immediately beyond it passes just below a ridgetop cabin. Over the next ¼ mile, slightly down to a ridge saddle, you can enjoy ocean views. From the saddle and its spur road, you can gaze east-southeast across miles of wilderness lands to broad, spreading Junipero Serra Peak.

Onward, you climb moderately, first up the ridge, then to the right of it. This stretch is the only spot in all my hiking in Ventana where I encountered feral pigs, though I suspect they range up and down much of the Coast Ridge Road. Near the top of your southeast ascent, you pass a minor road, on the left, then angle east through a stand of ponderosa pines. An easy stretch commences, and where it bends south (3860-1.5), we have our first view of rounded 4099′ Anderson Peak. About ¼ mile later, we have a second view, then descend toward it to a saddle, and from there climb up to **Anderson Peak's southwest ridge** (3930-0.9). This is only a few minutes past the start of a paved, gated side road, which climbs to a U.S. Air Force Optical Tracking Facility. This has a large-aperture telescope, which is used to track missiles launched about 125 miles down the coast at Vandenburg Air Force Base (America's west-coast missile-launch site), near Lompoc, California. You can't see that far down the coast, but from your ridge you do see quite a bit of coastline. You also see, to the northwest, Ventana Double Cone, and to the southeast, Cone Peak. You'd have to climb the latter to get a better coastline view.

As our road skirts Anderson Peak's south slopes, it enters Ventana Wilderness. Curiously, there are residents ahead and the road is maintained. The eastbound road stays on or very close to the actual ridge all the way to a road split, where you arrive at the Coast Ridge Road's **fifth locked gate** (3890-0.7). Left, a short spur road goes over to a private heliport on a broad, open part of the ridge.

Keeping right, we descend along the Coast Ridge Road toward unimpressive Marble Peak, which is merely an ordinary bump on our ridge. We reach a spur road south to a nearby cabin, and just 45 yards past it, when the road bends from east to south, reach the **north fork of the Marble Peak Trail** (3815-03). This climbs steeply to a nearby ridge and then quickly down to a junction with the south

fork. However, it goes across private property, so do not take it.

Not far south from the north-fork junction, we pass a junction with a descending road, on our right, and then traverse east across chamise-covered slopes to skirt just below a saddle by the peak's southeast corner. From it you'll see a trail, which may be hardly more than a deer path, descending to converge with our road. This is the **south fork of the Marble Peak Trail** (3770-0.4), and if unsigned it may be easily missed by unwary travelers heading northwest along the Coast Ridge Road. If you're heading in that direction, you'll see Marble Peak about a mile before you reach its southeast base. The peak stands out as a distinct, olive-green hill, due to its dense chamise cover, which contrasts with grasslands in the foreground. If you're bound for Indian Valley, Lost Valley or other destinations, consult Chapter 6's Route AS-2, which begins from the Arroyo Seco environs and heads west to this junction.

Now we'll stay at or close to the ridgecrest all the way to the road's end. The route stays fairly level for a southeast tack, but then turns east for a short drop to a saddle (3790-1.1). It resumes its course, and soon starts a longer drop to a forested saddle (3560-0.6), from which a spur road descends south down a secondary ridge to a residence. As you'll soon see, not all the Coast Ridge domiciles are cabins. From a minor summit just past the junction and until road's end, the vegetation is predominantly manzanita, chamise, warty-leaved ceanothus and scrub live oak, which offers no shade, but won't block your views to lands east and west of the route. The road makes a brief drop to a minor saddle with adjacent pine snags, and here you find another spur road (3470-0.8), this one going left. After climbing a bit, the road turns south to begin a fairly long descent to a saddle, from which it climbs up to a spur road that branches right, up to a residence, perched just above our road to offer excellent wilderness and coast views. Then in about 80 yards we reach a turnaround at a bend. Here you'll find the **sixth locked gate** (3380-0.8).

Onward, the only people likely to drive along the road are Forest Service personnel, and they do so only rarely. The road is somewhat maintained over to a junction with the **Bee Camp Trail** (3400-0.5), which is about 130 yards past the first saddle you cross after the gate.

Bee Camp Trail

When it's not signed, this trail can be easily missed. Among the brush, look for an old jeep trail descending southeast along a ridge. Only a few steps down it, the tread becomes perfectly obvious—and quite steep. After a ¼-mile, almost sliding descent, you brake to a halt near the base of a dry gully, then walk about 40 yards downstream to the base of a second gully. Here is scruffy **Bee Camp** (formerly known as Upper Bee Camp) (3190-0.3), which is locally adorned with blackberries, poison oak and, sometimes, litter. With luck, you can squeeze in two small tents; level space is minimal. During most of the year, water usually flows in the adjacent creek, but during the dry season it can dry up. Don't panic. Water lies just downstream. You can go on either side of the creek, but I prefer the left side. A use trail stays high and, about 80–100 yards from the creek, you can drop steeply to several small pools. In the driest times, you may have to go a bit farther. Back before the Marble-Cone fire, a use trail descended about a mile to Lower Bee Camp.

Today, the route is essentially cross-country, and unless a new trail is built, it's hard to imagine anyone wanting to continue down this very brushy canyon.

Ahead on the Coast Ridge Road, you can see that from the Bee Camp junction it rapidly deteriorates to abandonment, and from here it's called the Coast Ridge *Trail*. This 11.8-mile route to the end of the Cone Peak (alias Central Coast Ridge) Road is described in the opposite direction as Chapter 9's Route CP-1. I suggest you follow it only 10.3 miles, to the Gamboa Trail, and descend that trail 1.3 miles to Trail Spring Camp for your last night along the Coast Ridge. The next morning, climb 1.2 miles up the Cone Peak Trail to a ridge junction, drop your heavy pack, and climb the 0.3-mile-long summit trail to the peak's lookout. What finer way to conclude your trip! Backtrack to the junction and descend the Cone Peak Trail 2.0 miles southeast to the Cone Peak Road. The Cone Peak Trail is described in the reverse direction as Chapter 9's Route CP-2.

BS-5

Highway 1 to Coast Ridge Road via DeAngulo Trail

Distances
>3.8 miles to junction with Coast Ridge Road
>>0.7 mile along road to junction with Cold Spring Road
>>>0.6 mile along road to Cold Spring Camp and start of Big Sur Trail
>>>>4.2 miles along trail to Mocho Camp
>>>>4.9 miles along trail to Rainbow Camp

Map 13

Trailhead From the junction of Carmel Valley Road (County Road G16) in Carmel, drive 34.0 miles south along State Highway 1 to a road, on your left. This road begins 5.7 miles south of the Ventana Inn entrance road and about a 0.9 mile south of the large bridge across redwood-blessed Torre Canyon. If you're noting the highway's descending road mileages, you'll find the road about 200 yards south past the Monterey County Mile 39 marker. (Those driving north on Highway 1 will find this road 20.0 miles north of the Nacimiento-Fergusson Road junction and just 3.0 miles north of the Julia Pfeiffer Burns State Park entrance road.) There is room for several cars along the start of the road. Don't block this private road, since it climbs to a nearby residence. You'll find the trailhead on the road past a bend and a yard or two before a gate, which is less than 100 yards from the highway.

Introduction The DeAngulo Trail provides the shortest route to Rainbow Camp— 10.0 miles. But with a moderate-to-steep grade *averaging* 13.2%, it's quite a struggle with a backpack. Still, you save 5.0 miles over Route BS-3. The first 1.1-mile stretch—up to a private road—can be a very photogenic day hike. Averaging 16.7%, this steep stretch provides continuous views up and down the coast—when the fog's absent. In the fog, you'll just hear the crashing surf.

Description The DeAngulo ("day-an-GOO-low") Trail begins (elev. 600′) in dense, coastal shrubbery, which can be intimidating if a trail crew hasn't cut it back recently. However, the trail quickly climbs to grassy slopes, and you switchback steeply up, having ever-improving

The Big Sur Coast and the upper part of the DeAngulo Trail

vistas. These briefly diminish as you traverse gullied terrain with bays and live oaks, but then you switchback up open slopes again, and soon reach an ascending *private* road (1530-1.1), the same one you began from. The public has a right-of-way from this junction onward, but not below it.

You immediately round a ridge, curving from west to north, and have an easy climb north. Soon you pass just beneath the first of several homesites you'll see. Immediately past it you reach a junction (1580-0.2) in a redwood-shaded gully. Here a road starts a western descent, but you climb several short switchbacks for about 300 yards to reach sunnier slopes and a junction. From it a road starts northwest, but you traverse ⅓ mile southeast, passing a eucalyptus grove midway along this stretch. You'll also pass a couple of roads leading down to nearby homesites.

Your traversing road ends at the area's major road (1770-0.5), which descends southward to Highway 1. You turn left on it, and climb 80 yards north to a shallow saddle, from which a spur road curves east over to a homesite. Now you wind north up Partington Ridge, catching views of the ocean and the coast. The road up the ridge is mostly across grassland, and beyond it you enter a stand of live oaks and in 60 yards come to a junction (2090-0.5) with

an abandoned road. The main road continues northeast up the ridge, but you veer left and begin a descent north from it. Only a few yards from the abandoned road's end, you intersect a trail (1960-0.2). South, the steeply descending trail deteriorates as it approaches a private residence. I suspect this abandoned stretch exists only because so many descending hikers and riders have taken it, thinking it was the correct way down to the coast.

Northward, the trail switchbacks out of an oak woodland, across yucca-dotted slopes, and then up a grassy ridge. Here you get ocean views southwest down Torre Canyon and more views as you parallel the ridgeline steeply north. The Coast Ridge is now looming before you, temptingly close, but still a sweaty effort away. Take a break when at last your trail reaches the ridgeline at a saddle (2790-0.9), shaded by mature live oaks and ponderosa pines. Now comes a *very* steep ascent—about a 30% grade—on an old firebreak straight up now-brushy Partington Ridge. Fortunately, the ordeal is short-lived, and where the firebreak becomes even steeper, you branch left on a moderate, scenic, traversing ¼-mile ascent up to a junction with pine- and oak-shaded **Coast Ridge Road** (3520-0.4). From here, consult the second half of Route BS-3 to reach Cold Spring, Mocho and Rainbow camps.

Chapter 9: Cone Peak

CP-1

Cone Peak Road to Trail Spring, Ojito, Cook Spring, Madrone and Bee Camps via Coast Ridge, Gamboa, Ojito Camp, Cook Spring Camp, Arroyo Seco and Bee Camp Trails

Distances

1.5 miles to junction with Gamboa Trail
   1.3 miles along trail to Trail Spring Camp and junction with Cone Peak Trail
      1.5 miles along trail to Cone Peak
   2.9 miles along trail to junction with Stone Ridge and Ojito Camp trails
      0.9 mile along Stone Ridge Trail to Goat Camp
      0.5 mile along Ojito Camp Trail to Ojito Camp
2.5 miles to junction with Cook Spring Camp Trail
   0.4 mile along trail to Cook Spring Camp
3.7 miles to junction with Arroyo Seco Trail
   2.0 miles along trail to Madrone Camp
6.9 miles to junction with Rodeo Flat Trail
   2.8 miles along trail to junction with Arroyo Seco Trail
9.5 miles to junction with Lost Valley Connector
   1.6 miles along trail to junction with Lost Valley Trail
11.8 miles to junction with Bee Camp Trail
   0.3 mile along trail to Bee Camp

Maps 24, 23, 19 and 18

Trailhead First you must reach Cone Peak Road, which is also known—and indeed signed—as CENTRAL COAST RIDGE ROAD. The latter name is confusing in that North Coast Ridge Road, starting south from Ventana Inn, is officially signed as COAST RIDGE ROAD, implying it is the *entire* ridge road. The Forest Service attempts to keep this graded road open year-round, but after severe storms it may be temporarily closed.

If you're driving south on State Highway 1, from the Carmel Valley Road junction in Carmel you go 54 miles to a junction with Nacimiento-Fergusson Road. If you're driving north on Highway 1, you'll drive about 36 miles from San Simeon. This tourist town, in turn, is located about 41 miles north of where State Highway 1 splits from U.S. Highway 101 in San Luis Obispo. San Simeon, like Cambria 8 miles south of it, has a well-rounded choice of gas, food and lodging.

Highway 1 facilities closer to the Cone Peak trailheads include Kirk Creek Campground, Limekiln Beach Redwoods Campground and Lucia Lodge, respectively 0.1, 2.0 and 4.0 miles north of the Nacimiento-Fergusson Road junction. *Opposite the Kirk Creek Campground entrance is the start of the Vicente Flat Trail, Route CP-5. Park well off Highway 1, on a turnout immediately north of the trailhead; don't park in the campground.* This U.S. Forest Service campground is situated high on a bench, and there is no coast access. You'll find coast access—at privately operated Limekiln Beach Redwoods Campground, which also has a minimal supply of camper items, including food. Lucia Lodge has a restaurant, a very small store, gas pumps and telephones in addition to a few rooms. When business is slow, the place may be closed. *South of the*

Nacimiento-Fergusson Road junction lie Mill Creek Picnic Ground and Pacific Valley Center, respectively 0.4 and 3.2 miles away. The U.S. Forest Service picnic ground offers day-use coast access. Pacific Valley Center has gas and diesel fuel, a cafe and bar, a small store and a phone. About 2 miles south of these lie, in rapid succession, the additional attractions of Sand Dollar Beach, Plaskett Creek Campground and Jade Cove Beach.

On a clear day Nacimiento-Fergusson Road offers some fine coastline vistas as it climbs 7.3 miles to a crest intersection of Coast Ridge Road. *For east-side access along Nacimiento-Fergusson Road to this intersection, see the third paragraph of trailhead description in Chapter 7's Route IR-2, which includes mention of Ponderosa and Nacimiento campgrounds.*

On 6.6-mile-long Cone Peak (alias Central Coast Ridge) Road, drive 3.7 miles to a saddle to find the upper end of the Vicente Flat Trail, Route CP-4. You can also park here for the start of the San Antonio Trail, Route CP-3, which begins 0.2 mile farther up the road. At best, there is parking there for only one vehicle. In a shady gully 1.4 miles farther you'll find the start of the Cone Peak Trail, Route CP-2. Road's end, 1.3 miles farther, is the start of the Coast Ridge Trail, Route CP-1.

Introduction   Of the three stretches of Coast Ridge routes mentioned in this book (the other two being Chapter 8's Routes BS-4 and BS-5), this route is perhaps the most scenic. It is certainly the most rugged, composed of trail, road, and firebreak segments. The trail segments are generally well-graded, in contrast to the firebreak segments, which plow straight up and down the Coast Ridge. Fortunately, there are no major ascents or descents. On all three kinds of tread you'll encounter some rocky stretches, which are hard on the feet. Boots are highly recommended, even if you're walking only a few miles.

Trails branching off the Coast Ridge Trail go to lightly used camps. Bee Camp is the most distant from any trailhead, and it is also the least desirable. However, if you want to do all of the Coast Ridge Trail, you'll either have to spend a night there or face up to a 24-mile day. Trail Spring and Cook Spring camps, on opposite sides of the Coast Ridge, require nearly equal effort to reach. The former is a bit closer, but is definitely farther down from the ridge than the latter. It is also nicer, though certainly smaller. Of all the camps mentioned along this route, Ojito Camp is my favorite, but

you'd have to drop about 1700' below the ridge to reach it. The major effort required to climb back to the ridge will keep the camp from becoming too popular. Finally, there's pleasant, shady Madrone Camp, but it is more easily reached by ascending the Arroyo Seco Trail, Chapter 7's Route IR-2.

Description   From the trailhead (elev. 4110') the Coast Ridge Road enters Ventana Wilderness as the Coast Ridge *Trail*. Your traversing route, over 1000' below unseen Cone Peak lookout, takes you across steep slopes of metamorphic rock. This rock is prone to fracturing in small blocks, and you quickly encounter the result—talus—which in some spots totally buries the roadbed. After ½ mile, the abandoned road segment gives way to trail, which first makes several minor switchbacks down to a gully, then climbs moderately through a live-oak forest. In it grow sugar pines and Santa Lucia firs, which are seen in the Cone Peak area but not in too many other places in or near the wilderness. Several switchbacks then climb very steeply almost to a Coast Ridge saddle, which has snags interfering with an ocean view. What your trail provides, just ahead, is an excellent view to the east-southeast, down rugged canyon lands. After a couple of minutes, you climb to a similar view, and then immediately cross the crest. Over the next ¼ mile you have some ocean views, then you round a ridge and in 25 yards reach a junction with the **Gamboa Trail** (4620-1.5). If the trail sign is missing, the junction is easy to miss.

Gamboa Trail

This trail makes an essentially viewless, moderate-to-steep descent down to **Trail Spring Camp** (3800-1.3). This small camp, shaded by madrones and maples, lies on sloping ground a few yards below a junction with the steeply climbing **Cone Peak Trail** (Route CP-2). The camp can hold up to several tents, and you'll usually find water trickling in an adjacent broad, bouldery wash. Just up- and downstream, the flow is typically subterranean. If there isn't a trickle, you'll have to head cross-country down along the wash, going about ⅓ mile and dropping about 300' in the process just to get water.

Westward, the Gamboa Trail traverses in and out of over a half-dozen dry gullies, crosses some marble outcrops, and offers a glimpse or two of the ocean. The shady trail passes through a forest of live oaks, tanbark oaks and madrones, with a few Santa Lucia firs and a goodly number of sugar pines. These pines yield to ponderosa pines where we reach a dry saddle holding a junction with the **Stone Ridge and Ojito Camp trails** (3540-1.6). Here you turn right onto the Stone Ridge Trail, which can be indistinct and brushy in the upper part. Slopes gradually converge to form a gully, which nearly levels at its bottom. You may lose the trail along this descent, but from the base of the gully, the trail is quite obvious as it branches right, southwest, from it, for a switch-backing descent mostly along an adjacent ridge. After a total drop of over 1000′ in the ¾-mile descent from the junction, one that averages a *very steep* 26½% grade, you can then rest your sore knees after you traverse first 150 yards to a trickling creek, and then 100 yards beyond it to **Goat Camp** (2520-0.9). This tiny camp, beneath bays and oaks bordering a small, grassy bench, is about as remote as you'd want to get. You do have a view down the West Fork Limekiln Creek canyon and beyond to the ocean. If you want to continue farther, consult the last part of Route CP-4.

Your other choice from the saddle is to descend north to Ojito Camp. The trail down to it is even steeper, most of it averaging about 30% gradient. First you traverse north to a nearby saddle. Note that this ridge has two *parallel* saddles, with a minor depression separating them. This configuration is likely due to faster weathering and erosion of a nonresistant rock formation which is sand-wiched between two resistant formations. From the second saddle you plunge downslope, almost slipping and sliding until, 600′ lower, the trail eases off just above the floor of South Fork Devils Canyon. You could camp here, but rather, follow a sometimes faint tread just over 200 yards along a vigorous creek to **Ojito Camp** (2940-0.5). This two-tent site, shaded by madrones, bays and maples, rests above the creek's small pools on a bench composed mostly of marble boulders. This camp is even more remote than Goat Camp, and is a fine spot to just laze away the time. Also, you can do a fairly easy cross-country hike about one mile down the verdant canyon, to where the South Fork creek steepens to begin a mile-long, cascading descent to the Middle Fork.

From the Gamboa Trail junction the Coast Ridge Trail starts a scenic, arcing, rocky traverse that has views down to the usually peaceful ocean and across to a dramatic row of cliffs. You pass one cliff—a narrow, flat-topped ridge with a precarious summit block resting on

its far end—and then you quicky cross a Coast Ridge marble-rock saddle (4685-0.4). Now, rocks, vegetation and views change. You cross first gneiss, and then sandstone as you traverse—first north and then east—over to charred slopes with darkened snags. Here you have your first good view south up at Cone Peak's summit.

The trail curves north over to an adjacent gully, where it is replaced by an old road. This, in turn, climbs eastward to vault a nearby descending ridge, and then descends about 300 yards northward to a junction with the **Cook Spring Camp Trail** (4780-0.6).

Cook Spring Camp Trail

This "trail" is really an abandoned road, and it quickly forks. The left branch—not recommended—is *extremely* steep; the right branch, merely steep. On it you wind down to two-tiered **Cook Spring Camp** (4470-0.4), which is fairly spacious and is nestled in a stand of stately sugar pines. Associated with them are Coulter pines, which temporarily dominate over them after fires. Fortunately, this locale was spared from the Marble-Cone fire. From the camp's upper level, you can head 70 yards west over to seeping Cook Spring. I didn't map the abandoned road below the camp.

Onward, the Coast Ridge Trail touches its namesake in about 200 yards, and then stays on or close to it for just over ¼ mile, to where you cross some charred slopes with countless sandstone boulders. In this vicinity the road switchbacks left to climb around a minor, 4736′ Coast Ridge summit and then drop steeply northwest down a ridge from it. You could take this shortcut road, but a better route goes northeast along an open sandstone ridge. After 200 yards you'll meet a road (4680-0.5), but first continue a few yards onward to some nearby sandstone boulders, from which you obtain an excellent view northwest across The Rocks to spreading Junipero Serra Peak.

Leaving the inspiring view, you take the road, which arcs through a sugar-pine stand down to a junction with the shortcut road (4610-0.2). Now your road drops to a nearby saddle, quickly reaches a second one, and then descends to a third, where you'll find a junction with the **Arroyo Seco Trail** (4430-0.5).

Arroyo Seco Trail

This trail descends 5.0 miles to a trailhead near Memorial Park Campground, and Chapter

The Coast Ridge Trail just northwest of the Rodeo Flat Trail junction

7's Route IR-2 details the trail and its attractions up to your junction. You won't want to descend all the way only to hike back up it, but perhaps a few people may want to drop about 1400′ on a quite scenic stretch of this well-maintained trail down to **Madrone Camp** (3020-2.0). The camp is small, shady, and on sloping ground, and is best for a small party seeking creekside refuge on a warm day.

From the trail junction our road makes a steep but brief climb up the ridge, traverses along southwest slopes with ocean views below a summit, and then makes a brief but steep descent to a saddle. The route avoids the next ridge summit by curving around on northeast-facing slopes. When you again reach the crest, you cross it to begin a fairly long traverse across an area that suffered major fire damage, providing you with ample ocean views. Then you descend on a moderate grade to a nearby saddle, and from it the next ½-mile stretch, heading west, is a rocky, ridgetop firebreak. From a long saddle (4420-1.5) the firebreak reverts to road and angles slightly to the north side of the ridge. The rocky road first traverses through a stand of fire-scarred tanbark oaks, then bends northwest over to a saddle with an ocean view (4490-0.5). Now we head north, and after 200 yards our road branches right where a very steeply climbing ridgeline firebreak continues straight ahead. Our road first traverses north across burned terrain, and in places the roadbed is quite overgrown with yerba santa, which is one of several species that proliferates after conflagrations. Along here you should check yourself for ticks, although you may not have any.

After rounding a largely unscathed eastern ridge, our road rejoins the firebreak atop the Coast Ridge (4550-0.9). Over the next 120 yards, our descent along the firebreak is mostly a steep one, but then the ridge's gradient eases considerably. Here you may not see a junction

with a southbound road on your right. However, this abandoned, quickly fading tread could mislead southbound hikers. After heading 60 yards north down to a saddle, the firebreak climbs slightly and then turns northwest to traverse the ridge over to a broad, open saddle that has a junction with the **Rodeo Flat Trail** (4485-0.3).

Rodeo Flat Trail

Not a trail, this route leaves Rodeo Flat as a decent—even drivable—road, which heads north up to a junction with a nearby spur road that climbs to a sandstone summit. The "trail" then turns east, and after descending moderately for about a mile, reaches a ridge and degenerates into a very steeply descending firebreak. Near the bottom, the route becomes a jeep road, and it concludes with a 60-yard-long trail tread along a seasonal stream to a junction with the **Arroyo Seco Trail** (2480-2.8). Forks Camp is just 0.2 mile down-canyon, while Madrone Camp is 1.1 miles up-canyon—see Chapter 7's Route IR-2 for details. Few will want to descend waterless, essentially shadeless, and overly steep Rodeo Flat Trail. Its one redeeming feature is that it does have some inspiring views of the countryside.

The Coast Ridge Trail, still a firebreak, heads west from Rodeo Flat, and where it turns northwest to begin a fairly steep but not lengthy descent, you have a stunning panorama that extends from the ocean east across most of Ventana Wilderness. Views disappear as the firebreak approaches a gully, from which you climb 35 yards north to another ridge, where views resume. Your firebreak tackles the ridge head-on, climbing to a high point and then descending 160 yards west to a saddle (4330-0.7), where a road branches left. Straight ahead, the firebreak leads to another high point

(4366 on the map), this one the apex of a massive sandstone outcrop.

Back on the road, you veer southwest away from the saddle, and then wind down across brushy slopes before turning north-northwest. This stretch ends at a gully, from which you tack northwest and descend 110 yards to a seasonal seep (3980-0.7). During the wet months, this is the *only* source of water along the Coast Ridge Trail. During the dry months there is no water on the trail.

About 250 yards below the spring, the road reaches the ridge and reverts to being a firebreak. Minor, abrupt ups and downs are tempered by pleasing views. Just after the Coast Ridge Trail curves from northwest to west, it reaches a minor saddle (3835-0.6), and here the firebreak is blocked off. Straight ahead, you can easily follow the firebreak, which in fact is an upper variation of the Lost Valley Connector. You'll undoubtedly have gotten some good views of this ridge route well before reaching the saddle. If you're bound for the Lost Valley Trail, this variation is an acceptable route to it. However, by veering left from the saddle and descending a moderately steep road down to a lower saddle, you can reach the official start of the **Lost Valley Connector** (3540-0.6).

Lost Valley Connector

Unless it's been revamped, the start will be obscure. From the saddle, contour a few yards northeast until you see a trail's tread. The trail traverses over to a nearly level part of the firebreak (3610-0.3), where you join the previously mentioned variation. The firebreak then commences a scenic, though waterless and essentially shadeless, three-stage drop along a sandstone ridge. At the bottom of the third very steep stretch (2680-1.0) the firebreak veers northwest along a secondary ridge, but you continue along the main ridge, descending past manzanitas on a very steep trail down to a junction with the **Lost Valley Trail** (2276-0.3). You won't want to climb back up this route!

The Lost Valley Connector does provide a route to water, and with that thought in mind we head west along the Coast Ridge Trail toward another water source, Bee Camp. We undulate along the ridge, and from a second saddle leave it on a winding road down to a third saddle (3593-1.2), larger than the previous two and lying just west of the Coast Ridge. From it the road descends north-northwest back to the Coast Ridge and a fourth saddle (3460-0.2). From this vicinity a trail once descended west down a gully toward Lower Bee Camp, but the burned-over terrain is so choked with brush there is not a trace of trail. The water-deficient Coast Ridge Trail could use a new spur trail down to the former camp, but a major effort would be required to clear the brush down to it. Onward, our route—a firebreak or a rough road, depending on your criteria—makes a rolling traverse northwest to a junction with the **Bee Camp Trail** (3400-0.9). If it's not properly signed, you could easily miss it. However, you can guess its location, for the road quickly improves beyond the junction and in 130 yards reaches a saddle, from which it contours northwest away from a massive part of the Coast Ridge. See the last part of Chapter 8's Route BS-4 for a description of the descent to **Bee Camp** (3190-0.3) and what you can expect at it. If you plan to continue farther along the Coast Ridge, consult Route BS-4.

CP-2

Cone Peak Road to Cone Peak and Trail Spring Camp via Cone Peak Trail

Distances
  1.5 miles to junction with spur trail
  2.0 miles to junction with summit trail
    0.3 mile along trail to Cone Peak lookout
  3.2 miles to Trail Spring Camp and junction with Gamboa Trail

Maps 24 and 23

Trailhead See the Route CP-1 trailhead

Introduction No other trail of comparable difficulty reaches such electrifying views as those obtained from the Cone Peak lookout. With over a 1400' gain, the trail to the summit isn't easy, but by Ventana's standards it isn't difficult either. Most folks reach the summit in about an hour. If you're in the Cone Peak area on a clear, fog-free day, don't pass up the opportunity to view most of the Santa Lucia range and miles of the California coastline.

A summit view southeast along the southern half of the Santa Lucia Range

Description Starting from limited parking space in a shady gully (elev. 3720'), you take a closed road east up to a nearby saddle, and get your first views. Along your ascent views will be present more times than not, so the 360° summit panorama won't be a total surprise. The road climbs southwest, directly up a ridge, but we take an easier course, a trail, which first heads west before switchbacking to the ridge. On it, the trail climbs past brush, and you could discover that climbing in the afternoon on sunny days can have a drawback: the sun reflects off the ocean, heating you even on otherwise cool days. Actually, many summer days are cooler, for then fog is usually over the ocean, intercepting the sun's rays but, unfortunately, blocking coastline views.

Where the ridge steepens, the trail veers north, then switchbacks over to a nearby saddle (4030-0.5), from which you start a long, usually gently ascending, westward-curving traverse. In addition to ample views, this stretch offers plenty of shade, thanks to the bays and the live oaks. But on afternoons when the sun is reflecting off the ocean, temperatures can be high enough—even in winter—to activate pesky, face-swarming flies, which is another good reason to do a morning ascent.

You skirt the base of a nearly vertical cliff, then lose most views as vegetation thickens along a moderately graded stretch up to a saddle, which has a junction with a **spur trail** (4440-1.0). This spur goes 45 yards south along the ridge to a point, which offers a commanding view of the California coastline. Here, you're halfway to the summit, and for some folks the remaining 700+ feet of elevation gain won't be worth the effort.

Now comes the "fun"—short, steep switchbacks. The first set is mostly up a south-dropping ridge, which narrows to oblivion higher up. You then traverse northwest over to a narrow ridge, and here meet a junction with the **summit trail** (4830-0.5). Few people continue down an equally steep stretch of the Cone Peak Trail, so it will be described last.

Cone Peak summit trail

Taking a breather at the junction allows you to peruse the western half of the landscape. After your climb east to a spot just below the actual summit, the eastern half begins to reveal itself. Several short, tough switchbacks, climbing past some fairly rare Santa Lucia firs, conclude the climb to **Cone Peak lookout** (5155-0.3). A youthful, rugged mountain landscape surrounds you, and virtually all of Ventana Wilderness lies below you for your inspection. There are no prominent summits, other than Junipero Serra Peak, which lies along the east edge of the wilderness and breaks the northeast skyline. Southward, a ridge drops from the summit at an amazingly steep rate—about a 30% gradient—reaching the ocean in only 3.2 miles. This gradient is steeper than that of a ridge descending from Mt. Whitney to the west edge of Owens Valley—and that's *steep*. With binoculars on a very clear day, you just might see that peak and other peaks along the crest of the High Sierra.

From the narrow ridge with the summit trail junction, the Cone Peak Trail starts a steep, switchbacking descent and enters Ventana Wilderness. Views quickly fade as one becomes surrounded by a forest that contains a thriving population of sugar pines. Short switchbacks quicky yield to long ones, and these take you down to a crossing of a broad, bouldery creek bed. You can expect it to be dry except during heavy rains. After crossing it, you descend its gully and reach, just over ¼ mile from the last, a second broad, bouldery creek bed. Here you'll find **Trail Spring Camp** lying immediately below a junction with the **Gamboa Trail** (3800-1.2). The small camp, shaded by madrones and maples, lies on sloping ground, and it can hold up to several tents. You'll usually find water trickling in an adjacent broad, bouldery creek bed. Just up- and downstream, the flow is typically subterranean. If there isn't a trickle, you'll have to head cross-country down along the creek bed, going about ⅓ mile and dropping about 300' in the process, just to get water. To head either up or down the Gamboa Trail, consult the previous route.

CP-3

Cone Peak Road to Fresno Camp via San Antonio Trail

Distance
  1.5 miles to Fresno Camp

Map 24

Trailhead See the Route CP-1 trailhead

Introduction Fresno Camp and vicinity is one of the largest areas for camping in Ventana Wilderness, and so is ideal for large groups. The camp lies on the lushly vegetated floor of the San Antonio River canyon, which is reached in a half hour or so. Returning to the trailhead, you'll have a steady, moderate-to-steep climb, but still, most folks do it in an hour or less. From the camp you can make rewarding day hikes either up or down the canyon.

Description We begin on an abandoned road (elev. 3270'), whose bed is quite overgrown with brush that can harbor ticks, particularly in the wet months. In several minutes we reach a saddle, and now within Ventana Wilderness we exchange brush for a pleasing cover of tanbark oaks, live oaks and bays. Just after the route turns from east to north in a gully, the road is replaced by a trail, which makes a moderate-to-steep, 0.9-mile-long, switchbacking descent to the east edge of a floodplain. Welcome to **Fresno Camp** (2270-1.5). The chances of your being flooded out are virtually nil. However, perhaps once every 100 years or so, a titanic storm, heading north up the California coast, will produce so much rain that a wall of water will tear down the canyon you see to the west. The rampaging flood carries prodigious amounts of boulders and sediments, but since the canyon's floor widens in the Fresno Camp area, the current slackens there and much of the load is dropped. What this means for you is that the ground is quite bouldery and you'll have to choose your tent site carefully.

Fresno Camp has two developed sites. To reach the upper one, leave the San Antonio Trail where it touches the floodplain and traverse 120 yards northwest across it on a footpath to some maples. This site would be very pleasant indeed were there not so many boulders. However, just up the infant San Antonio River are two shady, spacious terraces that have far fewer boulders. For an interesting day hike, you can continue about 2 miles cross-country up the floor of the canyon to the headwaters of the San Antonio River, where several seasonal streams descend to it. This locality is roughly at 2800' elevation, and above it climbing becomes steep.

To reach the lower site of Fresno Camp, stay on the San Antonio Trail a minute longer. The site is on the left, beside the river. The ground here has lots of cobbles, not boulders, so pitching a tent isn't a problem. Boulders are scarce, since most were dropped at the upper site, where the canyon's floor widens. The lower site, in contrast, is located where the floor constricts and the floodwater regains it transporting capacity. This site, like the upper one, is quite pleasant.

Downstream, the San Antonio Trail is lightly used. From the lower campsite, the trail immediately crosses the river (if necessary, look just downstream for a good boulder-hop), and about 200 yards past the fifth crossing you'll arrive at the mouth of a western side canyon, about 0.8 mile below the camp. The canyon differs from others in that it is hanging. During or just after a storm, there's a waterfall, but the hanging wall is impressive even when there's no water coming over it.

About 150 yards past the hanging canyon, the trail crosses the river for a sixth time. After two more rather uneventful crossings, you reach the ninth, where the river is multi-branched, and you cross on large boulders. Now the trail begins to degenerate rapidly. From the tenth crossing, ¼ mile later, the tread becomes hard to follow, and in 250 yards you reach a beautiful, grassy cove. This is a fine place to camp. Downstream, the route is strictly cross-country. If you were to go about a mile you'd reach, where a south-flowing and a north-flowing stream join the river, the environs of abandoned San Antonio Camp. This camp is by the east border of Ventana Wilderness, and not far ahead you'd reach private land—the Avila Ranch.

CP-4

Cone Peak Road to Vicente Flat and Goat Camps via Vicente Flat and Stone Ridge Trails

Distances
  2.4 miles to Vicente Flat Camp
  2.5 miles to junction with Stone Ridge Trail
  6.0 miles along trail to Goat Camp
  6.9 miles along trail to junction with
       Gamboa Trail

Maps 24 and 23

Trailhead See the Route CP-1 trailhead

Introduction Except for a brief, initial climb, this route is downhill virtually every step of the way to Vicente Flat, and it's only about half as long as the next route, the *lower* part of the Vicente Flat Trail. The only drawback to the *upper* part is that it's a 1600′ drop, some of it steep. While this is not too bad going down, it's quite a grind going up, especially on a warm day, when you'll be soaked with sweat by the time you get back to your trailhead. So this trip is best in the cooler months of the year. Spacious Vicente Flat Camp has a number of campsites, and you can pick one to match the temperature: on the grassy flat in winter, beneath hardwoods in spring and fall, and among redwoods in summer.

The 6.9-mile-long Stone Ridge Trail connects the Vicente Flat and Gamboa trails. This trail is only lightly used, and it can be hard to follow in places. However, it ranks as one of the most scenic trails in the wilderness. Along it you have breathtaking views of Cone Peak, soaring ridges, deep canyons, and the California coastline.

Description At its upper end the Vicente Flat Trail starts from the south edge of a saddle (elev. 3190′). The trail may be obscure, but just climb steeply south up a ridge, and the tread rapidly becomes apparent. It veers left from the ridge and traverses over to a nearby saddle. This one, like the one you started from, is a landmark you'll readily identify lower down on this trail and along the Stone Ridge Trail. Leaving an ocean view through charred snags, you start a contour, and in ¼ mile reach a junction (3320-0.4). The former trail continued straight ahead and offered some fine views.

You, however, descend a series of short switchbacks, which soon yield to a steep, northwest-descending trail. While you're not concentrating on braking, look across the

gaping canyon. Hare Canyon is only about 3 miles long, but despite its short length, it rises from near sea level to well over 3000′. For its length, it is one of the deepest canyons to be found *anywhere*. Coulter pines cohabit along with the more common hardwoods—live oaks, tanbark oaks and madrones—all the way down to a nearly level ridge (2500-0.7), where the steep descent ends. Below the ridge, the scene grows shadier, and where we reach usually trickling Hare Canyon creek (2290-0.4) we're among redwoods. Along this intermittently flowing creek we descend west-northwest, crossing it in about ¼ mile. Then ¼ mile later, from a side gully we make a short, steep descent down to the creek, and cross it again. We now head southwest, and over the next ⅓ mile cross the creek seven more times.

From the last crossing we head south, and in a few minutes reach the upper limits of **Vicente Flat Camp** (1620-0.9). Here you'll find a shady redwood site on either side of the creek. Just ahead you enter Vicente Flat proper, a nearly level grassy flat the size of a football field; perhaps you should bring a ball or a frisbee. This flat is also a fine spot from which to take in the magnitude of the canyon's towering walls. Along the edge of the flat you'll find a sunny site or two. Note that two almost parallel trails skirt the flat. The lower one is a use trail, which takes you past a couple of somewhat shaded creekside sites before deadending at the official trail. This spot is only a few yards below the official trail's junction with the west-climbing **Stone Ridge Trail** (1620-0.1). The next route, CP-5, describes the lower part of the Vicente Flat Trail, from Highway 1 up to this junction.

Stone Ridge Trail

Although you probably won't want to hike the entire length of this highly scenic though infrequently maintained trail, you should consider hiking part of it. The trail starts with a winding climb past live oaks to the brink of an inner gorge (1780-0.3). Here you can get a feel for the magnitude of Hare Canyon. You'll also see a stretch of the Vicente Flat Trail traversing the steep opposite wall. Next, you climb to a grassy ridge and have impressive views up and down the canyon. Across mostly open terrain, you traverse slopes below a ridge composed largely of marble. You get plenty of views, including ones of the ocean by the time you reach a live-oak saddle on Stone Ridge (2030-1.1). For a sweeping view of the Pacific Ocean and the lower parts of Hare and Limekiln Creek canyons, head about ¼ mile along the ridge, to where it turns south and begins to drop.

Views are fewer along the next stretch. You traverse north through a live-oak forest, switchback once down a ridge, and then traverse a bit more. Then, more switchbacks take you down into a redwood domain, and after a short spell northward, you cross refreshing Limekiln Creek (1530-0.8). Within a 200-yard stretch below this point you can find shady creekside sites for camping.

The trail next makes a moderate but fairly short climb up the canyon's west wall, then switchbacks and traverses north to cross a minor ridge. This ridge marks your entry into a hanging canyon. Climbing west up its floor, you pass first redwoods, then bays, and then live oaks, the change in vegetation reflecting a rapid change in ground-water availability. Unless the tread is reworked, the route near the end of the shallow canyon will look like any of several deer paths. No matter—just climb directly southwest up to an obvious, nearly level ridge and start northwest along it. Tread rapidly reappears and you climb west briefly to a gully, beyond which you quickly emerge onto grassy slopes once again and you are treated to exciting, nonstop coastline views for almost ½ mile, until you reach a minor gap on a major ridge (2210-1.3). Besides the coastline, you see Hare and Limekiln Creek canyons from their mouths up to their ends at Coast Ridge. Cone Peak is readily identified as the apex above the latter canyon. To find a marble deposit larger than the one composing your ridge, you'd have to visit Pico Blanco, near the northwest part of the wilderness.

Heading northwest from the minor gap across grassy slopes, you have a less dramatic view of the western coastline, which is somewhat obscured by a ridge in the foreground. As usual, you enter live-oak cover, but then—surprise!—in the middle of nowhere is a smattering of mature ponderosa pines. You'll see a few more along your long, traversing route to the head of West Fork Limekiln Creek canyon. After winding into a number of shady gullies, some with redwoods, and curving around a number of sunny marble ridges, you reach a shallow gully (2160-1.3), this one distinctive

Cone Peak, from the Stone Ridge Trail

because of its exposed marble bedrock, down which water cascades in stormy weather. Just beyond it you reach and traverse a gentle, brushy open slope, where there is an active slump. In the future, during a very heavy rainstorm, this slump could completely slide into the canyon, leaving a major scar on the land. The trail across it can be obscure, and if you can't find it, you're better off traversing along the upper edge of the slump than along its lower edge.

About ¼ mile north of the slump, you enter the canyon's largest east-side gully, which is bouldery and redwood-shaded, though, unfortunately, usually dry. The climbing traverse north crosses a minor gully midway to another large one, this one usually with water. Now the trail turns west and goes almost 150 yards to a grassy slope. Here, where the trail bends northwest, you can descend a few steps southwest to isolated, bay-and-oak-shaded **Goat Camp** (2520-1.2), which has an ocean view framed by the walls of West Fork Limekiln Creek canyon.

From the camp you make a 100-yard traverse to a reliable creek, then traverse 150 yards more to the start of a *very steep* climb. This switchbacks about 500' up a ridge, and you'll want to stop a number of times to catch your breath, view the scenery, and take in the scope and depth of this coastal canyon. Next, you climb briefly northeast to the lip of a minor gully. The stretch of trail up it is not quite as steep, though because a fire raged through here, brush is thick, snags are fallen, and the tread may be hard to follow. If so, you can make a very steep ascent directly up to an obvious saddle, where you meet the **Gamboa Trail** (3540-0.9). Route CP-1 describes this 2.9-mile-long trail in a westward direction, and it also describes the 0.5-mile-long, incredibly steep trail from the saddle north down to Ojito Camp.

CP-5

Highway 1 to Vicente Flat Camp via Vicente Flat Trail

Distances
  3.4 miles to Espinosa Camp
  5.2 miles to junction with Stone Ridge Trail
    6.0 miles along trail to Goat Camp
    6.9 miles along trail to junction with
         Gamboa Trail
  5.3 miles to Vicente Flat Camp

Maps 23 inset, 24 and 23

Trailhead See the Route CP-1 trailhead

Introduction No other trail covered in this book offers such fine ocean views as does this one, though Chapter 8's Route BS-3 gives stiff competition. Overall, you'll do about 2000' of vertical gain before the trail starts its 300' descent to Vicente Flat. But despite taking about twice as long to reach that goal as via the previous route, you will arrive at Vicente Flat Camp quite refreshed because the trail is so well-graded. If you're camping at Kirk Creek Campground, then part or all of the trail to Vicente Flat makes a fine day hike. But in the dry months, fog often lingers along the coast, depriving you of ocean views, and then the trail is far less inviting.

Description The Vicente Flat Trail (elev. 190') starts opposite the entrance to Kirk Creek Campground, which rests on a bench above the Pacific Ocean, not along nearby Kirk Creek. Perhaps due to the creek's proximity, our trail got an alternative name, the Kirk Creek Trail. However, you don't head up along the creek; indeed, you never enter its canyon.

For the first 0.3 mile, your route parallels Highway 1 north, climbing slowly away from it, then the trail switchbacks to climb around the head of a gully, leaves brush behind, and switchbacks up grassy slopes. Leaving the din of traffic below, it heads toward a saddle, but fails to reach it, turning north instead. You traverse the grassy slopes one more time, then enter coastal brush, which will be the commonest trailside companion until you turn into Hare Canyon. Ticks can be present from about November through June, but usually aren't in great numbers. Their population is sustained by lizards, snakes (including rattlers), California quail, sparrows, rabbits, and rodents, particularly mice and ground squirrels. No wonder they don't die out.

You climb north to a gully, cross it below blocky cliffs, climb west to the snout of a ridge,

and then switchback to crest its shallow saddle. Just east of and above it the trail switchbacks, and where it rounds an upward extension of the ridge (1000-1.4) you have your first exceptional coastline view. You've been getting views almost every foot of the way, and will continue to do so ahead, but at this spot (and others) you see for miles both up and down the coast. If you're out for just a short day hike, this spot is a suitable goal.

You now enter Ventana Wilderness, and after ¼ mile, reach a ridge and encounter your first trees—bays—then traverse to a gully, skirting past your first redwoods. Onward, you climb out to a ridge, into a gully, and then out to another ridge, obtaining exceptional coastline views from both. After two more sizable gullies, you cross a gently sloped, grassy part of a prominent ridge, which has only fair views. The following ridge offers only a good view south, but the one beyond it—wow!—the panorama almost knocks you over (1610-1.5). Not only do you have commanding views up and down the coast, you have ones up Hare and Limekiln Creek canyons all the way to pointed Cone Peak and its western satellite, Twin Peak.

Descending from your spot on the ridge is the still followable tread of the Girard Trail, which drops to the mouth of Hare Canyon and a private inholding within the Los Padres National Forest, Limekiln Beach Redwoods Campground. For day hikers, this ridge spot is the second good place to turn around.

With most of the climbing behind, you now turn northeast for a leisurely walk past diverse vegetation that ranges from yuccas to redwoods. After crossing a major gully harboring redwoods but usually lacking water, you quickly encounter another gully. From it you walk just 50 yards out to a minor ridge, on which is nestled **Espinosa Camp** (1700-0.5). You could cram four small tents into this site, which offers a view of the ocean filtered by bays and live oaks. Note also a Santa Lucia fir, a scarcely distributed tree that seems out of place.

Though the camp is cozy and inviting, Vicente Flat Camp has far more to offer. Bound for it, you round a minor gully, then a notable ridge, and then come to a tantalizing, redwood-lined creeklet. Lying 400 yards beyond Espinosa Camp, this is the only reliable source

View northwest along the Big Sur coast, from ⅔ mile up the Vicente Flat Trail

of water until you reach the floor of Hare Canyon. You've been traversing high on this canyon's wall, which is composed mostly of marble. The abundance of marble on this trail and on the Stone Ridge Trail is probably the main cause for the dearth of flowing tributaries.

Beyond the creeklet you cross another nearby gully, contour northwest to a nearby, grassy ridge with an ocean view, and then start a fairly long traverse east. Along it at an ill-defined point you top out at about 1860' elevation, then descend a bit to a locale where three major gullies converge (1820-0.7). During a storm you'll find a small waterfall splashing on the trail where it crosses the middle one. Onward, you soon have a number of ocean views as you traverse on a usually gentle downgrade 0.3 mile out to ridge. You then mark a similar distance, traversing northeast past bays and tanbark oaks, barely losing any elevation.

From a dry, redwooded gully you next contour north, get your last ocean views through gaping Hare Canyon, and note the Stone Ridge Trail on the opposite wall.

You complete your hike by entering forest for a ¼-mile-long, moderate descent to the canyon's creek. Just before you reach the creek, you cross a sizable flat, which topographers completely missed while drafting the Cone Peak map from aerial photos. Likely, the dense stand of redwoods prevented them from seeing the ground. One specimen, just left of the trail, is a real beauty, having a 10' diameter trunk. A few yards up from the creek, you'll meet a use trail shortcutting northeast upstream to Vincent Flat Camp proper. The official trail continues a few yards up to a junction with the **Stone Ridge Trail** (1620-1.1). Consult the previous route for an excursion west up this trail or for a description of **Vicente Flat Camp** (1620-0.1), just to the east.

Part 2: State Lands of the Big Sur Coast

Chapter 10: Carmel River State Beach and Point Lobos State Reserve

Introduction

When you think of the world-famous Monterey Peninsula, certain attractions may come to mind: Monterey Bay Aquarium, Cannery Row, 17-Mile Drive, the peninsula's many golf courses, Carmel's six-dozen art and photography galleries, and the area's native Monterey pines and Monterey cypresses. Largely to protect these two endangered species, Point Lobos State Reserve was created back in 1933. It was later enlarged to 554 acres, then in 1960 expanded once again to include 750 acres of underwater habitat, thereby preserving native plants and animals both on land and off shore. The area, being very scenic, attracted so many tourists that it was being loved to death. Today, with over 300,000 visitors per year, entry is strictly controlled. There is only one entrance to this day-use-only reserve, and after 450 visitors have passed through, no more are allowed until others leave. The reserve opens at 9 A.M., and usually closes at 5 P.M., though when daylight is longer, it may remain open longer. To better your chances of getting in, arrive early and, if possible, try to avoid weekends, holidays and summer. *No pets are allowed.*

During the off season, when there are only a few people in the reserve, you're more likely to see birds and mammals. One mammal you'll see only during off season—specifically from about late December through January *and again* in March and April—is the gray whale, which stays very close to the coast as it migrates annually between cold arctic seas and warm Baja California lagoons. Regardless of when you go, *bring binoculars!* There is abundant animal life, such as California sea lions, harbor seals and sea otters, but they are rarely as close as you'd like them to be. For bird watchers, the place is a paradise.

When you enter the reserve, you can purchase a brochure that has a map and trail descriptions on one side, and history, natural history and regulations on the other. The map includes Carmel River State Beach as well as Point Lobos State Reserve, and since it is a large-scale map with abundant details, I haven't included a map of this area in the guidebook. The trails fall into two categories: ones along the coast or close enough to it to offer coast views, and ones across the peninsula, having few if any views. Tourists adhere to the roads or take the first kind of trails. Almost no one takes the viewless trails, but if

Left: McWay Creek's shoreline waterfall, in Julia Pfeiffer Burns State Park (Chapter 14)

A beach seasonally backs up the Carmel River

you are seriously interested in nature study, they warrant investigation. These trails could receive a lot more use in the near future, since *the reserve may soon be closed to all vehicles.* If that happens, the number of sightseers will greatly diminish. Like Yosemite Valley in the Sierra Nevada, this scenic, fragile area should not be overused.

To hike all of the reserve's trails requires about a 6+ mile effort, which is not a difficult day hike, even with lengthy stops. However, if you're seriously interested in nature, you could spend a whole day at just one local spot. Bring camera, binoculars, and guides to seashore life, birds and plants. If you don't have the proper guidebooks, you can purchase them at the reserve's information station.

Carmel River State Beach, like the state reserve, is also day-use only, and although there isn't a quota restricting its use, there is limited parking space. If you're staying in Carmel, the beach is not a far walk. The long southern part, south of the Carmel River, seems to attract quite a number of joggers. Dogs are allowed on leash only.

Carmel River State Beach

Carmel River State Beach, north of Carmel River

If you're not a Carmel resident, finding the northern parking area can be a problem. First, drive along State Highway 1 to Carmel's southernmost signal light, at Rio Road. This intersection is 0.3 mile south of the Carmel Valley Road junction. Take Rio Road about ½ mile west to Mission San Carlos Borromeo del Rio Carmelo (on the left, and often lined with tour buses). Turn left one block past the mission grounds, which is Santa Lucia Avenue. Since the road is easily missed, you could drive one block too far, in which case your road will fork *immediately,* giving rise to two parallel, north-trending roads, Junipero Avenue and Mission Street. On Santa Lucia Avenue, you head 0.4 mile west to a junction with Carmelo Street. Turn left and drive 0.4 mile south to the road's end, at the north beach's relatively small parking lot, which has a phone and restrooms beside it. A *very scenic,* slightly longer way to this lot is to continue west on Santa Lucia Avenue to an ocean view, about 250 yards farther. Here, where your road ends at Scenic Road, you see tempting Carmel City Beach stretching north. You turn left, and follow the narrow, twisting road, first south and then east, over to the south end of Carmelo Street.

The north beach is broad and sandy, and it stretches about 600 yards, arcing from a rocky point southeast to the Carmel River. This river originally was fed by drainages in northern Ventana Wilderness and its adjacent, northern lands. Today, however, San Clemente and Los Padres reservoirs divert most of this water for municipal use, so the Carmel River is a mere vestige of its former self. The significance for you is that for over half the year the river is too feeble to cut a channel through the sandy beach, but rather, seeps through it. Thus, during the tourist season, one can continue south along the beach without getting wet feet. About 0.1 mile south past the river, the beach becomes quite narrow. You'll note that the sandy beach has backed up the river to form a fairly permanent estuary. It is a good place for nature walks and bird watching.

Carmel River State Beach, south of Carmel River

The south end of Carmel River State Beach is almost a mirror image of the north end: it stretches about 600 yards, arcing northeast from near a rocky point to the south end of a bluff. A closed road runs along the length of the bluff, and this is the main route in the state beach. There is a ¼-mile-long stretch of Highway 1 parking along the south part of the beach, this stretch located about 1½ miles south of Carmel's Rio Road and about ½ mile north of Point Lobos' entrance. A road east to a highly visible Carmelite monastery effectively divides the parking stretch in two. On the Point Lobos State Reserve's map, this southern beach is labeled as Monastery Beach. Just 170 yards north of this stretch is Bay School, and from it a road heads 70 yards north, along the west side of Highway 1, to a sharp bend west. Here, where there is parking only for about three vehicles, is the start of a fence-line trail that goes 80 yards west over to the closed road. On that road you can walk 100 yards northwest to a turnaround loop, which is mentioned below.

Most folks prefer relaxing on south beach to walking or jogging along the closed road. It's a great place to take in a sunset, and on warm, sunny days the fairly broad beach is fine for sunbathing. Swimming is another matter. The surf is treacherous. Often, it appears mild, but then—out of the blue—a large wave leaps onto the beach, bowling over hapless waders and possibly dragging them in. Often there's a hidden trench just within the surf, and this complicates getting back to the beach. The water temperature is in the 50s year-round, which means you'll turn numb in a few minutes. If you're pulled out in an undertow, you don't have much time to rescue yourself or be rescued. So admire the surf and the bay from a safe distance.

If Carmel Bay were drained, you'd see an interesting topographic feature—a major canyon. This heads about 3½ miles west before turning northwest and growing deeper as it heads 12 miles along an active fault to a union with the much larger, southwest-descending Monterey submarine canyon. A major earthquake along this fault—or along some other faults in Monterey Bay—could produce a destructive tidal wave. Living near the sea does have its dangers.

For your convenience at the beach there are restrooms and a phone near its south end. The beach ends by curving about 160 yards northwest from the restrooms over to a bluff made up of well-cemented stream sediments—conglomerate. This rusty rock contrasts with light-gray rock of a granitic point just beyond it. In this general vicinity is a fence, which separates the state beach from the state reserve.

At the north end of the south beach, coarse granitic sand yields to a bluff of coarse granitic rock, which is laced with some prominent veins. A narrow ridge of rock is separated from the bluff proper by an equally narrow finger of Carmel Bay. You clamber around the head of this wave-cut finger to the bluff proper, where you have a choice of three north-heading routes. First, you can take a use path along the edge of the bluff. Second, you can head about 15 yards north through brush to a turnaround loop on the closed road, mentioned above. Third, from the turnaround loop, you can take a trail that climbs up brushy slopes to granitic outcrops. On this last choice, you go about 270 yards, meet a set of steps descending to the closed road, then go 210 yards more to its end by some homes, where Ribera Road dead-ends. Here is a second set of steps that descend to the closed road. (This is another possible trailhead, as is Calle la Cruz, a short spur off Ribera Road. However, I discourage use of both, since they are in a residential area.)

The nearly level closed road is well-suited for joggers. This goes about ½ mile north, passing beneath some expensive view homes, and then splits to start a loop. Follow either branch of the loop northward, each cut in about 150 yards by an east-west road, also closed. Ahead, you reach the north end of the loop in about 0.1 mile, on a bluff above the Carmel River estuary.

The use path along the edge of the bluff takes you, in several minutes, past a granitic outcrop, and then, in an equal time, to a larger, 30' high outcrop. Like others, this one is laced with veins, and you can observe their planar nature. Ahead, the use path's scenery is rather mundane. It lacks both good outcrops and a good beach, and the path may even lack a good tread. It is, after all, not a maintained trail.

Point Lobos State Reserve

The reserve's entrance is 2.2 miles south of the Highway 1/Rio Road intersection and 1.2 miles north of the Highlands Inn entrance road, Highlands Drive, in Carmel Highlands. I'll mention the reserve's trails more or less in the order you encounter them. All are briefly described in the brochure you get at the entrance station.

Carmelo Meadow Trail

Immediately past the entrance station, this short trail heads north to Whalers Cove. It lacks a trailhead parking area and views, and since one can drive to Whalers Cove, the trail is only lightly used. Bird watchers and botanists (at least in spring) may find Carmelo Meadow worth a visit.

South Plateau Trail

Like the Carmelo Meadow Trail, this trail begins immediately past the entrance station, but it heads in the opposite direction, to the reserve's south end. It is a viewless, winding trail mostly through a rather uniform stand of Monterey pines, whose shade and needle litter result in a rather sparse understory. This is supposedly a nature trail, and there should be pamphlets in the box at the trailhead. Unfortunately, the trail's proximity to noisy Highway 1 detracts from its ambience. This trail provides a way for hikers to get—with an assist from the Carmelo Meadow Trail—from the park's north-coast lands to its south-coast lands.

Drive west to a nearby road intersection. A service road heads south; you turn right, north, on a road winding over to Whalers Cove.

Granite Point Trail

This trail begins by traversing along the southern edge of Whalers Cove. Past a junction with south-heading Carmelo Meadow Trail, the Granite Point Trail curves north along the east shore of the cove. In a few minutes you reach a spur trail west out to nearby Coal Chute Point, which offers scenic views across Whalers Cove. On the Granite Point Trail, you continue a bit north and soon intersect an old road. West, it makes a brief descent to The Pit, a small cove. This spot is one of the reserve's few accesses to a sandy beach.

So far the rusty rocks you have walked across are part of the Carmelo formation, which around Whalers Cove is composed mostly of conglomerate—cobbles left by ancient stream beds at least 55 million years ago, when this migrating land was probably along Mexico's northern coastline. Beyond the

old road—today the Moss Cove Trail—the Granite Point Trail concludes with a circle around Granite Point. The light-gray rock you see here is the reserve's other common rock: granite. Technically, it's not a true granite, and geologists call it the porphyritic granodiorite of Monterey. Like all granitic rocks, it solidified from a molten state several miles beneath the earth's surface—in this case, below a volcanic range, which likely was situated in what is now Mexico. Since its solidification just over 100 million years ago, the porphyritic granodiorite has drifted to its current position, exposed during the migration by the erosion of overlying rocks. The term porphyritic means that this granite contains some large crystals (in this case, potassium feldspar) mixed in a matrix of more common, smaller crystals. Check this out for yourself. More likely, however, you'll be captivated by the numerous views attained from the brushy point.

Moss Cove Trail

This old road heading east from the Granite Point Trail is only lightly used. It crosses a marine terrace, which is a nearly flat stretch of land that lay under shallow water not too long ago. Early on this trail you'll spot—to the right—the Hudson House, which stands on a slightly higher terrace. Along the trail you're likely to see abalone shell fragments. The Ohlone Indians, inhabiting the general area for perhaps thousands of years, ate abalone, and there are about two dozen "refuse sites" in the reserve.

Because the trail is lightly used, it's a good one for nature lovers. You may find sea otters or great blue herons in Moss Cove, which is speckled with granitic islets, or deer grazing in the broad meadow you traverse. My best find was a burrowing owl, America's only ground-dwelling owl and a predator of ground squirrels. Near trail's end you can climb a low granitic point for additional views of marine life. Just past it you'll reach a fence, which prevents entry to "Monastery Beach" (the broad, sandy south-end beach of Carmel River State Beach). If you look closely you'll find, between trail's end and the fence, a small, low granitic outcrop with several mortar holes etched into it—a sign of former Indian habitation.

Immediately past the start of the Granite Point Trail, you come to the Whalers Cottage, on the left, the start of the Cottage Trail.

Cottage Trail

This trail climbs about 220 yards northwest up to the North Shore Trail, and at that end may still be signed, inappropriately, as the North Shore Trail. For hikers in a hurry between that trail and the Granite Point Trail, it offers a shortcut route, since it bypasses Cannery Point, a scenic and historic attraction you shouldn't miss.

North Shore Trail, east half

This fairly scenic trail runs well above the reserve's north shore, denying access to the shoreline. The only place you have access is along the west shore of Whalers Cove, near the trailhead. Here, by a picnic area and a fairly large parking area, is the only spot where divers can enter the water. Divers must first register at the entrance station before mingling with the sea otters and harbor seals in Whalers Cove. I saw these two mammals at a number of spots along the reserve's coastline, but nowhere closer than in Whalers Cove.

A diver at Whalers Cove

Most trail users go little farther than Cannery Point, since it offers fine views of Carmel Bay. Just up from the point, a spur trail starts west briefly over to a granitic headland. From it you can look west across Bluefish Cove and see where surf has cut a tunnel through the headland opposite you. The mostly forested North Shore Trail traverses high above the cove, first passing the Cottage Trail (see above) and then the Bypass Trail, which climbs to the nearby Whalers Knoll Trail (see below). You then quickly arrive at a junction with a short spur trail going out to a viewpoint on the tunneled headland. As the brochure states, the Guillemot Island viewpoint is the best spot to see western gulls, pigeon guillemots, Brandt's cormorants and pelagic cormorants when they're nesting in spring and summer. By the spur trail's junction you'll note Monterey

A sea otter in Whalers Cove

cypresses covered with what appears to be a parasitic fungus. The rusty growth on their branches is actually a harmless green alga, *Trentepohlia,* whose green pigments are masked by rusty colored ones. Here you're about midway along the North Coast Trail, and the western half, starting from an information station, is described below.

From Whalers Cove, drive back south to the main, westward-heading road. From the southwest corner of your road intersection, you'll find a trail going 10 yards west to a fork.

Lace Lichen and Mound Meadow Trails

The Lace Lichen Trail parallels the road west, going just over ⅓ mile to the Pine Ridge Trail. South, the Mound Meadow Trail goes just under ⅓ mile to the reserve's south-shore road, intersecting the Pine Ridge Trail midway along its course. The south half of this branch skirts along the east edge of Mound Meadow, a favorite foraging ground for local deer. While both trails are quite utilitarian, they do offer nature lovers peaceful, lightly used routes suitable for study or contemplation.

About ⅓ mile west of the Whalers Cove road, the main road splits into the two ends of a one-way loop.

Whalers Knoll Trail

There isn't any roadside parking for this trail or the next. However, you can park at the Piney Woods picnic area, walk briefly east up to the Pine Ridge Trail, and follow it about 300 yards north to the reserve's road split. Then take the Whalers Knoll Trail about 270 yards northeast to where it forks left. Straight ahead is the

Bypass Trail, which provides access to the nearby North Shore Trail. Climbing northwest, you'll quickly reach a shortcut trail that saves a few yards for those hiking between Whalers Knoll and Bluefish Cove. After a few minutes of moderate exertion, you reach the forested top of Whalers Knoll, then descend just a bit west to a clearing. Big Dome obscures part of the Monterey Peninsula, while pines and cypresses obscure views to the east. From the clearing, the trail switchbacks down to the west part of the North Shore Trail. Note that there are three approaches to Whalers Knoll: from Piney Woods picnic area, from Whalers Cove (either Cannery Point or the Whalers Cottage) and from the information station. The last choice is probably the most popular. All are of about equal difficulty.

Pine Ridge Trail

As mentioned just above, there is no roadside parking for this trail, so it's best to start by hiking briefly east to it from Piney Woods picnic area. Unlike the Lace Lichen Trail, this trail has some ocean views through the Monterey pines. The trail goes about ⅓ mile east to an intersection with the south-trending Mound Meadow Trail, then it concludes 270 yards later at the South Plateau Trail.

Depending on your available time, you can do one or more loops from the picnic area. The shorter of two south loops takes the Pine Ridge Trail east to the Lace Lichen Trail, then takes that trail south to a stretch of the reserve's road by the south edge of Mound Meadow. Then take the South Shore Trail northwest back to the picnic area. The longer south loop takes the Pine Ridge Trail east to its end, then the South Plateau Trail to the reserve's south end. Visit Gibson Beach, Pelican Point and China Cove, then head north along the Bird Island Trail to the turnaround loop of the reserve's road. Here, the South Shore Trail begins, and you take it back to the picnic area.

From where the main road splits into a one-way loop, drive briefly northwest to the reserve's "hub," centered on a small, sometimes staffed information station. If you're going to make just one stop, here's the spot. Four trails radiate from the parking area: North Shore/Cypress Grove trails, Sea Lion Point Trail and South Shore Trail.

North Shore Trail, west half

From the information station, a trail starts north and immediately forks. The North Shore Trail goes right, and after 150 yards on it you reach the Old Veteran Trail. This heads over to a nearby viewpoint above the tip of Cypress Cove. From it you can look across the tip of the cove to the Old Veteran Cypress, which has a massive trunk that makes it stand out from all the other cypresses. Northward, the North Shore Trail skirts past this cypress and soon reaches a junction with the Whalers Knoll Trail. If the junction is unsigned, you could walk right by it. However, you'll momentarily start a traverse above narrow Big Dome Cove, and from this vicinity you'll see the Whalers Knoll Trail switchbacking up brushy slopes. Its starting point then becomes obvious. For fair views of the western part of the reserve, climb the trail to its viewpoint. From it you're likely to hear the muted chorus of barking California sea lions, on Sea Lion Rocks, over ½ mile away.

Past the cove, the North Shore Trail passes through a cleft separating forested Big Dome from Whalers Knoll, and then makes a shady traverse east through the East Grove of cypresses to a junction with a short spur trail out to the Guillemot Island viewpoint. This was mentioned at the end of the east half of the North Shore Trail, described above.

Cypress Grove Trail

From the information station, a trail starts north and immediately forks. The left fork, Cypress Grove Trail, momentarily passes two restrooms, and then splits. This is a start of a loop through the Allan Memorial Grove of Monterey cypresses. Take the loop in either direction. The coastline is quite impressive, and you have views of it from two short spurs and from several spots along the trail. From the east spur you look across Cypress Cove at an imposing cypress-clad cliff, Big Dome. From the north spur, at North Point, you have, on clear days, a good view of Carmel Bay and the Monterey Peninsula.

Sea Lion Point Trail

This short trail west from the parking area appears to be the reserve's most popular one, and rightly so. With luck, you'll see all three species of resident marine mammals: California sea lions, sea otters and harbor seals. Shore birds are also common. And the rock outcrops—composed mainly of tilting beds of conglomerate (stream gravel) create a surrealist landscape.

California sea lions on Sea Lion Rocks

South Shore Trail

This short stretch begins by the south end of the parking area, heads west to Sand Hill, which is indeed sandy, and then turns north for a brief traverse north along a bluff over to the Sea Lion Point Trail. The South Shore Trail proper starts from this short stretch with a descent along stairs toward adjacent Sand Hill Cove. In this vicinity the trail dips close to the surf, which usually isn't all that rough, given the orientation of the coast, the wave-thwarting offshore rocks, and the protective nature of the cove. If you like seashore life, try the tide pools here, but be careful where you step—the conglomerate rocks can be very slippery.

The trail climbs a bit past the cove and quickly reaches a spot opposite the Piney Woods picnic area. About 100 yards past it, the trail skirts above the end of The Slot, and in a similar distance it reaches a roadside water faucet near the end of a false slot. From it the trail now heads east, and it soon reaches the Weston Beach/Mound Meadow environs, an open area with tap water and picnic tables. You often see deer in the meadow and gulls at the tables. The Carmelo formation in this area is composed of a sequence of thin, mildly dipping beds of sandstone and conglomerate, and the beach is another good spot for studying seashore life.

The trail turns southeast, and you quickly spy the start of the Mound Meadow Trail. Not far past it you pass another water faucet and then quickly arrive at a set of stairs down to the dark sand of Hidden Beach. If the rocks here were granitic, the beach would have light sand, as at China Cove's beach, mentioned in the next route. Now the trail turns south and winds along a bluff to the turnaround end of the reserve's road. To hike farther, start on the Bird Island Trail.

From the parking area by the information station, drive southeast and quickly reach the Piney Woods picnic area, which provides access to the previously mentioned Pine Ridge, Lace Lichen and Whalers Knoll trails. About 0.4 mile farther you reach Mound Meadow and find the Mound Meadow Trail starting north from the meadow's east side. The road then ends in ¼ mile, at a turnaround loop with parking spaces and an adjacent picnic area.

Thin, mildly dipping beds at Weston Beach

Bird Island is a home for hundreds of cormorants

Bird Island Trail

This trail (and its two spurs) is a favorite, for one sees a lot of diverse scenery and animal life with little effort. You first climb a set of stairs and then make a short, high traverse to the head

A steep set of stairs leads down to China Cove

of China Cove, where you'll find a long, steep set of stairs descending to a sandy beach. This beach and nearby Gibson Beach—both with white, granite-derived sand—are the only two in the reserve where you can safely splash around in the surf. But with year-round water temperatures staying in the 50s, you'll want at best only to wet your feet, perhaps to explore a nearby arch. Egrets frequent the cove, walking on the cove's dense stand of floating kelp blades ("leaves"), looking for tasty morsels.

Just past the stairs, you come to the south end of the South Plateau Trail, and a few paces north on it get you to a second spur, a set of stairs descending to Gibson Beach, which is larger than China Cove's beach. Private land of Carmel Highlands lies immediately beyond the beach.

The Bird Island Trail turns west here and skirts past some south-shore arches as it heads out to a nearby granitic bench. On the bench the trail makes a terminal loop. Bird Island is not the one just a stone's throw away, but the larger one behind it. Both serve as home for hundreds of cormorants, as do the smaller, adjacent islands. Out on the bench you have a view northwest along the islet-speckled Point Lobos coastline and a view south along the Carmel Highlands' coastline. The conspicuous headland to the south-southwest is Yankee Point, and stretching unseen from it are 1½ miles of coastline view homes, these yielding at a minor point to lands of Garrapata State Park, the subject of the next chapter.

Chapter 11: Garrapata State Park

Introduction

Created in 1983, this park is one of the most recent additions to the state park system along the Big Sur coast. State Highway 1 passes through about 2 miles of the park, paralleling the coastline, which, due to myriad coves and points, is perhaps about 4 miles long. The coastline's crenulated nature makes it exceptionally scenic, and the park has 16 highway turnouts which provide access to this very photogenic stretch. From about late December through January and from about March through April, visitors have an additional treat: views of gray whales. Migrating south to Baja California lagoons and then back north to arctic waters, the whales stay close to the coastline. While you can see them with the naked eye, you ought to bring binoculars or a spotting scope. Soberanes Point, near the park's south end, is a popular whale-watching spot. The point also attracts its share of surf fishermen.

Although the park's chief attraction is its coastline, it does have two respectable hiking trails, both east of the highway. The Soberanes Canyon Trail is the easier and more popular of the two, taking you into a fine stand of redwoods. Most of the Rocky Ridge Trail is overly steep for most folks, but it does have some excellent views. The first ⅔ mile of this route is relatively easy, and for those who don't want a taxing ascent, this initial part offers rewarding views down at the coast and up Soberanes Canyon to the Coast Ridge.

The park's north boundary is about 5.7 miles south of Carmel's Carmel Valley Road junction and about 2.0 miles south of Carmel Highlands' Highlands Drive junction. You'll find fuel, food and lodging in Carmel Highlands, but far more services are in the Carmel-Monterey area. The *day-use-only* state park has no facilities other than two outhouses, one between turnouts 13 and 14, the other between 15 and 16 (both outhouses are near Soberanes Point).

Map 1

Coast Access Trails

There are 16 State Highway 1 turnouts, each numbered unless vandalized. All but one are along the west side of the highway, the exception being turnout 14. (On map 1 each appears as a small hemisphere.) Northbound drivers wanting to pull off on the east side of the highway aren't restricted to just that turnout, since there are a number of places where the highway's east shoulder is wide enough for parking. The turnouts are numbered from north to south, the first being at Monterey County mile 67.2, the sixteenth at mile 65.3. The highway has mileage signs, which decrease southward to zero at the San Luis Obispo county line. The signs drivers should watch for are MON 65^{00}, MON 66^{00} and MON 67^{00} (MON stands for Monterey). Also COASTAL ACCESS signs at the north and south ends of the park alert you to this stretch of turnouts.

You come upon the first turnout immediately past a roadcut. Chances are that by the time you apply your brakes, you'll be at turnout two or three. Mile 67.0 lies between these two closely spaced turnouts. From the third an abandoned road starts northwest along Highway 1, passing adjacent turnouts two and one and then in about 100 yards reaching a spur trail. Immediately ahead, the road curves right and enters private land, so you take the spur trail 80 yards west to a granite viewpoint. North, the view is blocked, but south you see most of Garrapata's coastline plus Point Sur beyond it. There are at least three other use trails out to bluffs with similar views, the southernmost one beginning at the start of the abandoned road. I prefer the trail that begins about 200 yards from the start of this road, the trail curving south above a narrow cove to a point.

Bypass turnouts 4–7 (miles 66.9–66.4), since they offer dangerous routes down to the surf. From turnout 8 (mile 66.5), a steep, eroded trail descends to a bouldery beach in a small cove. From turnouts 9 (mile 66.3) and 10 (mile 66.2) trails—not as steep as the one from turnout 8—descend to the surf. At the end of the turnout-10 trail is an interesting hunk of granite in the process of being separated from the mainland. The seaward side of this block has some tidepools up to 25′ above the ocean. To sustain the tidepools' life, waves have to splash to at least their height quite regularly. (During and just after stormy weather, waves along Garrapata's coast splash up to 50′ high.)

Turnout 11 (mile 66.1) is the start of a steep, brushy, but basically safe descent to a lackluster cove—not worth the effort.

Turnout 12 (mile 65.9) is the northernmost of the turnouts serving the Soberanes Point-Soberanes Canyon area. From the east side of the highway, you can take a trail 130 yards up to a closed road and then walk 30 yards north on it to the trail's resumption. This is the Rocky Ridge Trail, which climbs 1.6 miles from this point. Most folks start this trail from turnout 13. From the west side of the highway, an official trail starts west and quickly forks. West, a short spur descends along the lowest stretch of Soberanes Creek, which has minor pools and falls. South, the main trail briefly descends to cross the diminutive creek. Given the size of the area it drains, Soberanes Creek should be a torrent, not the trickle it usually is. I suspect the redwoods up-canyon usurp most of the creek's water. Immediately beyond the creek, you have a choice of taking a trail out to coastal bluffs or staying on the main trail, which parallels the highway south to a reunion with the bluff trail.

This junction is just a few yards west of turnout 13.

Seventy-yard-long turnout 13, at mile 65.8, is probably the park's most popular one, since it is the starting point for the Soberanes Canyon and Rocky Ridge trails (both treated separately below), and a trail system centered on Whale Peak. This is hardly a peak at all, but rather just a conspicuous knoll separated from an adjacent, major ridge by a sizable saddle. Highway 1 tops out at this saddle, descending from it in both directions. You'll find the small, east-side turnout 14 just north of the saddle and the equally small turnout 15 just south of it. Turnout 16 (the last, at mile 65.3) is 300 yards south of turnout 15, and like turnout 13 is a popular one.

You can start a loop around Whale Peak from any of the above trailheads. If you're driving south, turnout 13 is a logical choice. From it, a heavily used trail starts a traverse southwest across a bench, and in 90 yards reaches a cluster of cypresses that hide an outhouse. In a slightly longer distance, the trail reaches a junction, where the loop actually begins. Left, a trail climbs south to Highway 1, reaching it near turnout 14. Right, a trail curves west out toward the north end of Soberanes Point. (From its north to its south end, this "point" stretches almost ½ mile.) Where the trail curves left for a southward traverse along the lower slopes of Whale Peak, a use trail branches west out to some rocks—a popular place for fishermen—and then meanders south along the bluffs before climbing briefly up to the main trail. From that junction the trail heads south over to Soberanes Point proper, then climbs, first east and then northeast, up to a junction. Between this spot and adjacent Highway 1 is an outhouse.

Two fishermen at Soberanes Point

Highway 1, Whale Peak and Soberanes Point, from the Rocky Ridge Trail

If you're starting a walk north from turnout 16, you'll reach this junction in about 240 yards. Midway to it, you'll pass a short trail that heads steeply down a gully to a sandy beach in a small cove. From the outhouse junction the main trail climbs north about 80 yards beside the highway to turnout 15, then climbs about 150 yards farther to another junction. From it, a short trail climbs southwest to a saddle on two-topped Whale Peak. Walk briefly along the crest to either summit. As at so many turnouts along the Big Sur stretch of Highway 1, this summit area is a fine spot to watch the sun set. North from the Whale Peak summit trail, the main trail immediately passes through the saddle, and then you descend, partly via stairs, to Highway 1 near turnout 14. You complete the loop around Whale Peak by descending about 150 yards north on a slackening grade to a junction on the bench between Whale Peak and turnout 13.

Rocky Ridge Trail

This trail begins from turnout 13, which is located at mile 65.8, a point that is 7.1 miles south of Highway 1's junction with Carmel Valley Road, in Carmel. The turnout is long enough to hold about a dozen vehicles, which on some days is not enough. From a gate on the east side of the highway, you walk east a minute along a closed road over to a nearby structure, then a minute farther to a crossing of Soberanes Creek. This is named for the Soberanes family, descendants of early Spanish settlers who later, under the Mexican land grant system, acquired over 35,000 acres of Salinas River land in the King City area. Just 30 yards beyond the creek, you come to the start of the Soberanes Canyon Trail, described below.

Keeping to the closed road, you head north, ducking into a minor gully and then into a larger one. As you climb out of it, you'll meet a trail on your left, which descends 130 yards to turnout 12. If you start your hike from this point, you'll save almost ¼ mile of easy walking. Just 30 yards farther north along the road, and about ⅓ mile from the main trailhead, the easy walking ends. The road ahead looks quite inviting, but in reality it quickly becomes overgrown, so you turn right and start a moderate climb up slopes. The trail climbs ⅓ mile southeast up to a steeply descending ridgecrest, and here, at about 410' elevation, you have good views of most of Garrapata's largely brushy coast lands and a fair view up redwood-blessed Soberanes Canyon. "Garrapata" is Spanish for tick, and there's a slight chance you might pick up one or more of these slow-moving, blood-sucking invertebrates as you hike past grass and brush, particularly in winter or spring.

If you're not a serious hiker, you'll want to turn back here, for the gradient of the ridge route ahead *averages* about 19%, which is definitely steep. But views of the coast and the canyon keep getting better, and hints of even better ones urge you on. After about 1.3 miles from the trailhead, you top a minor knoll, cross an adjacent, minor saddle, and then climb across slopes to a larger saddle. Trail yields to closed road just above it, and you almost top a north-trending ridge. This one has a U.S. Geological Survey bench mark on it, point 1435 on the map, and it is an excellent spot for a view-packed break.

With just over 1000' of steep climbing behind you, you face about 250' more, taking the road northeast across a saddle and then north up to its end on a north-descending ridge. At 1680' elevation you're 1570' above your trailhead and 1.9 miles from it. From your vantage spot you can see all the way from Point Sur north to the Monterey Peninsula and beyond it to the Santa Cruz Mountains.

Though the road ends here, you can continue eastward for some enlightening perspectives of California's central-coast lands. One path climbs directly up Rocky Ridge, while another skirts north-facing slopes for a ⅓-mile traverse to a shallow saddle. From it a use trail plunges about 1200′ in just under 1.0 mile to the end of the Soberanes Canyon Trail. The upper half of this descent averages a steep 16%; the lower half, an *extremely steep* 32%. That is almost too steep to stand on! Your body may be racked with pain should you descend this trail. A better descent route needs to be built—read on.

From the shallow saddle, several closely parallel cattle trails head northeast over to a nearby shallow saddle, and then climb briefly to a north-descending ridge. Here, 2.5 miles from the trailhead, you have your best views of the Monterey Peninsula. Onward, you can follow one or more cattle trails on or just north of grassy Rocky Ridge over to a major, broad, north-descending ridge. This is about 100 yards past a small grove of stunted redwoods, which grow just below the cattle trails. In this vicinity, you have a new panorama, which includes lands to the northeast. You'll see Fremont Peak crowning the north end of the Gabilan Range, which rises above the east side of Salinas Valley. You'll also see, to its left and in the far distance, a conspicuous summit, Pacheco Peak, about 50 miles to the northeast. This peak, like a line of others near it, is the eroded remnants of an ancient volcano.

From two posts on your ridge, you are about 3.0 miles from your trailhead, and you can retrace your steps to it. Onward, an abandoned road winds ¼ mile southeast down to a saddle, from which faint jeep tracks continue southeast up the main ridge, leaving park land in under ½ mile. What Garrapata State Park can really use is a trail segment connecting the saddle with the end of the Soberanes Canyon Trail. Moderately graded, such a segment would be about 2¼ miles long, and hikers would have a very scenic 7-mile-long loop trail that would be diverse in views, landforms, vegetation and animals.

Soberanes Canyon Trail

First see the first paragraph of the previous route for the trailhead location and the 260-yard walk along a closed road to the start of the Soberanes Canyon Trail. Your trail starts east along Soberanes Creek, and in a couple of minutes you pass a small population of mission cacti. Not a native to California proper, the mission cactus was brought north from Mexico by Spanish missionaries as early as 1769. The plants seen here were probably derived from a later stock planted by early settlers. About 0.4 mile from Highway 1, the trail bends northeast at your canyon's junction with a sizable side canyon. Here you'll see stunted, brushy redwoods mingling with creek-side willows.

From the bend you leave the sound of surf behind and note how redwoods increase in size and number. Within 0.4 mile you enter a shady forest of mature redwoods, and you'll stay within it—or briefly just above it—all the way to trail's end, 1.5 miles from the trailhead. After about 200 yards of redwood shade, the trail crosses Soberanes Creek, and over the next 0.3 mile it crosses the creek three more times. By the last crossing, a conspicuous use trail starts up along the south bank of the creek, while the official route starts up along the north bank. The latter quickly leaves the bank for a rollercoaster route up and down steep slopes, the last descent being from a south-dropping, bay-shaded ridge. There, a couple of short switchbacks take you down close to the creek, which flows more robustly here than at the lower end of the stand of redwoods (the creek apparently is sizably diminished by the trees' craving for water).

Near the creek a few short switchbacks climb steeply to a brushy ridge. These make up the last part of the overly steep descent route mentioned in the previous hike. I hope that someday this use trail will be supplanted by a first-rate trail up to a saddle along the east part of Rocky Ridge. In the meantime, to reach the ridge from this part of Soberanes Creek, you'll have to take the use trail. Ascending it is certainly easier on your body than descending it, but it is very strenuous. However, the canyon scenery is quite impressive, so you can take lots of breaks to admire it.

Chapter 12: Andrew Molera State Park and Point Sur State Historic Park

Introduction

Covering about 7.4 square miles, Andrew Molera is the largest state park along the Big Sur coast. Not surprisingly, it also contains the most trails, about 20 miles of them. Most of the mileage is along old roads, which will appeal to gregarious hikers, equestrians, joggers and bicyclists. *Please note that bicycles are allowed only on Trail Camp Trail, Creamery Meadow Trail and Ridge Trail.* From June through October many of the park's users are none of the preceding, but rather are surfers. They start from one of the park's first two Highway 1 turnouts or from the parking lot, and head to the beach near the mouth of the Big Sur River. All routes are about a mile in length, which seems a long way to carry a board. All are mentioned under the park's first route, the Headlands Trail. If you have a pet, you can take it on the roads and paths so long as you keep it on a leash.

As alluded to above, there are turnouts along Highway 1 through the park. In 1987 there were 19 turnouts on the southwest side of the highway (plus unsigned others on the northeast side). By 1993 there were only 8 turnouts identified on the park's *brochure*, but unfortunately they did not quite match the numbers at the turnouts in the *field*. Because of this mismatch and because the numbers may change in the future, I felt compelled to retain the 19 original turnouts in both the following text and on Maps 7 and 8. These are shown on the maps as black, numbered hemispheres. By noting the way the highway curves as it weaves through the park, you should be able to identify most or all of them. Be aware that most of these 19 turnouts once had spur trails through poison oak to lackluster stretches of the Big Sur River, and hence I am not describing them. Additionally, most have been officially closed. Remember that this book's numbers will not match those in the field. This is not a serious problem, since most park users will want to start from the parking lot, not from a highway turnout.

Particularly early in the morning, joggers can be seen pounding the pavement along Pfeiffer Big Sur State Park's roads, but they'd be better off driving to Andrew Molera and doing one of the following routes, which I've listed in order of increasing difficulty. 1) From the northwest end of the parking lot, run to the campground and beyond it to road's end, near the coastline—about 2 level miles, round trip. 2) From the middle of the parking lot, cross the adjacent Big Sur River (during the dry months, there's a footbridge; at other times you'll have to make a usually shallow wade). Jog southwest along a broad path to a nearby road, turn right on it and begin a 1.8-mile level loop around Creamery Meadow. 3) For added mileage take one or more of the following routes. Near the meadow's southwest corner, a broad trail goes 0.1 mile out to the surf, and from there you can take the Bluff Trail southeast. You can also reach this trail by heading up a short, steep road from the meadow's south edge. It climbs up to a bench, and you can branch right to the Bluff Trail on a path, which is just before the base of a steeply climbing road, the Ridge Trail. Take the rolling Bluff Trail to road's end at a junction with the Panorama and Spring trails. The latter descends to a nearby beach, if you need to cool off. The Bluff Trail plus its alternates add about 3.4 miles, round trip, to the basic Creamery Meadow loop. Strong, competitive joggers can tackle the Ridge Trail, whose first ½ mile straight up a ridge is too steep for most joggers. Follow the road up to its end, descend the Panorama Trail, and then traverse along the Bluff Trail back to the southeast corner of Creamery Meadow. This loop is a very good 10K workout, and total mileage from the parking lot is about 8.2 miles.

Those with a sedentary predilection will be happy to learn that one can take horseback rides along some of the park's trails. From April 1 through November 30, *weather permitting,* Molera Trail Rides offers morning, afternoon and twilight rides, all different but each visiting the ocean. For specifics, phone them at (408) 625-8664.

The park has a walk-in campground (fee required) situated about ¼ mile west of the parking lot. For most folks this is too far to walk in with all their gear. However, if you are traveling light or are willing to carry in all your gear, you'll be rewarded with one of the nicest campgrounds along the entire California coast. Be sure to bring a tent, or else by morning your sleeping bag will become saturated with condensed water vapor. Although you can stay overnight in the park's campground, the park is, curiously enough, *day use only.* No camping and no campfires are allowed anywhere else in the park. You can't camp in the parking lot, even if you do own a self-contained recreational vehicle.

Between the south boundary of Andrew Molera State Park and the north boundary of Pfeiffer Big Sur State Park, there's a 1.3-mile stretch of Highway 1 with additional services and lodging. From north to south, these are: River Inn and the Village Shops (motel, store, gasoline, shops), Big Sur Campground and Cabins, Riverside Campground and Cabins, Ripplewood Resort (cottages, store, gasoline), Glen Oaks Motel and Restaurant, and Fernwood

Resort (campground, motel, gasoline, groceries, dining room).

In contrast to Andrew Molera State Park, Point Sur State Historic Park is the smallest state park along this part of the coast, and it has restricted access, as mentioned just below in this chapter's first route.

Maps 7 and 8; also use Andrew Molera State Park's brochure (purchased at Pfeiffer Big Sur State Park), which has a large-scale map showing its trail system. See map 12's bottom left inset for the Point Sur area.

Point Sur State Historic Park

History buffs should consider visiting the Point Sur Lightstation, which in 1980 became a state historic site, then in 1984 became a state historic park. *Visitation is by guided tour only.* Tours are on Saturday, 10 A.M. and 2 P.M., and Sunday, 10 A.M. Get to the starting point about a half hour early. This is at a locked gate about ¼ mile north of the paved entrance to the point's conspicuous Point Sur Naval Facility. That entrance is 5.6 miles south of the imposing Bixby Creek Bridge and 2.6 miles north of Andrew Molera's entrance road. After paying a fee (in 1993: $5 for adults, less for kids), you'll be let through the gate and then can drive to a parking area at the base of Point Sur (this holds only 15 vehicles—*no RVs or trailers*). From it your guided tour climbs to the lighthouse and associated buildings.

The point tends to be windy, and from November through March can be quite cold. Dress appropriately, for you'll be exposed to the elements. The hike is not one for small children, who more likely than not will be put off by the weather and the 2½–3 hour guided tour. Pets are expressly prohibited.

The schedule of tours could be changed or increased in the future. Also, some tours may be canceled—for example if the weather is bad—while others may already be full. Therefore, the park service has set up a hot line with a recorded message: (408) 625-4419. It's a good idea to phone before driving to the trailhead. For other information, phone Pfeiffer Big Sur State Park at (408) 667-2315.

Trail Camp and Headlands Trails

The most easily attained view of the state park's coastline is from Molera Point, at the end of the short Headlands Trail. This is the park's only year-round *easy* coast-access trail, for it doesn't cross the Big Sur River; whale watchers, take note. From the northwest end of the parking lot head west along a riverside path, the Trail Camp Trail, which quickly broadens to become a road. In about 0.2 mile you reach a junction with a fire road, which climbs up to turnout 4 along nearby Highway 1. You then enter the park's spacious, grassy 0.2-mile-long walk-in campground. About 200 yards beyond its far end, your road reaches the start of a trail climbing up to the east side of the Cooper Cabin, in a eucalyptus grove. Onward, the trail continues 0.2 mile northeast to turnout 3. About 0.1 mile past this trail, the road meets another one, this one going close to the cabin's right and formerly going to the highway. Finally, about 200 yards farther, near an outhouse, a third trail strikes north, this trail also abandoned like the second one.

Soon the road ends, and a trail continues ahead. You may see two spurs over to the nearby river, and then you'll quickly reach the Headlands Trail, on your right. If you are interested in surf access, continue straight ahead on the main trail. Otherwise, head up the Headlands Trail's stairs to a bluff and follow the brushy route over to Molera Point. This is a good spot for whale watching when California gray whales are migrating south from late December through January and are migrating north during March and April. During most of the warm months, the marine mammals you're likely to see are an eccentric breed of *Homo sapiens:* surfers. Other marine mammals present are sea lions, harbor seals and sea otters.

Beach and Creamery Meadow Trails

Together, these two roads form a loop around Creamery Meadow. You can start the loop from two places. First, from the middle of the parking lot, cross the adjacent Big Sur River (during the dry months, there's a footbridge; at other times you'll have to make a usually shallow wade). Head about 140 yards southwest along a broad path to a nearby, northwest-trending road, which you can follow left or right. Right is the Beach Trail route. Left is the Creamery Meadow Trail route. Heading that way—southeast—you'll reach Creamery Meadow's east corner and a junction with a road that's occasionally driven by park vehicles. Just a few yards west on this road—the Creamery Meadow Trail—is a junction with a trail that parallels the northwest-trending road, staying just above it and out of sight of it.

The second start of the loop is immediately beyond the parking lot's entrance road. From a gate you continue 200 yards along the main road, passing two buildings before reaching a road branching right. This immediately crosses the river, and if on foot you'll get your feet wet regardless of the time of year. About 60 yards up the other side, a road branches left. This is the start of the River Trails (there is more than one trail). Continuing 35 yards straight ahead gets you to the junction with the northwest-trending road, and the start of the 1.8-mile loop around Creamery Meadow.

Since the Beach Trail is the shorter route to the coast, I'll mention it first. Take the northwest-trending road in that direction. It climbs a few yards up to the ground that the paralleling trail is on, and both meet in Creamery Meadow's north corner. The Beach Trail then heads southwest along the meadow's edge for ⅓ mile, staying close to the Big Sur River but separated from it by dense bank vegetation. The road then veers away from the river and narrows to a broad path before reaching the seasonally boggy southwest corner of Creamery Meadow. Here is the end of the Creamery Meadow Trail, which is a road coming from the east. Straight ahead, the Beach Trail goes 180 yards, passing just below a rocky end of a bluff midway to the surf. In stormy weather, waves surge halfway up this stretch of trail, strewing logs and litter about. Immediately before you reach the sandy beach, you'll pass the Bluff Trail, described below, climbing east to its namesake bluff, which is the edge of a marine terrace.

From Creamery Meadow's east corner a maintained road, the Creamery Meadow Trail, contours southwest 0.8 mile along the meadow's edge to a junction along its south edge, then continues 320 yards west beside it to end at the Beach Trail. Note that the south-edge junction, which marks the start of the Ridge Trail, is 1.0 mile from the parking lot regardless of whether you take the Beach Trail or the Creamery Meadow Trail. The Ridge Trail begins as a steeply climbing road, which makes a 120-yard ascent southeast up to the marine terrace. Atop it, one lateral trail branches south from the road, going 110 yards to the Bluff Trail. Just 35 yards farther along the road, a second lateral trail branches about 400 yards southeast to the same. This trail is unofficial, and park personnel discourage its use. That junction with the Bluff Trail is 0.4 mile east of the trail's start from the end of the Beach Trail near the mouth of the Big Sur River. Ahead, the road—the Ridge Trail—commences a steep climb straight up the ridge. To continue on the

Bluff or Ridge trail and beyond, see the next two routes.

Bluff, Spring and Panorama Trails

The Bluff Trail departs east from the Beach Trail only a few yards before that trail dies out on a sandy beach. The Bluff Trail first makes a steep 100-yard climb up to a bluff—actually, a marine terrace—on which it will stay for its full 1.8-mile length. You stay close to the edge of the bluff for ¼ mile, and then reach a lateral trail coming south from the nearby Ridge Trail, which you see climbing prominent Pfeiffer Ridge (locally it's called Molera Ridge). Your trail has widened to a road by now, and from it you make a gentle climb 0.2 mile straight ahead, away from the bluff, to a second lateral trail coming from the Ridge Trail. From the parking lot you can reach this second junction by any of several logical ways. Which one is the shortest? Surprisingly, all are about 1.32 miles long, plus or minus 100', so take any route you want.

So far, the vegetation along the marine terrace has been mostly grass and species of low coastal brush. At the use trail's reunion, the marine terrace is definitely sloping instead of nearly flat, and now coyote brush begins to take over. It will become the dominant trail vegetation well before trail's end and will continue to dominate all along the Panorama Trail. From the reunion, the Bluff Trail crosses a pair of actively eroding gullies, and then crosses several smaller ones as it rolls along the terrace. One wishes the road were along the edge of the terrace so you'd see the beach and the surf, but such a route is impractical, given the rapid rate at which the bluff is being eroded.

Near the end of the Bluff Trail, its tread almost disappears as it traverses across barren, rapidly eroding exposures of poorly cemented sandstone, perhaps the relict of an Ice Age beach. From it, the road dips into and climbs out of a gully, and then it ends at the brink of an adjacent gully. From here the **Spring Trail** starts a 0.1-mile descent to a nearby beach. During the stormy months, waves can erode the beach so much that it barely exists. However, from about April through November, the beach is sufficiently wide for sunbathing and for strolling about ½ mile along the coastline.

The 1.9-mile-long, view-blessed **Panorama Trail** begins where the Bluff Trail ends. It first drops into a major gully with a seasonal creek and then starts a protracted climb that averages 11½%, which is a little steeper than a moder-

The Spring Trail descends to an isolated beach

ate grade. The ascent is basically in two stages, the first part up to a ridge that has stunted, wind-cropped redwoods, some of them merely bushes. From a shallow depression in the ridge the trail heads southwest across a minor gully to a second ridge, briefly ascends it, and then traverses past blackberries and mints before starting the second major stage up through pervasive coyote brush. If you find the gradient a bit on the steep side, you can stop almost anywhere and enjoy a grand view northwest across parkland to Point Sur. Just 0.3 mile from trail's end, you reach a minor saddle on a descending ridge. Here, at 930' elevation, you have perhaps the park's best viewpoint, for now you also see coast lands to the south, including a broad marine terrace known as Pacific Valley, and also pointed Cone Peak.

The Panorama Trail now climbs northeast along a ridge, which more or less lies along the park's south boundary. A fence separates your trail from an adjacent, minor ridge road, on private land. The trail ends at the park's highest viewpoint west of Highway 1. Only the steep East Molera Trail, east of the highway, climbs higher. Here at 1050' elevation you have an extensive view of lands to the north and northwest. Rather than descend the way you came, a total distance of 4.6 miles, you can take the

Ridge Trail, a closed but maintained road, which starts a descent from the viewpoint. For diversity or expediency, you can take this road only 1⅔ miles to a junction, and then descend the Hidden Trail to the River Trail and follow it back to the parking lot. This is about ½ mile shorter than the 3¾-mile route via the entire Ridge Trail and either of Creamery Meadow's two routes.

Ridge and Hidden Trails

See the "Beach and Creamery Meadow Trails" description to get to the start of the 2¾-mile-long Ridge Trail, and then follow it 155 yards up to the second of two lateral trails over to the Bluff Trail. Keeping to the road, you make a steep climb, averaging 14% in grade, ½ mile up to point 451. Here views temporarily disappear due to tall coyote brush, but momentarily reappear as you start a slight descent along Pfeiffer Ridge (locally known as Molera Ridge). The road remains nearly level for about 250 yards, but then starts the route's second steep climb, averaging 17%. Fortunately, it's only ¼ mile long.

You top out at brushy point 703, where there's a hitching rail for horses. Here, 2.1 miles from the parking lot, you have one of the park's best views—a 360° panorama. You now see coast lands to the southeast as well as those northwest to Point Sur. You can look up the lower part of the Big Sur River canyon. Above it and east of you is a high point on a coast ridge, Manuel Peak. Just left of it to the east-northeast is another peak, Post Summit. However, the most dominating peak stands to the north-northeast, rising above the coast ridge: Pico Blanco. It's seemingly conical shape resembles a Cascade Range volcano, but

actually it's a huge mass of limestone, the largest in the Santa Lucia Range.

Most folks may be content to go no farther, but by continuing 0.1 mile farther, down to a junction with the Hidden Trail, they can put together a loop with diverse scenery. This 0.7-mile-long trail averages a steep 15% grade, and you may want to stop a time or two to rest your knees and admire the views. These disappear near the trail's end, as coyote brush gives way to live oaks. You end at the River Trails at a point about 0.7 mile from the parking lot. The "trails" here are only one tread, and it's a road. But westward, toward the parking lot, you reach a meadow and have a choice of routes, the direct path on the right being shorter than the road, which loops around the meadow. See "River Trails" for details.

If you're continuing along the Ridge Trail, you'll be glad to know that the steep climbing is over. Ahead the road averages only 5½% as it climbs 490' to an 1150' viewpoint. First you have a nearly level traverse along a ridge of grass and coyote brush, then you leave it for a moderate but short climb, which gets you back to the ridge. In 250 yards—and 2.1 miles from the start of your Ridge Trail—you reach a junction with the South Boundary Trail, which here is an abandoned road veering east over a low, nearby knoll. In 1.9 miles, this route, the lower part of it trail, ends at turnout 18 along Highway 1.

The Ridge Trail concludes by curving south and climbing first through a stand of stately live oaks, and then through a shady stand of redwoods. These then yield to oaks, which in turn quickly yield to coyote brush, which permits views as you do the last, fairly short stretch up to road's end and a viewpoint. If

Cone Peak and Pacific Valley are seen from high on the Panorama Trail

Point Sur, viewed from point 703, which is just above the upper end of the Hidden Trail

you're on a bicycle, you'll have to turn back here. Others can follow the previous route in reverse, first descending the Panorama Trail and then traversing along the Bluff Trail.

River and Hidden Trails

See the first two paragraphs of the "Beach and Creamery Meadow Trails" route for two equally long routes to the start of the River Trails. The River Trails starts as a good, level road, which goes 0.1 mile south to the edge of a large meadow. This often has deer at dawn and at dusk. Here you'll find a shortcut trail, which runs along the meadow's north side. Taking it saves about 140 yards. The road circles the meadow's perimeter, offering you fine views across it up to Pico Blanco, which pokes above a high coast ridge. From the meadow's east side, where the shortcut trail ends, you walk a couple of minutes beneath live oaks and past coyote brush gently up to a junction with the **Hidden Trail.** This 0.7-mile-long trail *averages* a steep 15% grade. The first 200 yards are easy, but then you confront a short but very steep stretch, which climbs up a live-oak ridge and onto coyote-brush slopes. Here, you catch your breath and admire your first good views, which include a glimpse of Point Sur. Ahead, the terrain is mostly open, and it offers generally improving views. When you do reach Pfeiffer (Molera) Ridge, after a 570′ climb, climb an additional 43′ by heading 0.1 mile west on the Ridge Trail up to point 703, where you'll have a 360° view. See the previous route description if you plan to go in either direction along the Ridge Trail.

Back at the bottom of the Hidden Trail, ½ mile into the River Trails route, follow the roadbed east, which quickly starts a short, fairly steep descent to the west part of a second meadow. From here, a trail heads northwest over to a nearby ford of the Big Sur River, and then climbs to a junction with the Bobcat Trail. Just a few yards east on it is the start of a very short spur trail up to Highway 1's turnout 6.

The main River Trail, still a road, starts east along the south edge of the second meadow. It skirts the base of an imposing fern-decked cliff, and here you'll see a trail, just north, paralleling our road. This "river trail" begins from the previously mentioned river-fording trail, starting from a high bank immediately above the river, and it traverses along the meadow's north edge. Past the cliff, the main River Trail curves south along the meadow's edge and, just within forest cover, reaches yet another junction. The main River Trail (a real trail—no bicycles, please) branches right here, making a shady, winding traverse past live oaks, bays and redwoods, rejoining the road after 0.3 mile. The slightly shorter road route first goes 180 yards east over to the river's bank, where you'll meet the meadow's north-edge trail. It then continues 280 yards along the bank to the River Trail's southeast end. Just 50 yards ahead, the trail tread diagonals across the Big Sur by the west edge of a small cliff, and then it climbs briefly to the Bobcat Trail.

I should point out that back on the south side of the Big Sur, there is a trail junction just 65 yards before the main River Trail rejoins the road route. From it a trail climbs steeply but briefly up a ridge, which surprisingly has several ponderosa pines on it, and then drops steeply to a redwood flat. Why the trail was built is a mystery to me, since although you avoid one river ford, you face one regardless of which way you head on a trail you meet on the flat. North, this goes about 110 yards to a ford of the Big Sur only a stone's throw east of the previously mentioned ford. East, this goes about 230 yards to the river, along which you walk upstream about 80 yards to where you ford immediately before a low mass of bedrock that protrudes partway across the river. This is the end of the River Trails system, and you've walked about 1½–1¾ miles along it, the mileage being inexact because of the wide assortment of route variations you can take to reach this point.

Here, note how the resulting constriction forces the river to flow faster. With extra scouring power, it has excavated the nicest swimming hole you'll find in the park. From about June through October, this usually warms by midafternoon into the 60s. Just across the river, a trail continues a few yards up to a large meadow, Coyote Flat, and crosses it over to Highway 1's turnout 11. This is a use trail. There are two official trails, which together circle the meadow. Both are branches of the Bobcat Trail, mentioned below. If you start north on the tread along the meadow's west edge, you'll reach the gate by Molera Trail Rides in 1.5 miles.

Bobcat and Cooper Loop Trails

For practical purposes, the Bobcat Trail begins at the parking lot's entrance road. Here, from a gate, you head 200 yards southeast along the main road, passing two buildings before reaching a road branching right. This road is the Creamery Meadow Trail, which dips to ford the Big Sur River and then climbs the opposite bank to reach a nearby junction with the River Trails, the previous route. You keep on the main road, reaching its end at a corral about ⅓ mile from the gate.

At this spot the Bobcat Trail officially begins, and in 0.1 mile it reaches a junction. Right, a lateral trail heads south to the nearby river, follows it a bit upstream, and then crosses it. This trail climbs to the south bank, and up there is another junction, this one with a trail traversing along the north edge of the meadow. Ahead, the lateral trail quickly ends at a road, the main River Trail. This junction, mentioned in the previous route, is the one in the west part of a second meadow.

Just a few yards east along the Bobcat Trail, you'll meet a short trail climbing up to Highway 1's turnout 6. About 0.1 mile farther, you come alongside the highway, parallel it past redwoods and then across a minor gully before diverging slightly from the highway to reach the tip of a large meadow. The route touches the riverbank, winds through the meadow, and then makes a brief, shady traverse back to the riverbank. Here, about 1.2 miles from the gate, are two closely spaced junctions with the River Trails system. A trail west crosses the river on a diagonal, reaching the other bank at the west

edge of a small cliff. The trail then goes 50 yards downstream, to a junction where the main River Trail and its alternate road route converge. The second trail leaving the Bobcat Trail heads southeast across a bend in the Big Sur, this ford only a stone's throw east of the previously mentioned ford. This trail will end at ours in about ¼ mile, where it crosses a fine swimming hole.

The Bobcat Trail next heads briefly east along the Big Sur, crosses a seasonally trickling creeklet, and then heads briefly north up the east side of the creeklet's gully. The trail starts a curve southeast, and in 0.1 mile reaches the northwest edge of a large meadow, Coyote Flat, and forks. The left branch stays along the meadow's north edge, paralleling the adjacent highway, which isn't too interesting. However, about 110 yards along this route you'll reach former turnout 11, which is just before a conspicuous cluster of redwoods, and then about 240 yards farther, you'll reach larger turnout 12. Just beyond it, at the meadow's east end, this branch rejoins the more inviting right branch.

The right branch follows the meadow's edge, first south and then east. At the trail's bend, it crosses a use trail coming directly across the meadow from turnout 11. From this junction a trail descends a few yards southwest, crossing the Big Sur where a low mass of bedrock protrudes partway across it. Constricted flow has resulted in the development of the nicest swimming hole you'll find in the park. Most folks will reach this from turnout 12 rather than via 1.5 miles along the Bobcat Trail. This spot marks the end of the previous route, the River Trails system.

Onward, the south branch of the Bobcat Trail arcs along the meadow's edge, gradually veering from the river before it joins the north branch almost ¼ mile later. The trail then makes a shady traverse 80 yards southeast to a river ford. From the other bank, the trail is known as the Cooper Loop Trail, and true to its name, it quickly forks to create a loop. Both branches are just over ⅓ mile long, and both take you past redwoods, the right, southern branch more so. Where they converge on the riverbank, you're about 2.2 miles from your start by the gate. A use trail continues up the river's southwest bank, essentially dying out midway along a ⅓-mile stretch to the South Boundary Trail's river ford. If you're not hiking this trail, the ford's location can be obscure. It's roughly midway along a short southwest-flowing leg of the river. Should you wish to take the trail, read on.

South Boundary Trail

Having an obscure trailhead and being overly steep and generally viewless, this route receives little use. However, it does take you to some of the finest viewpoints in the park, and it gets you to them in a shorter distance than does the Ridge, Bluff or Rattlesnake Trail. The 1.9-mile-long South Boundary Trail begins from Highway 1's turnout 18, which is found just over 2.0 miles east of the park's entrance road, at a spot about 0.2 mile west of the park's boundary. The trail winds southeast over to a fairly broad ford of the Big Sur River and then continues about 40 yards east, sometimes as an invisible tread across river boulders, to an old stream channel. Follow this about 120 yards northeast, to where the trail turns south, running between two long, parallel logs. You'll find other trails in this area, including ones coming from private land just a stone's throw to the east, but you head south across the river terrace to the base of a steep slope.

There you'll find a conspicuous trail, which switchbacks up past redwoods and quickly ends at an abandoned road. This begins by switchbacking, and then it parallels the park's "south" boundary southwest for 0.2 mile before relaxing its fairly steep grade. The obvious route then rambles west, but curves to return to the boundary for a short, steep stretch. The road touches the boundary at a gate, and on the other side, on private land, is a well-maintained boundary road.

You are now 1.2 miles from the trailhead, and you've thankfully got 800' of elevation gain behind you. Ahead, the road traverses over to an adjacent gully and just past it makes a short, steep drop before traversing over to a larger gully, this one with a spring-fed, concrete cistern. Who knows what wildlife drinks its slimy water; better not trust it. Now you face a fairly steep climb, gaining 300' in elevation by the time you cross an open, viewful knoll. The Ridge Trail—a much better road—lies 90 yards to the west and slightly below the knoll. Two of the park's best views lie to the south. Go ⅔ mile up the Ridge Trail to the first viewpoint, at this road's end, and then about 0.3 mile quite steeply down the Panorama Trail to a second viewpoint, which is at a shallow saddle where the trail veers away from the park's obvious border.

East Molera Trail

You can begin this from two spots. To reach the start of the longer route, head 0.1 mile down from the park's entrance road, where it forks, branch right and quickly reach the parking lot's entrance. From here you'll have to backtrack on foot or horseback up to the fork and then take the service road just a few yards past a barn, where there's a signed trailhead but no parking accommodations. The trail immediately curves southeast, momentarily parallels the highway, and then tunnels under it. Now on an old road, you briefly parallel the highway again, to where the road is somewhat blocked off. Here you'll see a trail crossing your road, and you turn left, up it. The second trailhead is to the right, just a few yards below, along Highway 1. This spot is about 0.3 mile southeast from the park's entrance road. Unfortunately, there's no parking here either, so you'll have to use either a turnout about 0.1 mile before it or one about 0.1 mile after it (that one being signed turnout 5). Walking from either turnout to the second trailhead still saves you about 0.3 mile of walking compared to a start from the first. You'll find the second trailhead just a few yards northwest of a conspicuous gate across a road. From here, the route up to a redwood saddle (elev. 1549 on the map) is 1.6 miles long.

You head up the trail, cross the old road in a few yards, and then climb about 90 yards back up to the road. You could have stayed on the road, this alternate being a bit longer but also a bit gentler. From the upper end of the short trail, which is by a water-storage tank, you climb moderately, first under live-oak shade, but mostly across open grassland. Then, immediately before the road bends left to start a very steep ascent, another road branches right from it. This traverses into the redwood-shaded gully you've been paralleling, and then it traverses about 280 yards over to a very large oak. A poorer tread begins a descent from here, followed quickly by a short climb to an obvious, grassy knoll—a fine spot for a picnic. Don't bother continuing along the tread, which rambles down toward Highway 1.

On the main track, you gear down for a major effort. You'll climb about 950' to a redwood saddle, averaging a very steep 20% grade. Unfortunately, that's just an average. The first 0.2 mile averages 25%, and a brief stretch of it is even 30%! The tread is rubbly, and on your descent, you could easily slip there.

Once you've gotten past the first 0.2 mile, you can begin to enjoy the ever-improving views. You reach a ridge, switchback to climb directly up it, and then, after a steep climb east,

Pico Blanco, from the ridgecrest just east of the redwood saddle

reach a lesser ridge. This rewards you with a view of the main ridge, which by this point is a much needed incentive. Several minutes later you reach another minor ridge, and from it see the redwood saddle, barely 200 yards away. Your very steep ascent to here has been exacerbated by a lot of brush growing on the tread, some which you must push through. Although I didn't pick up any ticks on this ascent, you might.

Now the grade slackens as you wind across grassy slopes up toward the saddle. The tread dies immediately below it, so walk directly up to the stand of redwoods, which seem blatantly out of place. At them you stand face to face with towering Pico Blanco. For a better view of the terrain, take a path about 300 yards east along the ridge to a cluster of mature live oaks. From that vicinity you have unrestricted views, including ones northeast up the South Fork Little Sur River canyon, east up toward Post Summit, southeast along the Big Sur to Pfeiffer Big Sur's lands, and of course south and southwest across most of Andrew Molera's lands to the ocean.

You could continue onward, for a ridge-hugging former fire road follows a winding, open course a little over 2 miles to the park's boundary and then enters Forest Service land for an additional 1¼ miles up to Post Summit. It then traverses about 1¼ miles over to the Mt. Manuel Trail. However, the upper stretch to Post Summit and the Cabezo Prieto crest east from it were severely torched in the Marble-Cone fire, and the scrubby vegetation that has grown since then is so dense as to make the road essentially impenetrable.

Coast Road Spur Trail

In addition to all the previous trails, there's another official one, which I call the Coast Road Spur Trail. It begins about ¼ mile up the Coast Road, which in turn begins opposite the park's entrance road. From a bend in the Coast Road, the spur trail heads about 200 yards south along a ridge before dying out just above Highway 1. The trail does have ocean views, but you can get these from both the highway and the Coast Road, so this short trail seems superfluous.

On summer days, swimmers and sunbathers flock to this large pool at the end of the "Gorge Trail"

Chapter 13: Pfeiffer Big Sur State Park

Introduction

For many people, "Big Sur" is synonymous with Pfeiffer Big Sur State Park. This park, about 1¼ square miles in size, is not actually along the coast, but rather lies about a mile or so inland. Perhaps the park's most popular activity is camping; folks don't come here to hike. But if they want to, there's one challenging trail that'll give them their money's worth. This is the Mt. Manuel Trail, which begins in the park, but lies mostly in adjacent Ventana Wilderness. It is described earlier in this guide as Chapter 8's Route BS-1. Few people hike its entire 13-mile length, which is about twice as long as all the park's trails together. Please note that pets aren't allowed on any trails.

The entrance to Pfeiffer Big Sur State Park is along State Highway 1, 26 scenic miles south of the Carmel Valley Road junction in Carmel, and 28 equally scenic miles north of the Nacimiento-Fergusson Road junction near Kirk Creek Campground, at the south end of this book's coverage. Within the park is Big Sur Lodge, which offers rooms, a store and a restaurant. The park also has a large campground. With 217 sites and two group camps, you'd think it could handle the crowds. On most fair-weather days *and* holidays, it can't, so if you want to be guaranteed a site, make reservations well in advance through MISTIX by calling their toll-free number: (800) 444-PARK (444-7275).

In the 1.3-mile stretch of Highway 1 north of the park's north boundary, which is 0.5 mile north of the entrance road, there are additional services and lodging. From south to north, these are: Fernwood Resort (campground, motel, gasoline, groceries, dining room), Glen Oaks Motel and Restaurant, Ripplewood Resort (cottages, store, gasoline), Riverside Campground and Cabins, Big Sur Campground and Cabins, and River Inn and the Village Shops (motel, store, gasoline, shops).

Just 1.5 miles south of the park's entrance road is the Big Sur Post Office plus a store and a gift shop. Immediately past these is Begonia Gardens, a tourist attraction. About 0.6 mile beyond it, only 0.1 mile before Highway 1's summit, is the entrance to deluxe Ventana Inn. About 0.6 mile past the summit is Nepenthe, which serves lunches and dinners from an ocean-view terrace (they claim you can see 40 miles of coastline, but fog usually prevails). Finally, 0.7 mile past Nepenthe is Deetjen's Big Sur Inn, which has lodging and serves breakfast and dinner.

Maps 8 and 12; also use the park's brochure, which has a large-scale map

---

Pfeiffer Falls Trail

This is the most popular trail in the park, for it is short, it passes some of the park's finest redwoods, and it takes you to the park's only significant waterfall. You have a choice of two starting points. Just past the entrance station, you'll take a road veering right, over to nearby Big Sur Lodge. From this vicinity, you'll notice a road climbing northeast. The Pfeiffer Falls Trail begins just 30 yards up this road, on the right side. In 40 yards the road forks and you keep right, driving up to a small parking area immediately before a sharp bend in the road. The second, more popular trailhead begins here, at the bend, and it saves you 0.15 mile of uphill climbing.

At the second trailhead you'll see a 6' diameter cross section of a redwood that was about 1000 years old when felled. This was an average-sized tree—hardly a record breaker, even by the park's standards. Here, in the coast mountains of *central* California, few trees exceed 10' in diameter, 250' in height, or 1500 years in age. In the coast mountains of northern California, redwoods thrive better. There, trees with the above statistics are quite common, and the larger ones are 15–20' in diameter, 300–370' high, and 2000 or more years old.

The Pfeiffer Falls Trail begins from this second trailhead by going 100 yards to a junction. From it, the Valley View Trail (see below) branches west, immediately crossing trifling Pfeiffer-Redwood Creek. You can take that trail to Pfeiffer Falls, but it is about ¼ mile longer than the 0.4-mile-long main trail, and it involves extra climbing. Most folks take the easier route up the creek. In 160 yards this reaches a junction with the west end of the Oak Grove Trail (see below). You then bridge the creek four times, progressing up the shady, moist canyon to a junction with the west segment. From here, two sets of stairs take you to a viewing platform of the 60' high lower fall. The upper fall, of similar height, is partly obscured by a sycamore standing in front of it.

From the junction at the base of the stairs, you can continue your loop. In under 0.2 mile, this stretch first bridges a seasonal tributary and then climbs out of the redwood forest to an oak-shaded junction with the Valley View Trail.

Valley View Trail

Just 100 yards up the Pfeiffer Falls Trail, this 0.7-mile-long trail branches west. It leaves a shady forest floor, which is carpeted with redwood sorrel and some Pacific starflowers, and climbs quickly to drier slopes supporting scotch broom and live oaks. About 300' higher and almost ½ mile from the junction, you reach a second junction. Going to the right, you'd descend in under 0.2 mile to a junction at the base of two sets of stairs. The Valley View Trail, however, branches left and climbs to a ridge clad in brush and scraggly live oaks. This you follow to a viewpoint located ¾ mile from and 500' above the trailhead.

At the brushy viewpoint you have a sweeping panorama that extends from Point Sur, 7¼ miles to the northwest, over to the gap (elev. 980') crossed by Highway 1, 2½ miles to the southeast. You'll note that the valley below you is quite straight. This is because the Big Sur River, which cut a wandering course through Ventana Wilderness, reached a linear, northwest-trending fault in the state park. Rather than proceed directly to the sea, the river turned northwest along the zone of fractured, erodible rocks created by the fault, and in time the river excavated the valley you see today.

Oak Grove Trail

This trail starts at a junction just 260 yards up the Pfeiffer Falls Trail, and from there it traverses 1.1 miles southeast to the Mt. Manuel Trail. It then coincides with this major trail (Chapter 8's Route BS-1) for a 0.4-mile descent to a closed, paved fire road, which in turn descends 300 yards to a road junction beside a trailhead parking lot. To reach that lot, first go left at the fork immediately past Big Sur Lodge, and drive 0.7 mile past picnic areas to a road branching right, into a huge picnic area. The picnic-area road immediately forks, and you veer left and park just a few yards from the base of the closed, climbing road.

I found the southeast part of the Oak Grove Trail the most interesting, so I'll describe the route from that end. First, you climb southeast up the closed road, then curve north and momentarily reach a junction. Ahead, the road continues as a "gorge trail" (see below). You start west on a dirt road, which immediately passes a homesteader's cabin and turns north for a climb to the park's water supply. From this turn, immediately past the cabin, the Oak Grove/Mt. Manuel trail branches northwest, and in about 230 yards it winds in and out of a shallow gully to arrive at a junction with a former "Fitness Trail."

The Oak Grove/Mt. Manuel trail makes an initial switchback east, then climbs northward past brush, offering views of the local terrain. It then heads up a shady ridge clad with some of the finest specimens of live oaks the park has to offer. At the upper end of this minor ridge, the two trails split, the Mt. Manuel Trail climbing 4.8 miles from this junction to a scenic viewpoint.

Northwest, the Oak Grove Trail winds in and out of two gullies, which are shaded by sycamores, maples and bays, this vegetation contrasting with the chamise of intervening slopes. You then leave views behind as you enter an oak forest. You duck into three more gullies, and then curve north into a redwood forest, where your trail ends with a short climb to the Pfeiffer Falls Trail.

Gorge Trail

See the first two paragraphs of the previous trail for the trailhead and the initial 300 yards of the "gorge trail." Actually, there are two gorge trails, and neither is an official, maintained trail. Both are popular *de facto* footpaths, and both may have short stretches inundated in times of high water. During such time you won't want to enter the gorge. No dogs are permitted on either trail.

From the junction by the homesteader's cabin 300 yards into the route, the west-bank trail continues straight ahead, along the paved road, which ends in 330 yards, where a bridge formerly spanned the Big Sur River. Just 5 yards before the road's end, a trail branches left, descending in 55 yards to a seasonal footbridge across the river. From here you can climb up to the nearby north part of spacious Big Sur Campground. The west-bank trail continues about 300 yards upstream, reaching a fair pool just before hitting a headwall. It's dangerous to climb over the wall, though nimble hikers can climb around its base. A safer alternative is just to wade upstream, though the best solution is to take the east-bank trail.

This trail starts from the north tip of the campground and also goes about 300 yards before running into difficulty. By early summer, some folks have usually built a stepping-stone traverse across a shallow stretch of river, from which you clamber on giant boulders to the edge of an olympic-size pool. This lies at the mouth of a minigorge, and the only way you can safely continue up-canyon is to swim the length of the briskly refreshing pool. (On warm spring and fall days, the temperature rises in the afternoon to the mid or high 50s; on hot summer days, to the low or mid 60s.) The pool vies with Pfeiffer Falls as the park's most popular attraction. On hot days it can be crammed with dozens of swimmers and sunbathers.

Unless you like exploring, you won't want to go beyond the pool. Above it, the river's course quickly turns east, and the river, flowing through a deep, narrow canyon, is shaded in the afternoon, when the water is warmest and the time when most folks like to sunbathe. I hiked only about ⅓ mile above the pool, and in this stretch found one fair-size swimming hole. In this short stretch I probably made about a half-dozen river crossings. These are typically about a foot or two deep, and the current is too weak to sweep you away. However, there is abundant opportunity to slip on the bouldery bottom and crack your skull—don't travel alone. Judging by flotsam stranded on the banks, one can see that the river easily rises 10′ above its normal level during rampaging floods. Don't enter the gorge if there's even a hint of rainy weather.

Nature Trail

This is about ¼ mile long, and it has a dozen posts. Unfortunately, when I hiked it there were no trail leaflets available. Perhaps you'll have better luck. It ends in a small grove of redwoods growing in the wedge immediately west of where the park's road forks into the campground branch (veering right, across the adjacent bridge) and the picnic-grounds branch (straight ahead, winding along the river). The nature trail crosses the latter road at a spot just 50 yards beyond the fork and 35 yards before a driveway to an adjacent ranger station. From trail's west end you can take two very short trails. The all-season route (right) goes up to the nearby end of the bridge, and then resumes at its far end, dropping you to a visitors' parking area immediately before the Big Sur headquarters. The dry-season route (left) goes a stone's throw to the river, crosses it by a seasonal footbridge, and then ends at the visitors' parking area.

The Nature Trail begins opposite a parking lot for a picnic area that is about ¼ mile east of the road fork mentioned above. This lot in turn is just past a larger lot, which also serves a picnic area, plus the park's Campfire Center. A restroom lies between the two lots, and from the far lot a trail descends a few yards to the river, where there's a seasonal bridge taking you to the campground, ending between sites 6 and 9.

The virtually level Nature Trail starts in an oak woodland and ends in a redwood forest— two of the park's five major plant communities, the other three being chaparral, grassland and riparian woodland. You can investigate these other communities by first driving to the large parking lot immediately before a service-road/fire-road fork, which is the trailhead for the Oak Grove, Gorge and Mt. Manuel trails. You'll find chaparral (brush adapted to fire and drought) along the Oak Grove Trail between the homesteader's cabin and the Mt. Manuel

Pfeiffer Beach is one of the best beaches along the Big Sur coast

Trail junction, grassland in the field just beyond the parking lot, and riparian woodland along the river. Along it are alders, maples and sycamores. Look for a truly impressive sycamore—hard to miss—between the lot and the river.

Buzzards Roost Trail

At 3.1 miles this semiloop route is easily the longest of the park's trails, and likely the least hiked. If it had good views, it might be more popular. This is a trail for those who like shady, forested hikes. The official start is from a visitors' parking area immediately before the Big Sur headquarters. Reach the lot by taking the campground's road. This first crosses the Big Sur River and then immediately curves left to avoid plowing into Highway 1, on the opposite side of a fence. From the curve you quickly reach the lot, on the left. The Buzzards Roost Trail begins by first traversing under the campground road's and Highway 1's bridges to quickly arrive at a junction with a closed road. This road begins from the highway, 0.1 mile to the southeast. On your return, if you miss this junction, you'll then have to backtrack that distance. Avoid this oversight by looking for the Highway 1 bridge.

On the road you traverse almost 0.2 mile along the river, soon climbing by either of two splitting paths to their reunion. In about 60 yards you reach a junction. Straight ahead, a trail winds about 300 yards to end at a climbing road. This closed road quickly descends to two spacious group sites, which can be reserved when they're open from the Memorial Day weekend through September. In the opposite direction the road goes about 0.3 mile before forking in a grassy flat. Private land lies ahead.

From the junction beyond the reunion, the Buzzards Roost Trail climbs briefly, then back-tracks 0.4 mile southeast through a redwood forest to another junction. Here is the start of a 1.7-mile loop. You can go either way. The 0.6-mile-long right-branching route is more direct, switchbacking up to Buzzards Ridge, then heading 100 yards south along it to skirt just below the actual summit. If the summit had a lookout instead of an antenna, the trail would be more attractive. Straight ahead, the longer route traverses for 0.4 mile before making a 0.7-mile climb to the summit. The last 230 yards are along well-vegetated, generally view-less Buzzards Ridge.

Pfeiffer Beach

Perhaps you'd like to stroll along a beach, rather than through a forest. Well then, ½-mile-long Pfeiffer Beach is for you. To reach it from the Pfeiffer Big Sur State Park entrance road, drive 1.1 miles southeast up Highway 1 to a saddle with two roads. The southern, ungated one is Sycamore Canyon Road, and you take this narrow, winding paved road 2.2 miles to its end at a parking loop. If you're driving north on Highway 1, you'll meet Sycamore Canyon Road 1.1 miles northwest down from the Ventana Inn entrance.

From the parking loop, which has nearby vault toilets, a trail strikes 150 yards west, reaching the beach near its east end. Directly in front of you are some dramatic, very photogenic rocks, the largest having a set of three adjoining arches that are being enlarged by the crashing surf. The line of rocks breaks up the surf, resulting in shallow tide pools behind them, which are safe for wading. The diminished surf allows a broad, sandy beach to exist, which is good for walking or, when the sun is out, sunbathing. During the warmer months, surfers may abound along stretches where rocks don't disrupt the surf. Wet suits are necessary, for the water temperature stays in the 50s all year long.

Chapter 14: Julia Pfeiffer Burns State Park

Introduction

The trails of this 3¾-square-mile park are used by only a small fraction of Highway 1's visitors, and most of those who do hike take the short Waterfall Overlook Trail. However, the park has far more to offer than that. You can take either the Fire Road or the Tan Bark Trail up to the Tin House, a great viewpoint for a picnic. Better yet, ascend one route, descend the other, then walk about 0.8 mile along Highway 1 back to your vehicle. When its last mile is renovated the Ewoldsen Trail will offer a third—and picturesque—route to the Tin House.

From late December through January, and again in March and April, migrating gray whales pass close to the surf, and at times you can view them from the Waterfall Overlook or from Partington Landing, at the end of the Partington Cove Trail. Along the Waterfall Overlook Trail, no pets are allowed, and nowhere in this *day use only* park can you light fires except at two environmental campsites, which are mentioned under the Waterfall Overlook Trail description.

Highway 1 winds about 2.7 miles through the park, from about Monterey County mile 35.4 north to mile 38.1. For the park's trails, there are essentially three parking areas. If you're driving from the south, you get to the southernmost one by turning in on the park's short, signed, McWay Canyon entrance road at mile 35.85. There is a small fee to be paid at a self-service entrance station. The road quickly splits, the left branch going over to an adjacent parking lot with restrooms, and the right branch immediately bridging McWay Creek and curving to an overflow parking lot. The Waterfall Overlook Trail begins from the west side of the bridge; the Ewoldsen Trail begins from the upper end of the main parking lot.

The second parking area is a very conspicuous, popular vista point on a bend at mile 37.0. Use this for the start of the Fire Road,

which begins 70 yards to the east and has only minimal parking space near its gate.

The third parking area is at Partington Creek Bridge, roughly mile 37.8. Park at either end of the bridge. The Tan Bark Trail starts from the east end, though there's also a lateral trail joining it from the west end. The Partington Cove Trail begins at that end, signed as a fire road.

Gas, food, lodging and camping aren't found locally. For services available north of the park, consult the introduction in the previous chapter. For services south of the park, and for coast access south of the park, consult the trailhead section in Chapter 9's first route.

Maps 13, 14 and 17; also use the park's brochure, which has a large-scale map

Waterfall Overlook Trail and Spur Trails

The Waterfall Overlook Trail is the park's most popular trail and, with a length of 0.2 mile, it's one of its shortest. From the west end of the bridge crossing McWay Creek, you descend a few steps and reach a spur trail, veering left. This goes 50 yards southsouthwest to the Pelton Wheel, housed in a small room. A sign explains the history and mechanics of this vintage hydroelectric plant.

Saddle Rock and McWay Creek's fall, from the overlook

The Waterfall Overlook Trail keeps right and traverses about 140 yards southwest to a tunnel beneath Highway 1. On the other side of the tunnel, the trail splits, the Waterfall Overlook Trail paralleling the highway 160 yards over to trail's end, the waterfall overlook. At one time, a trail descended to the beautiful, sandy beach nestled in the idyllic cove harboring the McWay Creek's 60' waterfall. Today, the area is closed, to protect both people and habitat,, and persons descending to this area are subject to citation.

From the split at the tunnel, a trail follows Highway 1 briefly south, and then from a roadside gate it drops to a nearby road. If you were to follow this closed road 150 yards up to its start, you'd find it on the south side of a small highway roadcut about ¼ mile south of the park's McWay entrance road. From the trail's end, the road descends to a quick end beside two environmental campsites that are nestled on a cypress-cloaked bench that overlooks Saddle Rock. Reservations can be made only by mail—up to 8 weeks in advance and no later than 10 days before your starting date. Write to: California Department of Parks and Recreation, Attention: Reservation Office, P.O. Box 942896, Sacramento, CA. 94296-0420.

Ewoldsen Trail

Part of this 3.1-mile-long trail was burned in the 1985 Rat Creek fire, and the trail was closed. In 1993 all but the last mile to the Tin House—mostly a brush-and-oak high traverse—had been reopened. Below this traverse is a scenic 4¼-mile semiloop hike past redwoods, oaks, chaparral and grass that offers one of the finest vegetational samplings to be found along the Big Sur coast.

From the main parking lot the trail goes through a forested, creekside picnic area to just below the back side of a dilapidated barn, where it bridges McWay Creek. It then continues shortly to a junction, 0.2 mile from the trailhead, from where the Canyon Trail heads 0.1 mile along the creek to a bench below a small waterfall in a serene setting.

From the junction the Ewoldsen Trail initially climbs steeply, then traverses in and out of a side canyon, briefly climbing above redwoods before traversing north across steep slopes to a junction by a bridge across McWay Creek. Here, 1.0 mile from the trailhead, you can begin a loop. The left-hand trail climbs 1.0 mile to a ridgecrest junction, while the right-hand trail climbs 1.1 mile to it. Both contain steep stretches, and so the author prefers perspiring up the shadier, slightly less steep right-hand trail. This continues about 0.4 mile up McWay Canyon's redwood-shaded floor before climbing steeply west, then moderately south, to a bend on a minor ridge that affords a dramatic view—weather permitting—of the Big Sur's coastal lands. Live oak now dominates a generally viewless, comfortable ascent to a junction at a shallow saddle on a ridgecrest. When opened, the remaining part of the Ewoldsen Trail will climb about 0.3 mile northwest up this ridgecrest, then traverse largely open, brushy slopes with ranging coast vistas before ending at the Tin House about 0.7 mile later.

From the saddle junction the loop route starts southwest along a nearly level stretch of marble-rock ridgecrest, from where an alluring, quickly ending use trail drops southwest. You follow the ridgecrest, which soon becomes grassy as it turns south and drops steeply almost to the brink of a dropoff—the top of a huge, temporarily stabilized landslide scar above Highway 1. The steep descent southeast along the edge of this scar is atop a three-foot-wide ridgecrest—*absolutely no place for small children, careless hikers or the faint-of-heart*. The descent tapers among brush, and after a brief traverse you leave the ridge for a winding, generally moderate, largely oak-shaded descent down to the bridge by the start of the loop. Retrace your steps.

A view southeast, from low on the Fire Road

Fire Road

From the vista point at Highway 1's mile 37.0, walk 70 yards east to the start of the gated road. This first climbs steeply 140 yards up to a redwood glade, and then makes a similar ascent from it to a nearby ridge. This spot, like the highway's vista point, offers inspiring views up and down several miles of coast. The gradient now relaxes to moderate, although to its 2020' high point, which is 1580' above the trailhead, the 2.2-mile climb averages a moderate-to-steep 13½% grade. The trail weaves in and out of gullies and then, about 0.8 mile from the trailhead, reaches a prominent ridge. This spot, one third of the way to the Tin House, is a worthy goal in itself, for you have excellent coast views plus views up Partington Creek canyon to the Coast Ridge.

You now turn north for a diagonaling climb up the canyon's east wall. Soon views all but disappear as you enter a forest mostly of tanbark oaks plus some redwoods. About 1.6 miles into the route, the road switchbacks. It briefly climbs south, switchbacks again, climbs too steeply east, makes a final switchback, and then traverses ¼ mile over to a ridge, the road's

high point. Here, at a spot just above the Tin House, you meet the upper end of the Tan Bark Trail. With just 0.2 mile left to go, you follow the road, first on a brief traverse southeast, and then on a longer descent west down to the Tin House and adjacent grassy ridge lands, which offer a fine view northwest along the coast. Up here you'll find the upper end of the Ewoldsen Trail, mentioned above. If the weather is sunny and the wind is not strong, this locale is a great spot for a picnic.

Tan Bark Trail

This 3.3-mile trail provides a longer route to the Tin House. Because it's longer than the Fire Trail, one would assume it's better graded. However, it's almost as steep, since it starts lower and climbs higher, challenging you with a 2000' climb. The trail actually drops about 200' in its last ¼-mile stretch to the Fire Trail, which you then follow 0.2 mile to the Tin House. So why take it? Well, the route is through a luxuriant forest, which on warm days is reason enough. True to its name, the Tan Bark Trail is mostly through a forest of tanbark oaks.

The trail begins at the east end of the Partington Creek bridge, and after about 280 yards, mostly across the base of talus slopes, it is joined by a lateral trail of similar length. This starts from the west end of the highway's bridge and ends immediately after bridging rather miniscule Partington Creek. Given the size of the drainage, one would expect it to be larger, but redwoods lining the creek levy a hefty

On fogless days the Tin House environs can be a great spot for a picnic

water toll. The first prominent redwoods lie just up from this junction, and collectively they're called the Babcock Family Grove.

Redwoods line the creek all the way to a trail junction about 0.3 mile farther. Ahead, a use trail quickly dies out at the creek. The main trail turns east up an alcove, the site of the Donald H. McLaughlin Memorial Grove, and then the route curves south to a quick switchback. You then follow two switchback legs, the first northeast into a gully, the second out of it and south to a point about 1 mile from your trailhead. Now the trail heads 1¼ miles northeast to a junction, the first half of this stretch paralleling the unseen Fire Road, which is about 200' higher up the slopes.

The junction is at a saddle on a minor ridge you reach after crossing a luxuriant redwood glade with a usually reliable creek. An abandoned trail climbs northeast, but you climb southeast, quickly reaching a bench beside the creek. From both, the trail climbs south and in about ⅔ mile you may spot another abandoned trail, this one also climbing northeast. About 230 yards farther, just below a prominent ridge, you meet a trail that climbs part way up the ridge. This trail is on private property, so *do not take it*. The Tan Bark Trail tops out at this junction, and it then stays just below the prominent ridge until its end at the Fire Road, ¼ mile later, the junction being only several yards before the road turns the ridge.

Partington Cove Trail

This short, fairly popular route, signed as a fire road, starts from the west end of the Partington Creek bridge, and it descends rather steeply ¼ mile to a small flat beside the creek. Upstream, a spur trail goes east to a nearby outhouse. Downstream, the route goes 35 yards west to a junction. Straight ahead, a trail continues about 120 yards to a narrow beach at the head of Partington Point's west cove. An interesting site along this trail stretch is a small cluster of stunted redwoods, which grow within 70 yards of the surf. Supposedly they never grow this close to the ocean because they can't take the salty air. But here they are!

Most people turn right at the junction, taking a path that immediately crosses Partington Creek and then quickly ducks through a 40-yard-long tunnel over to the east cove. The trail continues along the cove to a point, a fine spot to take in a sunset. This cove is the site of Partington Landing, operated in the 1880s by John Partington, who felled the canyon's redwoods and oaks, and then loaded the products on ships docking at this cove. These were taken to San Francisco, where the redwood was used for construction, while the bark of the oaks was used for leather tanning (hence the name, tanbark oak). Today, the landing is used by scuba divers. If you are skilled in this sport and would like to explore the cove's clear waters, contact Pfeiffer Big Sur State Park at (408) 667-2315.

Topographic Maps

Except for Chapter 10's Carmel River State Beach and Point Lobos State Reserve, all of the places described in this book are shown on the following 25 pages of topographic maps. The index map, below, shows these pages, each identified in *black* with an appropriate map number. These maps are parts of U.S.G.S. 7.5' topographic maps, which are also shown on the map below. These 14 topographic maps are drawn in *gray,* and they are listed in the index map's upper right corner.

The scale of the book's 25 maps is about 1:42,100, which equals 1.50 inches per mile (1.0 inch equals ⅔ mile). Each full-page map is 5' of latitude high by 3¾' of longitude wide (a 7.5' topographic map is 7.5 x 7.5). Each full-page map covers an area of 5¾ by 3½ miles; each two-page spread covers 5¾ by 7 miles.

North is at the top of the page. Declination is about 15°E.

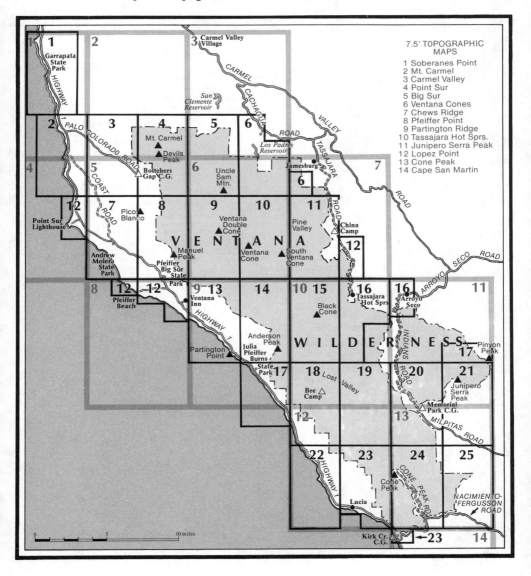

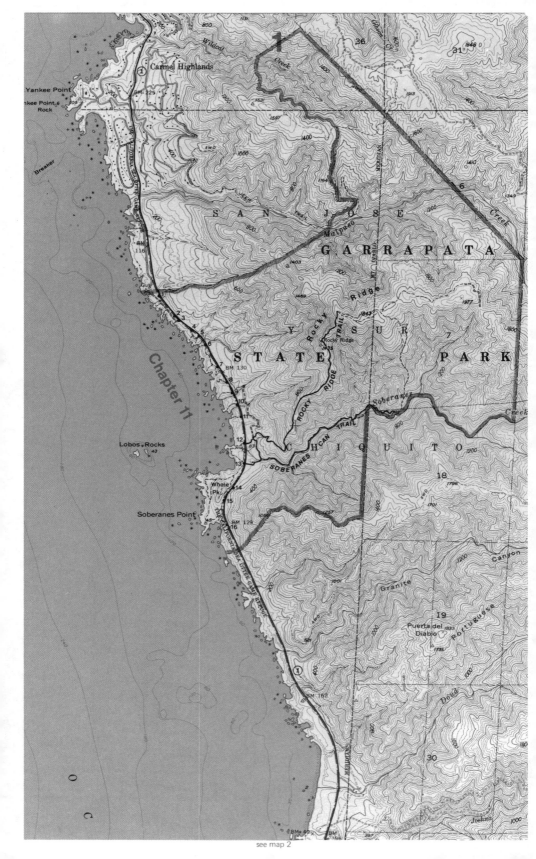

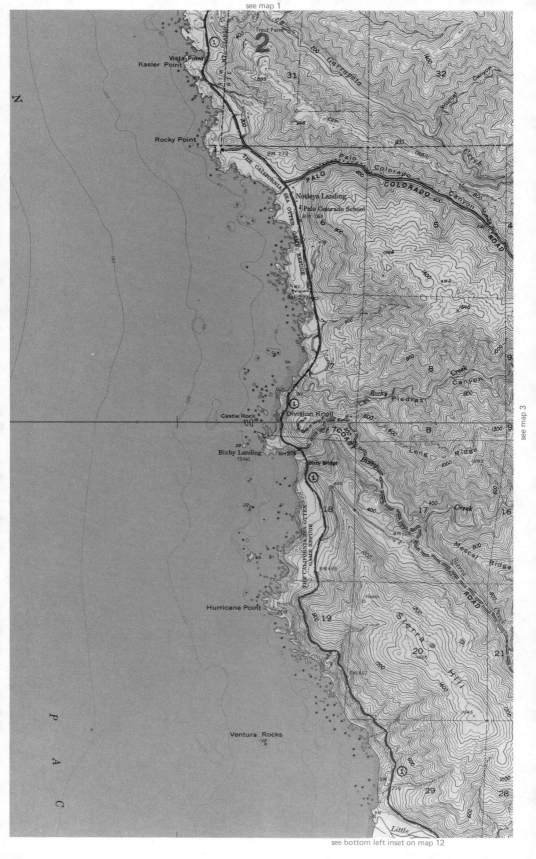

see map 3

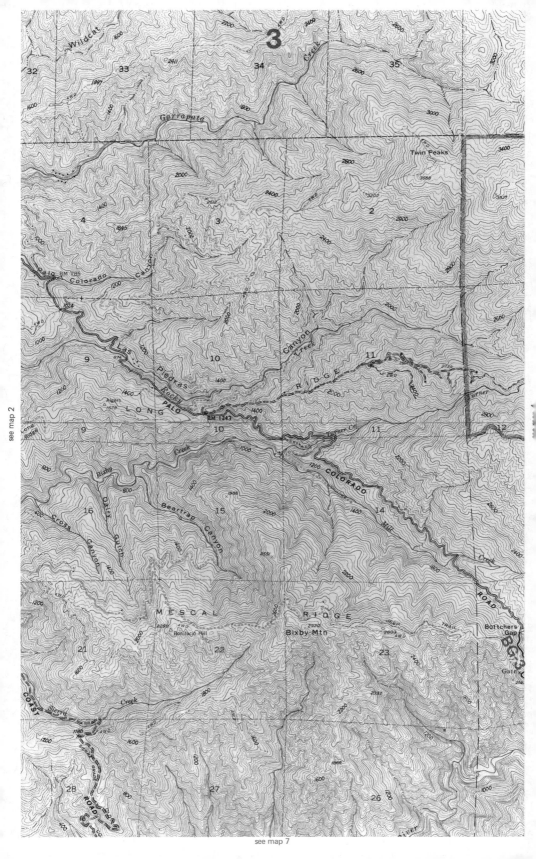

see map 2

see map 7

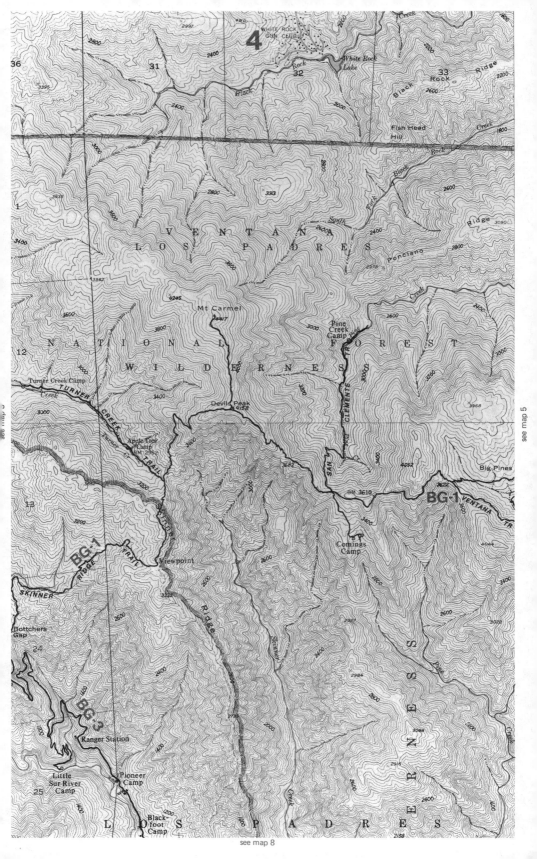

see map 5

see map 8

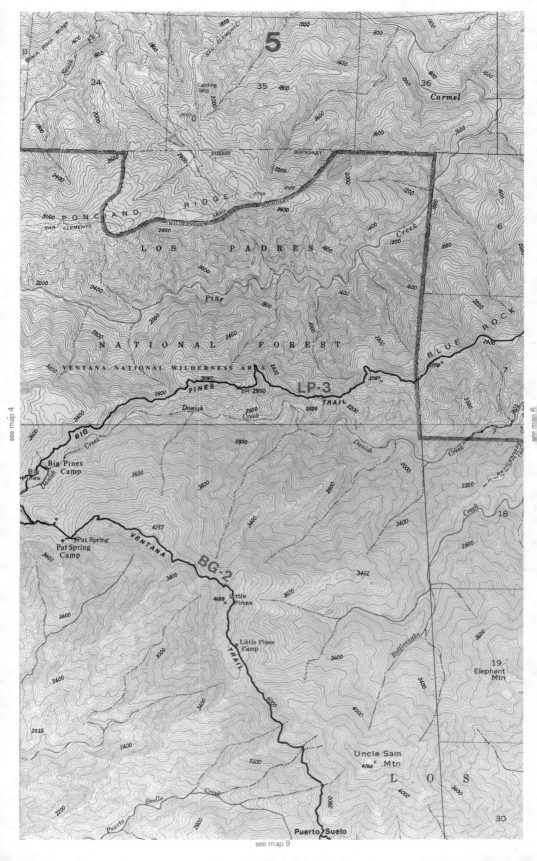

see map 4

see map 6

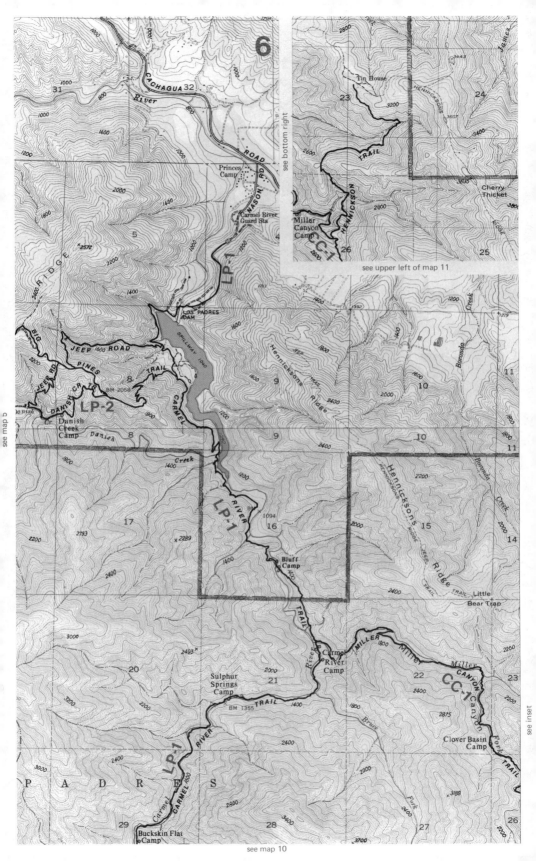

see bottom right

see upper left of map 11

see map c

see inset

CACHAGUA 32

River

NASON RD.

ROAD

Princes
Camp

Carmel River
Guard Sta

LP-1

RIDGE

LOS PADRES
DAM

SPILLWAY

BIG

JEEP 1600 ROAD

PINES

JEEP RD.

DANISH CR.

TRAIL

CARMEL

LP-2

BM 2058

Danish
Creek
Camp

Danish

Creek

LP-1

RIVER

BM

Bluff
Camp

TRAIL

RIVER

Sulphur
Springs
Camp

TRAIL

BM 1355

LP-1

RIVER

CARMEL

Carmel

PADRES

Buckskin Flat
Camp

Tin House

HENNICKSONS

TRAIL

HENNICKSON

Miller
Canyon
Camp

CC-1

Cherry
Thicket

RIDGE

Hennickson

Ridge

Hennicksons

Ridge

JEEP

TRAIL

Bonanza

Creek

Bonanza

Creek

Little
Bear Trap

Carmel
River
Camp

MILLER

Miller

Miller

CANYON

Canyon

CC-1

Brace

Fork

Clover Basin
Camp

Fork

TRAIL

see map 3

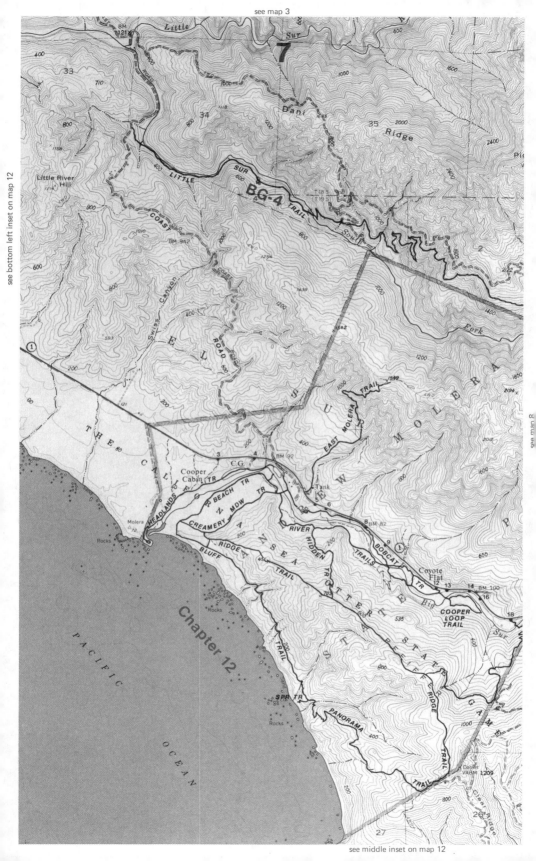

see bottom left inset on map 12

see map 8

see middle inset on map 12

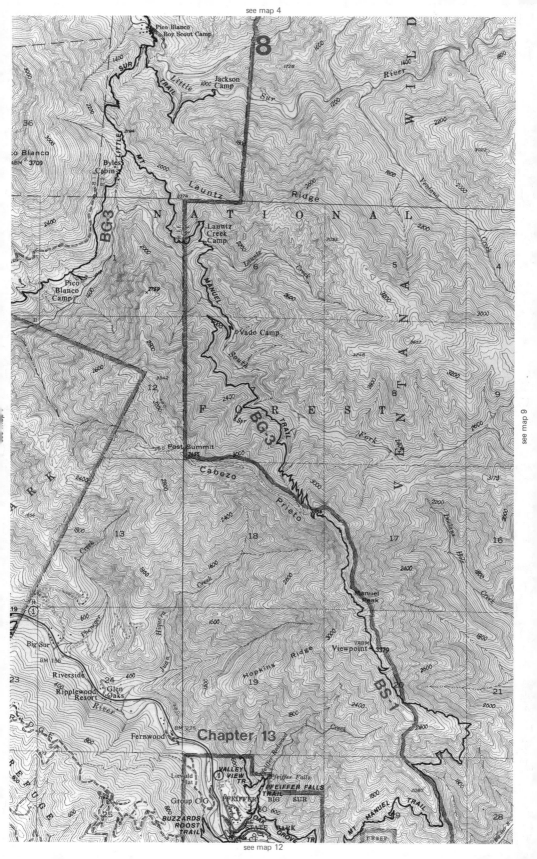

Chapter 13

see map 9

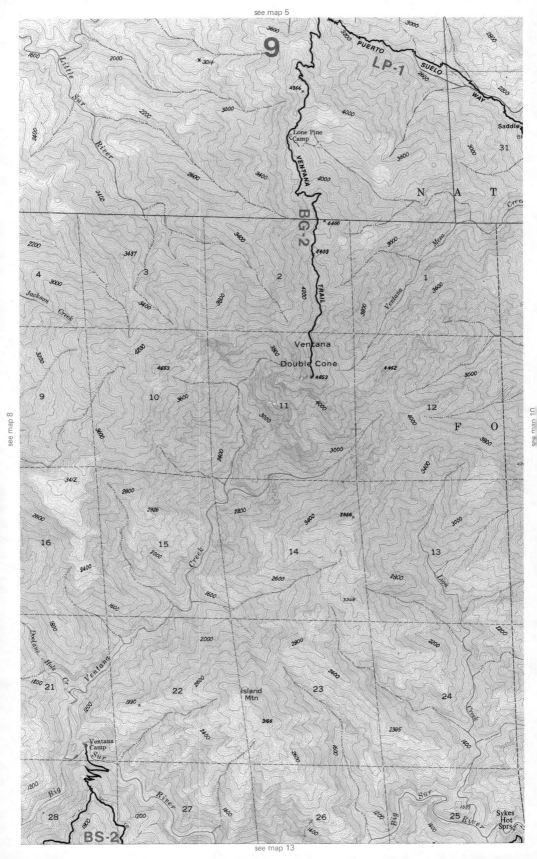

see map 8

see map 10

see map 6

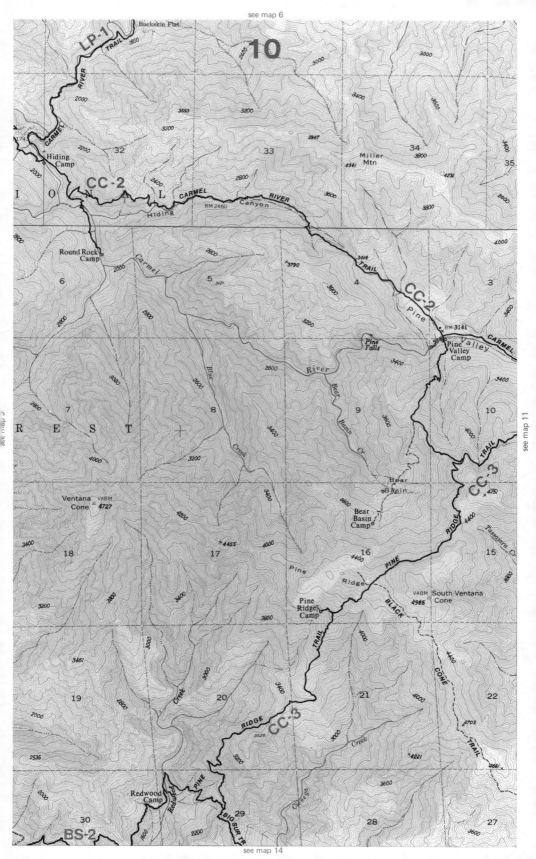

see map 11

see map 14

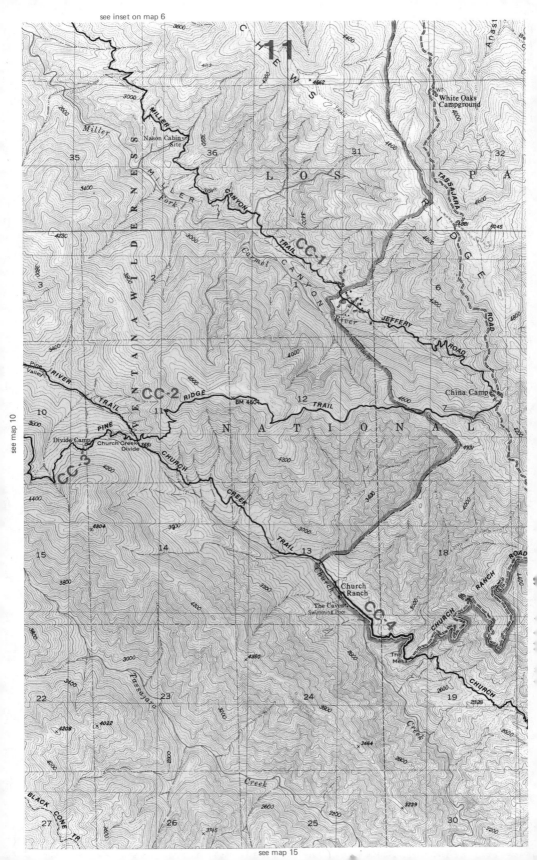

see map 10

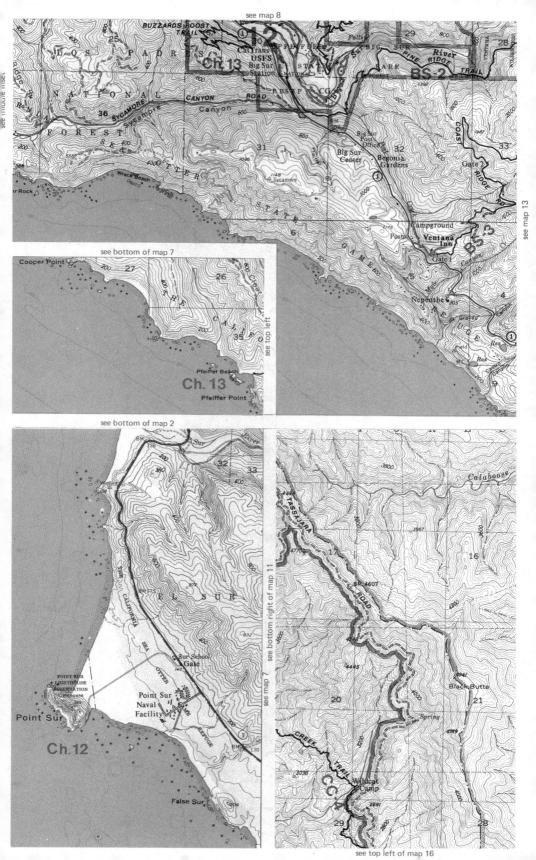

see map 13

see bottom of map 7

see top left

Ch. 13

Pfeiffer Beach

Pfeiffer Point

see bottom of map 2

see bottom right of map 11

see top left

POINT SUR
LIGHTHOUSE
RESERVATION

Point Sur

Ch. 12

Sur School
Gate

Point Sur
Naval
Facility

False Sur

Black Butte

Wildcat
Camp

see top left of map 16

see top of map 12

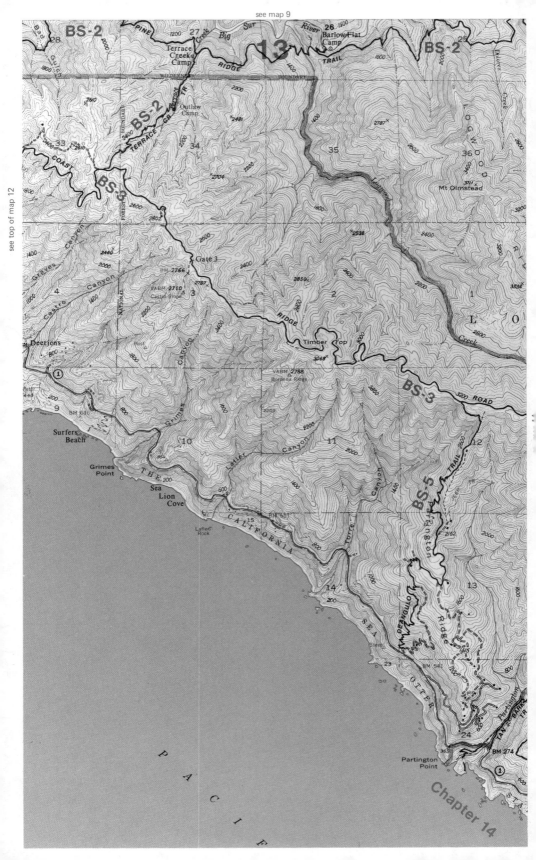

BS-2

28

BS-2

PINE

Terrace Creek Camp

Big Sur River

26 Barlow Flat Camp

25

BS-2

RIDGE

TRAIL

13

WILDERNESS BOUNDARY

BS-2

Outlaw Camp

TERRACE CR. TRAIL

FOREST BOUNDARY

33

34

2481

35

36

Mt Olmstead

2787

COAST

BS-3

2802

2600

LOGWOOD

2704

Gate 3

BM 2766

2538

2850

Graves Canyon

Castro Canyon

VABM 2710 Castro Slope

2787

3

2

RIDGE

1

L I O

Deetjens

NATIONAL

Post

Timber Top

3068

Creek

1

VABM 2788 Borgena Ridge

BS-3

ROAD

BM 616

Surfers Beach

Grimes Point

Sea Lion Cove

Grimes

9

10

11

12

BS-5

Laffler Canyon

Torre Canyon

Partington

TRAIL

2762

Ridge

THE

200

CALIFORNIA

Laffler Rock

15

14

13

SEA

DE ANGULO

Steep

23

BM 541

OTTER

24

Partington Point

BM 274

P A C I F

Chapter 14

1

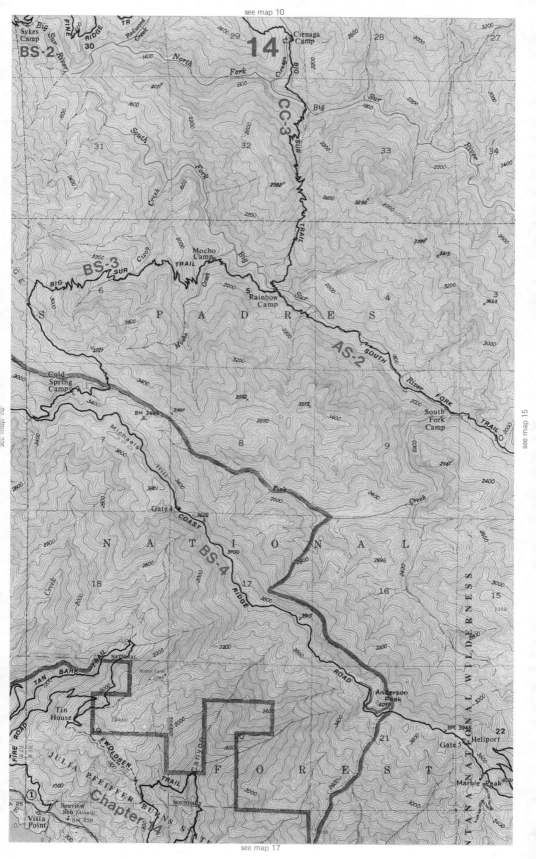

see map 15

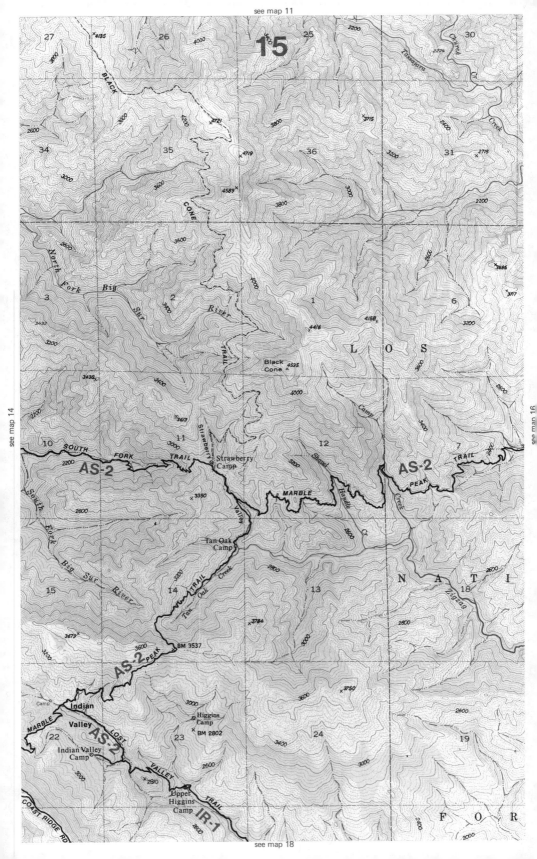

see map 14

see map 16

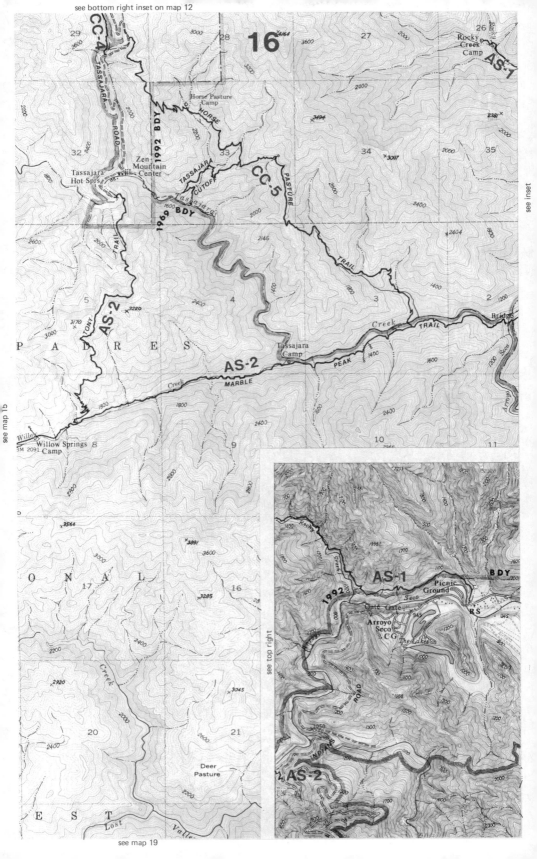

see bottom right inset on map 12

16

Rocky Creek Camp

AS-1

Horse Pasture Camp

1992 BDY

Zen Mountain Center

Tassajara Hot Sprs

TASSAJARA CUTOFF

CC-5

PASTURE

1969 BDY

Tassajara

TRAIL

P A D R E S

AS-2

TONY

AS-2

Tassajara Camp

MARBLE

Creek

PEAK

Creek

TRAIL

Bridge

Willow
Willow Springs Camp
BM 2091

8

9

10

11

O N A L

17

16

20

21

Deer Pasture

E S T

Lost Valley

see map 1b

see map 19

see inset

see top right

AS-1

1992

BDY

Picnic Ground

Gate Gate

Arroyo Seco CG

The Lakes

RS

INDIAN ROAD

AS-2

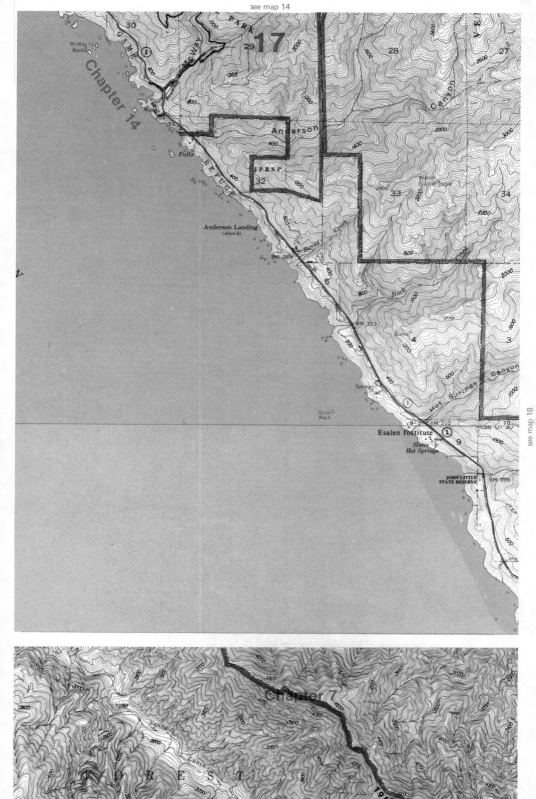

see map 18

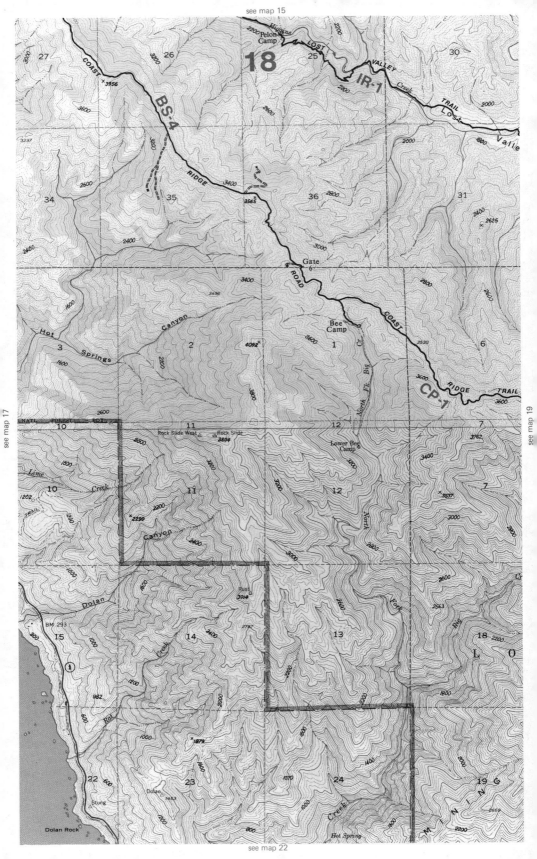

see map 17

see map 19

see bottom left of map 16

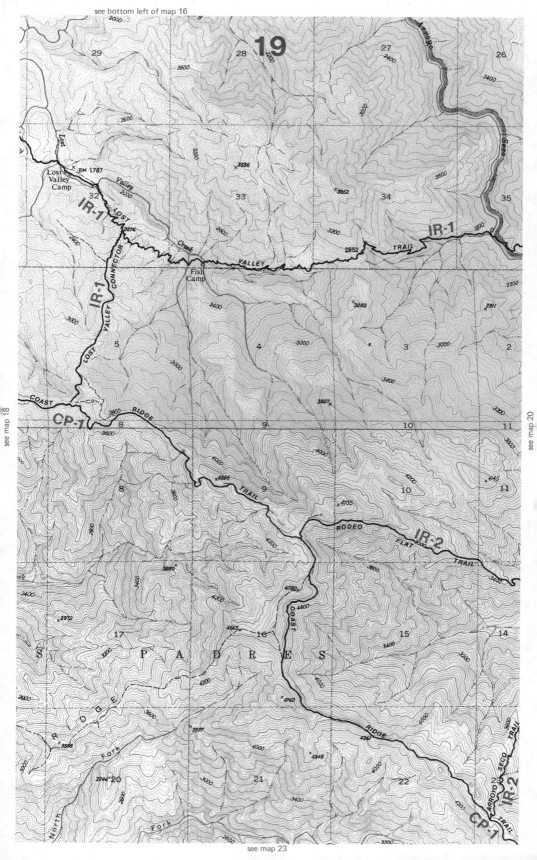

see map 18

see map 20

see map 23

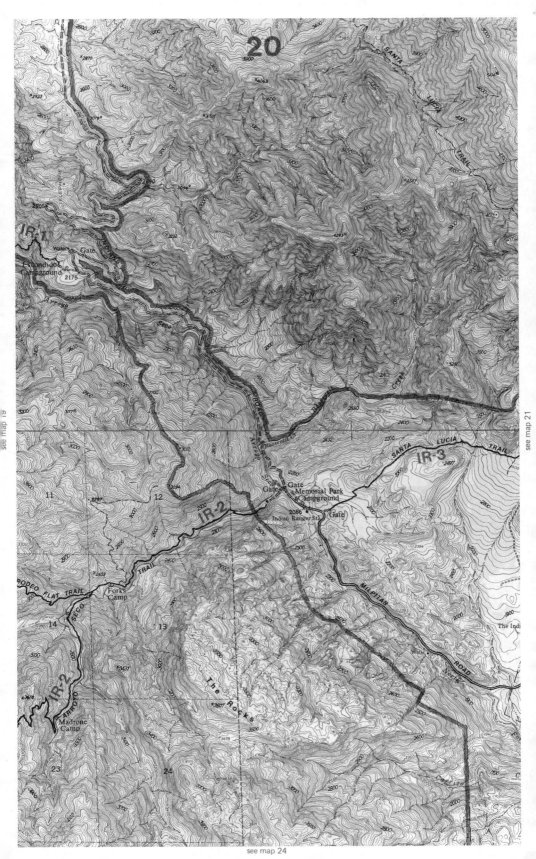

see map 19

see map 21

IR-1

Escondido
Campground

Water Gate

SANTA LUCIA TRAIL

IR-3

SANTA LUCIA TRAIL

Memorial Park
Campground

Gate

Gate

Gate

Indian Ranger Sta.

IR-2

11

12

RODEO FLAT TRAIL

SECO

TRAIL

Forks
Camp

MILPITAS

The Indi

14

13

ROAD

North

IR-2

The Rocks

Madrone
Camp

23

24

see map 24

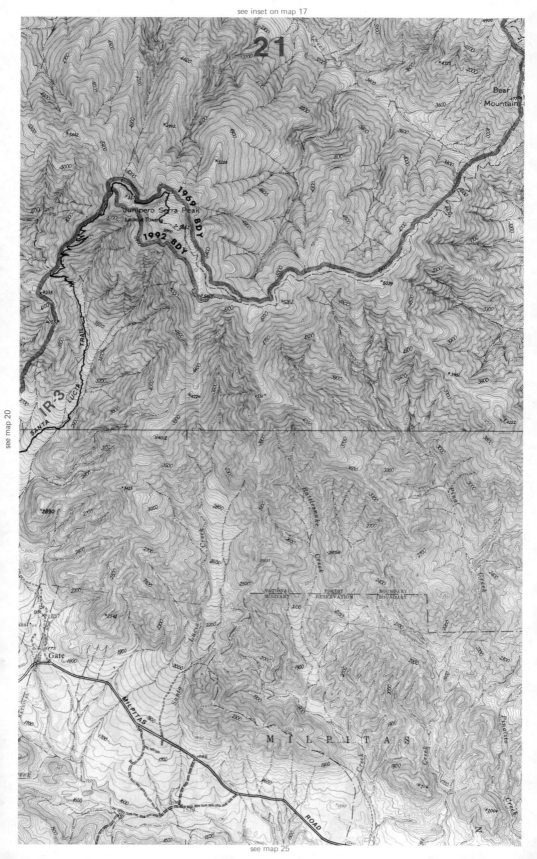

21

Bear Mountain

Junipero Serra Peak
Lookout Tower

1969 BDY

1992 BDY

SANTA LUCIA TRAIL

IR-3

see map 20

NATIONAL FOREST BOUNDARY
MILITARY RESERVATION BOUNDARY

Gate

MILPITAS

M I L P I T A S

ROAD

Rattlesnake Creek

Pinedra Creek

see map 25

see map 18

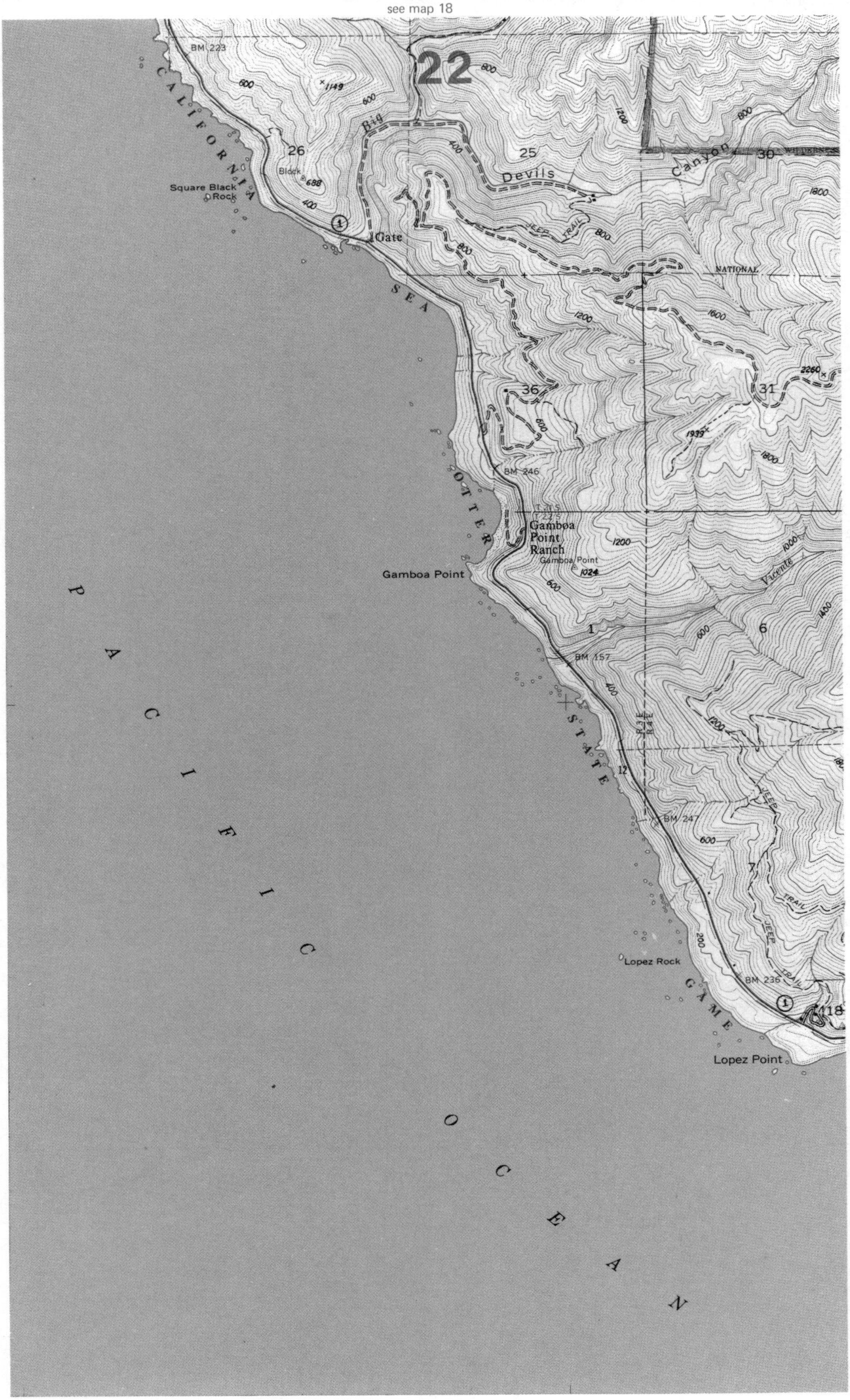

22

see map 23

BM 223

1149

600

600

800

1200

CALIFORNIA

26

Black 688

25

Devils

Canyon

30 WILDERNESS

800

Square Black
Rock

400

400

Gate

400

600

JEEP

TRAIL

800

1800

NATIONAL

SEA

800

1200

1600

31

2260

OTTER

36

600

1939

1800

BM 246

THIS

2275

Gamboa
Point
Ranch

1200

1000

Gamboa Point

Gamboa Point
1024

Vicente

PACIFIC

600

1600

1

6

BM 157

STATE

400

1200

12

JEEP

400

BM 247

600

TRAIL

200

GAME

Lopez Rock

BM 236

1118

Lopez Point

O
C
E
A
N

see map 19

see map 22

see map 24

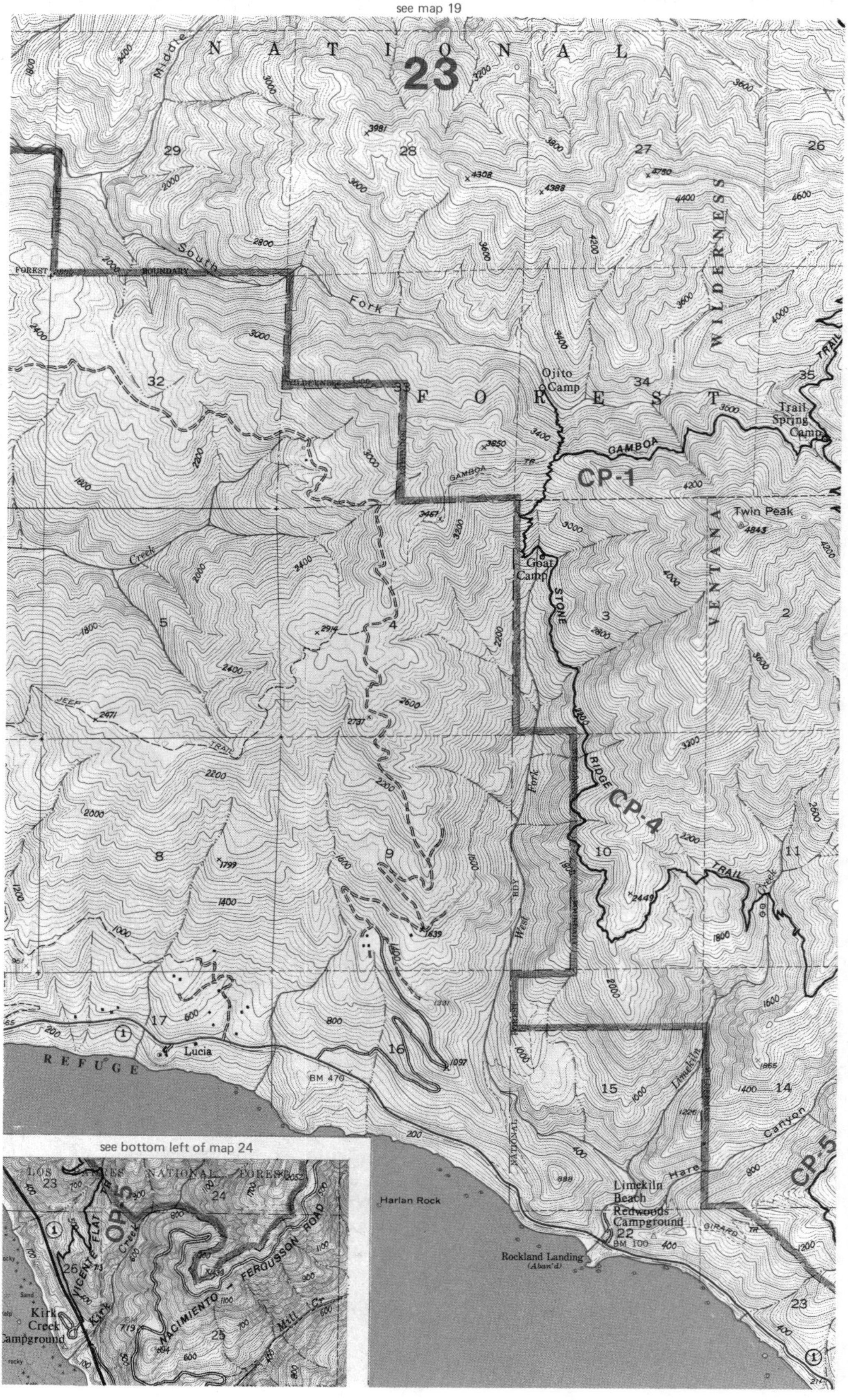

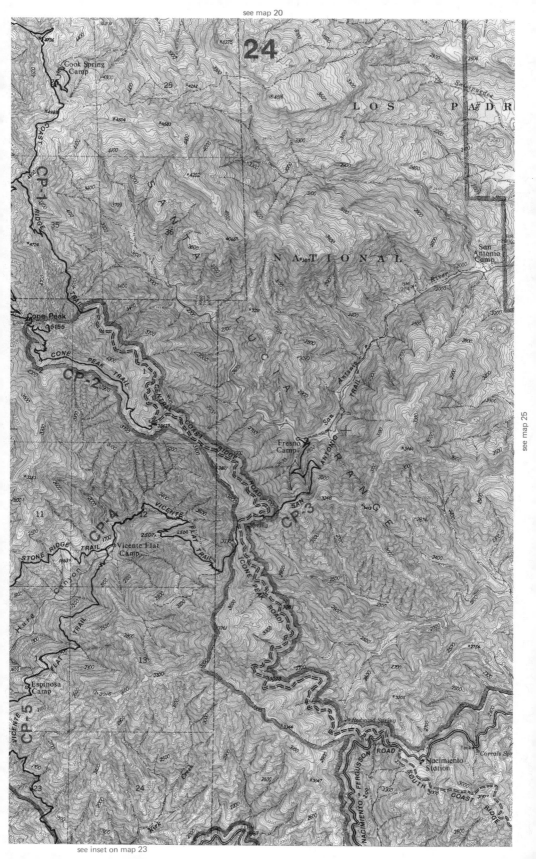

see map 25

see map 21

see map 24

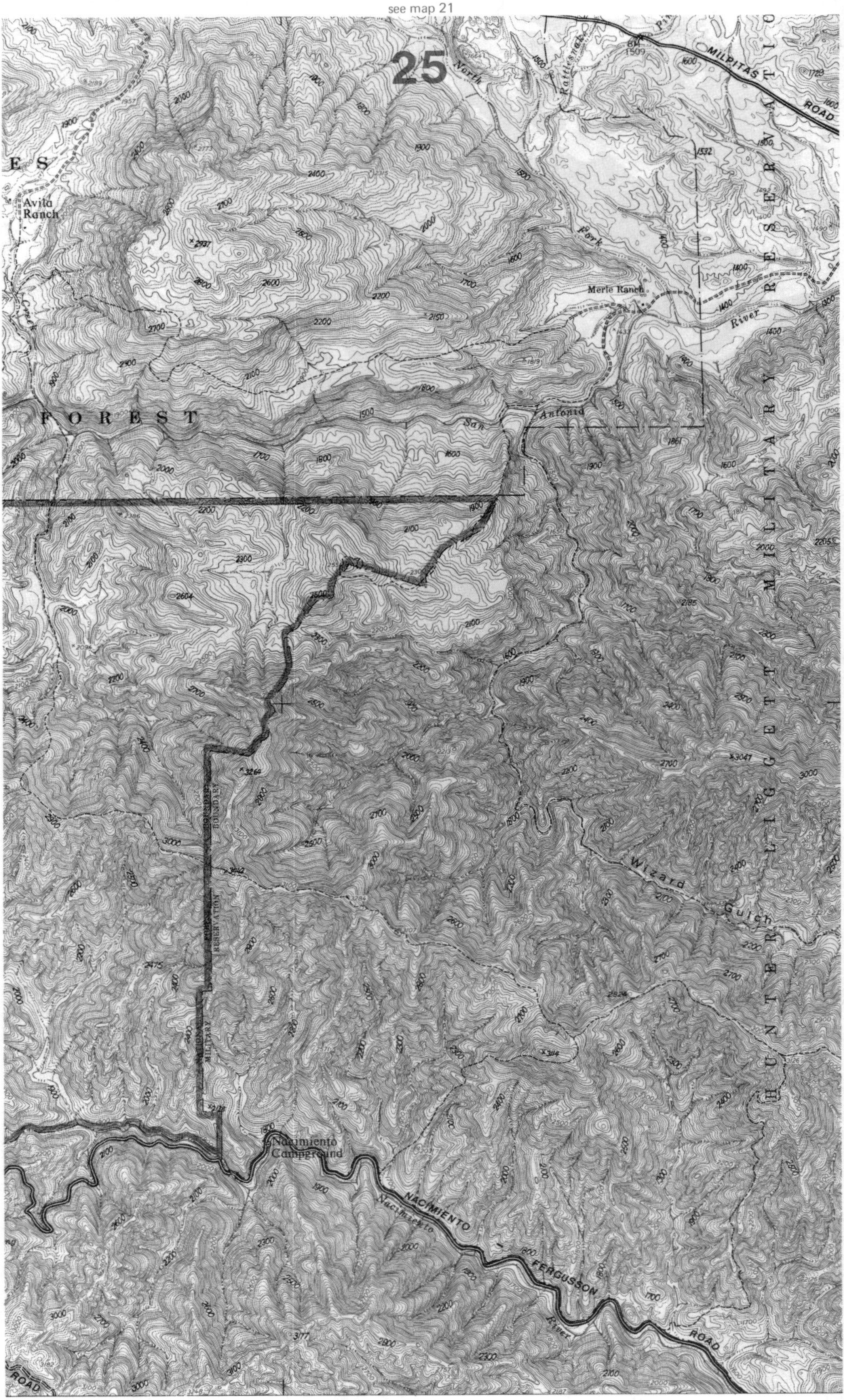

25
MILPITAS ROAD
North Fork
Avila Ranch
Merle Ranch
San Antonio River
FOREST
HUNTER LIGGETT MILITARY RESERVATION
Wizard Gulch
MILITARY RESERVATION BOUNDARY
Nacimiento Campground
NACIMIENTO FERGUSSON ROAD
Nacimiento River

Selected References

Periodicals

Fremontia. California Native Plant Society, 909 12th Street, Suite 116, Sacramento, CA 95814. *This brief, quarterly journal has some excellent articles on California's native vegetation. There are many articles on chaparral and oak plant communities, which make up most of the Big Sur Country.*

Geological Society of America Bulletin. Geological Society of America, 3300 Penrose Place, Boulder, CO 80301. *In my opinion, this monthly periodical provides more useful information on California's geology than any source other than the U.S. Geological Survey. Each year you can expect to find several articles that are relative to California's central Coast Range.*

Series

Nature Study Guild, P.O. Box 972, Berkeley, CA 94701. The following are part of a series of very useful, economical, truly pocket-size paperbacks. Most weigh only two ounces, and all of the following, other than the *Redwood Region Flower Finder,* cover species in California, Oregon and Washington. The following titles (and a few others not relevant to the Big Sur Country) are distributed by Wilderness Press, 2440 Bancroft Way, Berkeley, CA 94704.

Keator, Glenn, and Jeanne C. Koelling. 1978. *Pacific Coast Berry Finder.* 62 p.

Keator, Glenn, Ruth M. Heady and Valerie R. Vinemiller. 1981. *Pacific Coast Fern Finder.* 62 p.

Russo, Ron, and Pam Olhausen. 1987. *Mammal Finder.* 94 p.

Russo, Ron, and Pam Olhausen. 1981. *Pacific Intertidal Life.* 62 p.

Watts, Phoebe, and Sarah Ellen Watts. 1979. *Redwood Region Flower Finder.* 60 p.

Watts, Tom. 1973. *Pacific Coast Tree Finder.* 62 p.

United States Geological Survey, 345 Middlefield Road, Menlo Park, CA 94025. (Order books and open-file reports from U.S. Geological Survey, Books and Open-File Reports, Federal Center, Box 25425, Denver, CO 80225; order maps from U.S. Geological Survey, Map Distribution, Federal Center, Box 25286, Denver, CO 80225.) The U.S.G.S. Menlo Park branch produces the most—and certainly some of the best—maps and literature on the Big Sur Country. Most of these publications, however, are too technical for non-geologists. Here is a sample of relevant publications, which have references that list many other sources of data.

Greene, H.G., and others. 1973. *Faults and Earthquakes in the Monterey Bay Region, California* (Miscellaneous Field Studies Map MF-518). 4 sheets plus separate text.

Nilsen, Tor H., and Samuel H. Clarke, Jr. 1975. *Sedimentation and Tectonics in the Early Tertiary Continental Borderland of Central California* (Professional Paper 925). 64 p.

Pearson, Robert C., Philip T. Hayes and Paul V. Fillo. 1967. *Mineral Resources of the Ventana Primitive Area, Monterey County, California* (Bulletin 1261-B). 42 p.

Ross, Donald C. 1977. *Maps Showing Sample Localities and Ternary Plots and Graphs Showing Modal and Chemical Data for Granitic Rocks of the Santa Lucia Range, Salinian Block, California Coast Ranges* (Miscellaneous Field Studies Map MF-799). 3 sheets plus separate text.

Ross, Donald C. 1984. *Possible Correlations of Basement Rocks Across the San Andreas, San Gregorio-Hosgri, and Rinconada-Reliz-King City Faults, California* (Professional Paper 1317). 37 p.

Ross, Donald C. 1976. *Reconnaissance Geologic Map of the Pre-Cenozoic Basement Rocks, Northern Santa Lucia Range, Monterey County, California* (Miscellaneous Field Studies Map MF-750). 2 sheets plus separate text.

Seiders, V.M., and others. 1983. *Geologic Map of Part of the Ventana Wilderness and the Black Butte, Bear Mountain, and Bear Canyon Roadless Areas, Monterey County, California* (Miscellaneous Field Studies Map MF-1559-B). 1 sheet with accompanying text.

Index

Ventana Wilderness
1998 Update

(compiled by Jeffrey Van Middlebrook)

p. 8: As of mid-1997 many of the more popular routes were overgrown in sections and washed out in other sections. Some of the trails were nearly impassable and others were outright dangerous to attempt except for the most experienced and daring hikers. The USFS said that their timetable and budget do not allow for any significant trail clearings/openings/restorations until well into late 1998 and beyond. Years of heavy rains and fires coupled with USFS budgetary constraints have rendered travel in much of Ventana Wilderness a troublesome obstacle course.

pp. 33-34: The section of trail to Mt. Manuel's summit from Launtz Creek Camp has been eradicated by two consecutive years of severe storms and fires. The USFS has officially designated this part of hike #BG-3 as closed until further notice. The wilderness manager of the USFS said that it will be 1998 at the earliest before any attempts are made to clear and restore this section of hike #BG-3. He also advises that nobody attempt to hike this section because of the high risk of taking a serious fall from the washed out sections of trail above vertical cliffs.

pp. 38-43: For most of the distance of hike #LP-I the trail is overgrown with poison oak to such an extent it is virtually impossible to avoid contact with it. The USFS needs to clear and restore this trail, but they give no indication if or when such work will be done. Also, given the extent of encroachment by poison oak and other shrubs onto the trail, it's impossible to avoid picking up ticks. A recent trip down this trail resulted in each member of our party picking up dozens of ticks per mile covered. The only relief from the poison oak and ticks came during the 32 river and tributary crossings required between the Los Padres Dam and Hiding Camp.

pp. 54-55: Most of the trail from Pine Valley downriver into Hiding Camp is grossly overgrown with poison oak, and therefore ticks are also unavoidable. (Hiding Camp is the first crossing of the greater Carmel River about 0.5 mile after passing the Round Rock Camp Trail junction heading northwest away from Pine Valley. toward Los Padres Dam). Hiding Camp is a very obvious riverside table of stable gravel deposits. There are picnic tables and fire pits strewn helter-skelter along this narrow but long shelf that is shaded by trees. The Puerto Suelo trail begins from this area.

pp. 81-82: From the Oak Grove Trail-Mt. Manuel Trail junction to the summit of Mt. Manuel there is a trail-closed advisory by the USFS. Though the USFS says that it's possible to attain Mt. Manuel's summit, there are a few sections of the trail hundreds of feet above the Big Sur River gorge that are severely washed out and there is a substantial risk of taking a serious if not fatal fall into the gorge. Restoration work is under way but the USFS can give no timetable for the completion of the work.

pp. 83-87: Gone is the crude dirt parking area that veteran Ventana hikers would recall, replaced by a paved, lined and curbed large lot. Circumscribing this lot are new USFS buildings used as employee housing, tourist information and modern toilet facilities for hikers. There is a two-dollar entrance fee for parking, with a 14-day limit.

The Pine Ridge Trail begins at the southwest corner of this parking lot and parallels the new fenceline that delineates a grazing pasture used by the USFS. Hikers follow this fenceline for about 150 yards, at which point the fence turns away from the trail and one encounters the abandoned and fenced off fork of what was the trail prior to the construction of the new parking lot. Beyond this point the Pine Ridge Trail remains unchanged, save for seasonal variations the result of rains and fire.

For the first two miles of this trail's rapid ascent it's heavily overgrown with genista and some poison oak. In the wake of three successive heavy winters this trail is strewn with large fallen redwoods, cedars and oaks. New trail courses have been beaten down around the smaller obstacles, but in a few locations the size of the fallen trees has created aggravating challenges for the hiker, especially those carrying heavy packs. The worst such location is at Terrace Creek, where it looks like a war zone of felled redwood giants. The hiker is forced to go off-trail and scramble over huge tree trunks in order to regain the trail's normal course.

The next of these major locations of fallen trees is at a point about a mile before reaching Sykes Hot Springs. In 1987 the remainder of the hike from Sykes to Redwood Camp was heavily overgrown with brush, and ticks were plentiful, but there were no major obstacles or washouts.

Note: Regarding washouts, the author makes note of a significant washout (p. 84, paragraph 3) that poses fatal possibilities in the event of a fall. This slide area has not been improved since the initial publication of this guide; indeed it has become even more dangerous to cross, especially when wet. A serious warning must be given the inexperienced hiker as to this slide's deadly potential. To take children over this route would be taking an unconscionable risk! I would not dare to take anyone over this slide without a climbing rope and hardware in order to rig a safe belay. Someone may die trying to cross this.

p, 99, CP-2: Most of this short but lofty trail was recently free of overgrowth and washouts, save for two minor washouts halfway to the nearly mile-high summit of Cone Peak. At both of these washouts the potential exists for a rather long and injurious cascade down a very steep mountainside. Great attention to foot placement through these two sections is required.

p. 129: The telephone number now reaches the California Division of State Parks, not MISTIX, and you can reserve through them.

As of mid-February 1998, record storms have made many trails, and even roads to trailheads, impassable. Before going to the area, phone the Forest Service in King City (831) 385-5434 or Big Sur (831) 677-2315.

Please refer to the first page of this guidebook for an important notice.